PERSPECTIVES ON THE ECONOMY OF MANIPUR

Perspectives on the Economy of Manipur

Essays in Honour of
Prof. H. Nabakishore Singh

Edited by
E. Bijoykumar Singh
Damodar Nepram

AKANSHA PUBLISHING HOUSE
NEW DELHI • GUWAHATI • VISAKHAPATNAM

AKANSHA PUBLISHING HOUSE
4649-B/21, Ansari Road
Darya Ganj, New Delhi - 110 002
Ph.: 23263193 / 9811582579 / 09435116718
Fax: 011-23263193
Email: ektabooks@yahoo.com
www.akanshapublishinghouse.com

Perspectives on the Economy of Manipur

First Published 2010

ISBN 978-81-8370-220-1

PRINTED IN INDIA

Published by Akansha Publishing House, New Delhi and Printed at S.N. Printers, Delhi.

Prof. H. Nabakishore Singh

Prof. H. Nabakishore Singh is a pioneer in the study of Economics in Manipur with a wide range of experience from being a teacher to Research Officer in the Secretariat Planning Department, Government of Manipur. Prof. H. Nabakishore Singh (born October 1, 1934), s/o late Heigrujam Tomba Singh and late Anirei Devi of Imphal matriculated from Johnstone High School, Imphal (now a Higher Secondary School) under Gauhati University with letters in Compulsory Mathematics, Mechanics and Geography in 1950. He passed the Intermediate of Arts Examination from (the then combined) D.M.College, Imphal, under Gauhati University securing the 4th position in the University in 1952. He graduated from Cotton College, Gauhati (now Guwahati) with honours in Economics in 1954, passed M.A. in Economics in 1956, and LLB examination in 1958 securing the 5th position in the University, all under Gauhati university. He was awarded Ph. D. in Economics by the same university in February 1970 on his thesis: 'The Industrial Policy of the Government of India since Independence up to the end of the Third Five Year Plan', under the guidance of the late Prof. S. Sarangpani of Gauhati University.

After serving for one year and four months in Imphal College, he joined the D.M.College of Arts & Commerce as Lecturer in Economics on August 2, 1958 and was promoted as Senior Lecturer in 1966. He also served as the senior most Research Officer in Secretariat Planning Department of the Government of Manipur for two years on deputation and was also a member of the State Planning Board for several years. He joined the JNU Centre for PG Studies, Imphal as Associate Professor on Sept.1, 1978 and was later absorbed in the Manipur University when it was established on June 1, 1980. After joining the Economics Department of the Jawaharlal Nehru Centre for PG Studies, Imphal in 1978, he became associated in various capacities as an academician, administrator and policy maker with the development of Economics teaching and economic policy in Manipur. He became Professor in Economics of Manipur University in 1984. He was also a member of the Academic Council, Senate and Syndicate.

During his service in the University, he produced under his supervision and guidance seven Ph.D. degree holders and several M.Phil. degree holders in Economics. He retired from his service as Dean of Social Sciences on September 30, 1994. After retiring from the service he spends his time writing text books and guidebooks for school and college students more as a hobby and social service than as a line of business.

Contents

Introduction

This collection of 18 essays on various aspects of the economy and society of Manipur is being brought out in honour of Dr. H. Nabakishore Singh, Retd. Professor, Economics Department, Manipur University who had played a key role in popularising this discipline in Manipur and giving the current character of the Economics Department in Manipur University. Dr. Nabakishore belongs to the generation of teachers who considered teaching as the most important duty of a teacher. After having brought out a collection of essays on the economy and society of Manipur in honour of Dr. M. Iboton Singh, Retd. Prof., some of his former colleagues and students felt that another volume should be brought out to honour Dr. Nabakishore who was a pioneer in this discipline in Manipur. This was the genesis of this volume. The eighteen essays cover four broad themes viz rural and agricultural development, population growth and its quality, public finance and trade. These essays carry forward the issues raised in the earlier volume regarding various aspects of the economy of Manipur. The current volume thus will enhance the depth and quality of the debate.

Krishnamangol in "Patterns of Participatory Development in Manipur: A New Strategy" examines the participatory development system and sets out appropriate strategies for promoting the process of participatory development in Manipur. In the new concept of participatory development, the process of participation exists at different levels and in different forms such as the village society/ community organizations, panchayats, non-governmental organisations, cooperative institutions etc. This suggests a set of policy measures which need to be formulated to create willingness of the people and favourable conditions for participatory development system in Manipur. While the state-led model for participatory development is necessary to achieve people's cooperation in development, there is still the need for decentralisation for planning at district and block levels in order to build up a strong institutional base for strengthening the process of participatory development in the state. In the new strategy of participatory development proposed, the state-led model of development programmes and people's participation in development are sought to be combined in the decentralized planning process. This requires strengthening the district level planning agency in different districts in Manipur. In the new paradigm of participatory development, district planning can provide a lasting solution to the conflicts among the state-sponsored participatory institutions like the panchayats, NGOs and other government agencies. The presence of such district level planning machinery or agency is necessary for government institution and participation of people in the economic development system in order to develop the productive potential in such important areas of agriculture and rural development including small and village industries which provide a number of basic-needs of life. In these broad-based areas of development, people's initiative is also necessary for decision-making. Participatory development institutions like the panchayats, NGOs etc. can be entrusted to identify and formulate the various development programmes. The District Planning Board should have the planning authority to strengthen democracy in the state. There can be lower level committees also under it to initiate planning from below. Thus it is argued that the decentralised model of planning can be an effective system for promoting a new participatory system of development in Manipur.

Menjor & Silvia's essay "An Approach to Agricultural Development with Sustainability" discusses the issue of sustainability of economic development. They argue that the growth of agricultural productivity in the state has become unsustainable. The essay outlines the measures which will render agricultural development in Manipur sustainable.

The issue of sustainable agricultural development in Manipur should involve strategies such as tackling poverty, development of minor irrigation, mini watershed programmes, extension services, drought management, livestock management, institutional management, marketing, and commercialisation. Their argument is that agricultural development can be made sustainable only when several policy measures are initiated simultaneously to impact on the decision-making matrix of rural areas.

Ibotombi in "Problems and Prospects of Rural Economy of Manipur" examines the rural economic scenario of Manipur in order to suggest ways and means for a healthy rural life. A predominantly rural economy like that of Manipur cannot develop without a vibrant rural sector. The aspects taken up are occupational structure, rural unemployment, agriculture, animal husbandry, horticulture, non-farm rural economic activities and rural administration & development programmes. The major constraints to rural development are inefficient rural administration, shortage of resources and their uneven distribution.

Priyoranjan in "Institutional Impediments to development in the Hill Regions of Manipur" discusses the nature of development in the tribal and hill regions of Manipur and examines some of the institutional hurdles that are holding back many of the development efforts since Independence. The issue is of high importance as lack of development of the tribal areas has been posing a serious threat to the integrity of the state. He highlights the core features of the socioeconomic status of tribal regions of Manipur based on macro level data and shows how population growth, environmental degradation and fund flows are distorting the economic base of the tribal village. He argues that tribal polity, social orders and the property rights regimes are in a state of transition in Manipur. The fractured belief systems of the tribes are not yet in a position to create the conditions of impersonal exchange and efficient economic and political markets. Violence as a means of protecting resources rather than creating resources is likely to continue for quite some time. This prediction should not be ignored by policy makers in dealing with the spiralling violence not only in Manipur but in other backward areas of the country.

Biren & Romen's essay "Agricultural Growth in Manipur State" examines the constraints faced by agriculture sector in Manipur such as lack of irrigation facilities, continuous fragmentation of land and widespread jhum cultivation. Several measures are also suggested for improving agricultural production in Manipur, the most important being the suggestion for identification and scientific use of agricultural land in the hills.

Narendra *et al.* in "Persons with Disabilities in Manipur: A Statistical Analysis" study the incidence of disabilities in Manipur reflecting on the quality of population. The present study was initiated to compare district-wise variation of prevalence rate (PR) of persons with disabilities per 1000 people with respect to sex, residence, literacy status, economic status, type of workers and type of disability. Analysis is based on secondary data of Census 2001 for Manipur. Disability affects directly the ability of the Person to benefit from the process of development. The magnitude of disability varies significantly over the six parameters out of the seven considered. However no rural-urban variation of disability is observed. Since some contradictory findings are found, an in- depth study is suggested to identify the prognostic factors behind the phenomenon.

Kumar's essay "Demographic Transition in Manipur" highlights demographic developments during 1981-2001. How high population growth affects a backward economy is well known. He attributes the declining sex ratio in Manipur to sex ratio at birth supplemented by under-enumeration of female and counting of male population more than once. However the dynamics of sex ratio at birth as a determinant of declining sex ratio needs to be seen in the context of amniocenteses and related interventions. The fertility rate shows the inefficiency of family planning programmes in the state. The fertility data of NFHS are correlated with unemployment rates for both usual status and current weekly status in rural and urban areas. He argues that there is ample scope for reducing the population growth rate further particularly in the valley.

In "Some Aspects of Gender Equity in the Patriarchal Setup in Manipur" Umavati examines the issue of gender equity in Manipur using both primary and secondary data. She argues that contrary to the the situation in other patriarchal societies in India and abroad Manipur presents a totally different scenario. The classification of sex preference shows that equal preference dominates in every age group. Equal preference is dominant even among illiterate respondents. The childhood experiences of the respondents also confirm equal treatment. She concludes that the position of women in Manipur is far better than their counterparts in other parts of India with regard to practices such as female foeticide and female infanticide. The basis of gender equity is very much in existence in the mindset of the people. This aspect should not be ignored while we try to promote opportunities for women in education and employment that would enhance their voice and decision-making role in the family in particular and the wider society in general as well. Policies based on less gender inequity will be more meaningful than policies based on acute gender inequity.

Anand's essay "Fertility and Fertility Preference by Wealth Index in Manipur: Experiences from NFHS-3" analyses the effect of wealth on the current marital fertility and fertility preference of Manipur using data from National Family Health Survey-3 (2005-6). He found a high degree of negative association between income and fertility preference. Poorer families are found to have higher probability of having more children than richer families. Less educated women are more likely to have a higher number of children ever born as compared to women who have attained higher education. These findings corroborate the importance of economic development and education in controlling population growth.

In "Civil Service Reforms in the North Eastern States: With Special Reference to Manipur", Damodar critically examines the various policy measures for improving the quality of public service delivery in the context of Manipur. Though the wage bill has been contained to some extent, the quality of services has not improved due to the absence of any system for rewarding good work and penalising bad work. The only incentive for government employees in far flung rural areas is the chance to indulge in absenteeism. It has emerged as a major block in the delivery of public services throughout the state. As remedial measures he argues for a serious attempt to involve the stakeholders for whom public services are meant and provision of good governance.

Debendra in "Efficiency of Resource Mobilisation in Manipur"examines how efficient Manipur has been in mobilising its resources using ratio of tax and non tax revenues to SDP, cost of collection of taxes, the difference between the budgetary estimates and the actual revenues realised from different own tax and non tax items . It is important because resource mobilisation for development has become a crucial component of any development strategy. On all counts Manipur's resource mobilisation efforts have been found lacking. An interesting aspect of the paper is the description of the pattern of inefficiency also.

In "An Examination of Revenue - Expenditure Linkage: A case study of Manipur" Jaman examines rigorously the long run and short run relationship between public expenditure and revenues using three variables model formulation comprising public expenditure, revenues and NSDP of Manipur. The long run relationship among the variables is examined by using Johansen co-integration test. Multivariate Co-integration (VAR) and Vector Error Correction Model (VECM) are used to establish both short run and long run relationship between public expenditure and revenues. The long term relation observed did not suggest any impact either from expenditure to revenues or from revenues to expenditure. But a short run relation is observed running from NSDP to expenditures and revenues indicating that changes in expenditure policy have no affect on real NSDP growth in the short run. The missing link between expenditure meant for economic growth and the actual economic growth both in the long and short run needs to be examined rigorously to restore credibility to the system.

Jhaljit in "Water Supply in Imphal City: Demand, Supply and Sustainability" takes a holistic view of the issues relating to water supply in Imphal and its sustainability. In the context of Imphal the demand management strategies have limited scope. The real problem is that of inadequate and erratic supply. Any attempt at this stage to restrict or squeeze the demand will amount to compromising on quality of life and health. The two broad ways for enhancement of water availability are strengthening the public water supply system in terms of its coverage, improvement in its performance (adequacy and reliability factors) and making better and more effective utilisation of the other options like roof water harvesting, the ponds, river and canals. Beyond the basic requirement of water for life and health, water can be looked up as an economic good and pricing and allocation done accordingly.

In "Border Trade at Moreh-Tamu Sector: Bane or Boon for Manipur," Bhupendro argues for a holistic vision of border trade in Manipur. Not only goods but also bads are entering the border trade. Border trade has not been able to play its expected leading role in Manipur. Formal trade has not grown as fast as the growth of informal trade due to over-regulation, limited size of trade basket, overvaluation of Myanmares currency in the official exchange rate coupled with the absence of rule of law and proper infrastructure in the state. He argues for the need to incorporate the social cost of the unfolding border trade as part of India's Look East Policy. The HIV/AIDS epidemic in Manipur is closely associated with the illegal border trade which has encouraged cultivation of Opium in Manipur and other neighbouring states. The proliferation of smuggling activities involving small arms along the border has given a lease of life to the endless cycle of violence. The state of law and order has dissuaded many would- be- investors from making any investment in the state. Thus the employment and income generation aspect of border trade will provide at best only a partial picture of the role of border trade in the state economy. Policy makers will be committing a big mistake if the negative aspects continue to be ignored any longer.

Priyokumar's essay "Trade and Industrialization in the Post-Liberalization Period in Manipur" attempts to examine the linkage between the emerging pattern of trade and the industrial development in the state particularly in the post-liberalisation period. The emerging pattern of trade has been lopsided. The volume of imports has far exceeded the volume of exports. From essential items to luxury items the state is dependent on imports. The emerging pattern of trade does not favour the state as far as transfer of knowledge, technology and financial resources are concerned. It discourages industrialisation and the state has become the captive market of outside products. There is a need for rapid industrialisation for getting the state out of the low level equilibrium. If the emerging pattern of trade deindustrialises Manipur, one has to identify the pattern of trade compatible with industrialisation.

Sanatomba in "Inter-sectoral Linkages and Implications on Growth – The Manipur Experience" discusses the intersectoral linkages in Manipur and the contributions of these sectors to growth during 1994-2005. He argues that decreasing share of trade in the state economy and non significant association with industry will deprive the state of the opportunities provided by India's Look East Policy. Manipur has become more of a transit point. The opportunities provided by the opening up of South east Asian markets should be capitalised upon to establish medium and large industries which have so far failed to take off , inter alia, due to the small size of market.

Komol in "New-Wave of Globalization and Hill Village Economy in Manipur: An Observation" examines globalization as a process by which the whole world becomes a single unit. It originates with the market and religion. In the recent past, the driver of globalization has changed from market to electronic communications. The villages are now exposed to the new wave of globalization which can reach the remotest corner of the world, which the earlier form of globalization could not reach. This paper highlights the impact of globalization in the tribal villages. How the new wave of globalization enters into the tribal hinterland and its consequences in the primitive society are discussed. The important role of Christian Missionaries in the tribal villages is also discussed.

Isworchandra in "Understanding Economic Liberalization in Manipur" provides a synoptic view of economic liberalisation and structural reform programmes. Comparing pre-liberalisation economy of Manipur with the post-liberalisation economy, it is argued that liberalisation has brought growing casualisation and informalisation of labour force. It subserves the interest of the advanced capitalism of the core economy of the mainland and is biased against the underdeveloped peripheral economies. Huge inflow of cheap products from mainland India and southeast Asia in the post liberalisation era virtually led to the closure of many manufacturing units in the state. Peripheral state economies like that of Manipur have been serving as a captive market for capitalist class based in more advanced states. The negative aspects of border trade too need to be understood dispassionately.

Together these essays will hopefully enhance the quality of discussion and debate on various aspects of the economy. That perhaps has been the objective function of the contributors. Policy makers will also have something to develop further to give a realistic touch to economic policies. Future economic policies will be based on better understanding of the reality. During the preparation of this work Dr. Thokchom Biren Singh expired and in his death we have lost an enthusiastic scholar ever ready to help in any endeavour. The editing of his paper had to be done with the help of the co-author L. Romen Singh, co-opted by the editors.

We wish Dr. Nabakishore a long and healthy life to serve as a role model for younger generation of teachers. The importance of such a role model is more clear at a time when education at all levels is passing through a period of flux.

We would be failing in our duty if we do not put on record the encouragement and patience of Mr. M.P. Misra of Akansha Publishing House who has done yeoman's service in bringing works on the North East to international readers. May he be blessed with many more active years of life!

E. Bijoykumar Singh
Damodar Nepram

Acknowledgements

This volume in honour of Prof. H. Nabakishore Singh is a product of the inspirations that he had instilled in many, besides those who were his admiring students, colleagues, well wishers and those who take keen interest in the field of development issues. Many had prodded, in fact insisted upon us, to bring out this book and we sincerely acknowledge them all for motivating us.

We are grateful to the Department of Economics, Manipur University and specially Prof. L. Tombi Singh, Head of the Department of Economics, Manipur University for actively encouraging us throughout the endeavour. The tedious work of going through the papers, revisions and reformulations were made much more fruitful with valuable inputs from L. Krishnamangol, H. Isworchandra and L. Sanatomba. We are also thankful to N. Nungshitombi for her patient assistance in typing the manuscripts. We are also grateful to M.P. Misra of Akansha Publishing House, New Delhi who has taken keen interest in seeing the book published. Lastly, we hope that this volume inspires many more and further what Prof. H. Nabakishore Singh stands for.

Editors

Our Contributors

Dr. L. Krishnamangol Singh is a Selection Grade Lecturer in Economics and Member, Core Committee, Imphal College, Imphal, Manipur. He was also formerly Secretary, Family Planning Association of India, Manipur Branch. His area of specialization is Development Economics and International Trade.

Dr. Kh. Menjor Singh is Joint Director, Department of Higher Education, Government of Manipur. He was initially working as a Reader in the Department of Economics, C.I. College, Manipur. He has published a number of books on issues ranging from WTO to Co-operative movement in Manipur.

Dr. Ng. Ibotombi Singh is a Reader in Economics and Member, Core Committee, Imphal College, Imphal, Manipur. He specializes in Rural Development and Labour Economics.

Dr. Ch. Priyoranjan Singh is an Associate Professor in the Department of Economics, Manipur University. He specializes in Agricultural Economics.

Prof. R.K. Narendra Singh is Professor and Head, Unit of Biostatistics, Regional Institute of Medical Sciences (RIMS), Manipur.

Dr. W. Kumar Singh is a Reader in Economics, Y.K. College, Wangjing, Manipur. He specializes in Demography and Public Finance.

Dr. Th. Umavati Devi is a Selection Grade Lecturer in the Department of Sociology, G. P. Women's College, Manipur. She specializes in gender issues.

Dr. Ksh. Jhaljit Singh is an Associate Professor in the Department of Economics, Manipur University. His area of specialization is Environmental Economics.

Dr. Damodar Nepram is a Senior Lecturer in the Department of Economics, Churachandpur College, Manipur. He specializes in Public Finance and Labour Economics.

Dr. Thokchom Biren Singh is a Senior Lecturer, G. P. Women's College, Manipur. He is working in Agricultural Economics.

Dr. L. Debendra Singh teaches Public Finance and Econometrics at Thoubal College, Manipur. He had worked on the financial aspects of Manipur for his Doctoral degree. He is actively involved in research activities and has attended many seminars and conferences.

Dr. N. Sharat Singh is a Lecturer in Thoubal College, Manipur. He specializes in Demography and has published many articles in both national and international journals.

W. Jibol Singh is Senior Lecturer and Head, Department of Statistics, Biramangol College, Manipur.

Dr. N. Bhupendro Singh is a Lecturer in the Department of Economics, NIT Silchar, Assam. His area of interests are Econometrics, Agricultural Economics, Trade and Development.

Dr. Ksh. Anand Singh is an Assistant Professor in the Department of Statistics, Manipur University. His area of specialization is Demography.

Dr. Th. Priyokumar Singh is a Lecturer in the Department of Economics, D.M. College of Commerce, Manipur. He specializes in Trade and Development.

Dr. Samsur Jaman is a Lecturer in the Department of Economics, Jiri College, Manipur. He specializes in Public Finance and Econometrics.

Dr. L. Sanatomba Meetei is a Lecturer in D. M. College of Commerce, Manipur. He specializes in Industrial Economics, Trade and Development.

Komol Singha is a Senior Lecturer in Economics, Royal University of Bhutan, Gaeddu College of Business Studies, Gedu, Bhutan. He was initially working at St. Joseph's College, Kohima.

H. Isworchandra Sharma is a Research Scholar in the Dept. of Economics, Manipur University where he is working on Rural Non-farm sectors of Manipur.

Silvia Lisam is a Lecturer in the Department of Economics, D. M. College of Commerce, Imphal. She specializes in Agricultural Economics and is currently doing research in agricultural labour in Manipur. She did her post graduation from the Department of Economics, Panjab University, Chandigarh.

L. Romen Singh is a Research Scholar in the Dept. of Economics, Manipur University. He is currently doing research in the topic 'The role of silk industry in the economy of Manipur'.

Ch. Memchanu is a Research Scholar in the Department of Statistics, Manipur University.

1

Patterns of Participatory Development in Manipur:

A New Strategy

L. Krishnamangol Singh

Introduction

It is observed that people's participation exists in various forms in different parts of the country (India) including Manipur. It is also well known that the voluntary actions for community development were initiated either by individuals or by groups or by institutions in different parts of the country even prior to Independence. Till today, voluntary endeavours as participatory institutions have crucial role to play in various fields of development in a country or state where the progress of rural transformation is still embryonic due to a variety of reasons. Interestingly, the concept of "participatory development" has gained much popularity in recent years. Initially, the central approach to participatory development was based on the concept of self-reliance. Thus, the mobilisation of the community resources and efforts of the rural poor were the main factors for promoting the process of participatory development. The concept was also used in the context of the collective action for the use of common property resources (CPRs) like land, water, forests, etc. in different parts of the Less Development Countries (LDCs). The institutions of people's participation are found in various forms such as the conventional form of panchayati raj institutions, village level, organisations, non-governmental organisations and other people's institutions. These institutions play different roles in various fields of development in less developed regions or states like Manipur. Thus, the main purpose of the present paper is to examine the participatory development system and set out appropriate strategies for promoting the process of participatory development in Manipur.

Participatory Development: Genesis and Reality

The central idea of participatory development can be traced back to the community organisation and collective action among the rural poor. In the past, our planners recognised the rural poor as the main focus of rural development. The strategy was the need for involvement of the rural poor in decision–making and implementation for the rural development programmes. The participation of the rural poor in rural development programmes and mobilisation of the local resources by the community organisations came to be known as participatory development in most of the Third World Countries or Less Developed countries in the late 1970s. According to a study (Obaildullah Khan,1980:57), participatory development drew attention to the concept of "self- reliance" at the individual, community and national levels. In his view, the concept of "self-reliance" does not imply autarky and it requires interactions among the actors at the three levels (i.e. individual, community and national levels) so that the outcome of the participatory development process is "interdependence rather than dependence of one on the other". In some other studies, the term "collective action" or "group action" was used to mean participatory development. However, the term "participatory development" was not explicitly mentioned in the theory of collective action. In recent years, the term "participatory development" has been popularised in many circles. In their study on Participatory Development: People and Common Property Resources, Chopra *et al.,* (1990) examined the process of participatory rural development in Sukhmoi village in U.P. (India). The study explored the significance of collective action or group action in the management of common property resources (CPR) for rural development and suggested the concept of participatory development as an alternative institutional mechanism for people's participation or community participation in decision making process for rural development. Thus, in examining the relevant literature on participatory development, it is found that the "concept" has been evolved from the theory of collective action and cooperation rather than the individual action. Therefore, it would be quite essential to touch briefly on the theory of collective action in order to understand the real meaning of participatory development. The theory suggests that individual action cannot yield the common goal. It would be appropriate here to note that the collective action is action by more than one person intended to achieve a common goal or satisfy a common interest i.e. a goal or interest that cannot be obtained by an individual (Wade, 1987). But there are many writers who argued that the theory of collective action could not work without an external agent (or authority usually the state to enforce the rules of the common) Hardin (1968) drew attention to the "tragedy of commons" and suggested that it is essential to give an external agency usually the state to regulate the common interest. The presence of the State authority or regulation will also check the "free riding tendency" which may destroy the common interest. In his "Logic of Collective Action", Olson (1965) came to the conclusion that "unless there is coercion or some other special device to make individuals act in their common interest, self- interested individuals will not act to achieve their common or group interests". Thus, there is the need for enforcement of set of rules to achieve the common goal. But, it is observed that there are success stories in the development efforts carried out in the Indian villages without the support of the government or outside agencies (Wade, 1987). Thus, the genesis of the concept of "participatory development" lies in the various strands of thought on the theory of collective action or group action. We may now briefly examine the basic philosophy behind the evolution of the concept of participatory development. The history of the human society is the history of participation in various socio-economic systems. Marxists believe in the evolution of the stages of development leading to the emergence of socialism in which the state would play a leading role in the socio-economic development of the system. In the early stage of development, there was the model of community participation or collective participation called the "commune" which broke down due to the lack of institutions or authority to govern the system. It is also well known that there is the individual nature of participation in economic activities, which is central to the human culture and civilisation. This form is very common, which exists side by side with the cooperative structures or group endeavour. There is still the social institution of group action or community participation in the management of resources like land, forests, water, etc. in tribal communities including the hill areas of Manipur. Thus, it is difficult to evolve a general theory of participation in the development process. On the other hand, there has been a lot of development literature dealing with the process of modern economic development. Thus the development policies framed so far in most of the LDCs including India have bypassed a large section of the society both in the rural and urban areas. And, the various rural development programmes are now being questioned as they have bypassed "people" at the grass-roots level. As already noted, Chopra *et al.* (1990) provides a clear idea of the evolution of the concept of "participatory development". The study reveals the shortcoming of the planning process and emphasised the community approach to development rather than the individual one. The community approach is focused on the village community. According to their study, participatory process is a new social-economic force for sustained development at the village level. The study further reveals various forms of people's participation in development or institutions of participatory development. Thus, participatory development has been redefined to mean the process of participation or integration of people with decision making institutions. Today, such a process of development is known as participatory development. The foregoing discussions suggest the following essential points: (i) People's participation exists in Indian society in various forms, (ii) Initially, the participatory development implies the existence of the participation of the people in villages or community development without the help of government, and (iii) Also, the participatory development institutions exist with the support of the government. The concept was developed as an alternative to market or as an institution of the people in development. The decision making for development was at the level of people. But it is difficult to achieve the highest stage of participation or reach the mature stage of participation due to the lack of appropriate institutional support of government. In certain cases of community management of resources, there is also the authoritarian nature of participatory development which is historically governed by costumes and traditions. This is found in the hill areas of Manipur, where the Tribal Chief directs the rules of participation. Again, many schemes of participatory development in the field of agriculture and rural development, health, education etc. are carried out or implemented without proper rules. And, the traditional rules followed by the people are conflicting in the absences of legal support, resulting in the short period of the participatory system of development. Thus, many of the non-governmental organisations which were quite successful for sometime slowed down in the long run. As already noted, the authoritarian regime still exists in the name of community participation in development. Another problem is that if all "development institutions" are participatory, there will be no role of the government. Again, the nature of participation of the people in the "private sector" is different from the participation of the "public sector". That is to say, public sector is different from the "private sector" which was clearly defined in the initial stage of the formulation of economic policy of the country. It is argued that in the private sector, there is the element of exploitation and reward of individuals. In this system, the concept of "producer" or "labour" is used. Again, the Indian system of "public sector" is not related to the concept of participatory development. It is well known that public enterprises are run by the government and their objectives are for the common good. Thus, the concept of "participatory development" relates to the people's sector in various forms of community organisations, village organisations, non-governmental organisations etc. Today, the concept calls for the reorganisation and support of the government to create conditions for people's participation in development. It is here that the concept of participatory planning or participatory development planning is used. Therefore, those who are excluded from development should be given opportunities for participation in development process. In this context, the Indian planning process is now participatory because it seeks to achieve the objective of inclusive growth and development, which is almost parallel with the concept of participatory development. Therefore, in participatory development, there is the need for recognition of the government for any type of participatory institution. But, the nature of participation should be in the form of group, community, class, institutions etc. Thus, "participatory development" is an alternative strategy of development. In this concept, the initiative of development rests on the people. Today, the nature of participation has assumed different dimensions. While there is the participation of the individuals in the private sector for their livelihood and profit motive, there has also emerged a new paradigm of development in which private individuals participate in development programmes sponsored by the government. This model is generally known as Public Private Participation or PPP model. This system is at the highest stage of participation and may not be relevant for the purposes of participatory development at the people's sector. Again, this type of participation relates to the highly organised sector in which the government collaborates the development programmes with the capitalists or MNCs. But, the PPP model alone cannot grapple with the broad-based issues of development. Therefore, the participatory development model needs to become "people - centred" approach to development. This suggests that the decision-making and implementation of the programmes /schemes of development should be entrusted to the people with the support of the government. In this new model, the government needs to play an active role in initiating conditions for involvement of general mass of the population in the participatory development process.

New Participatory Development: Critical Issues

We may now briefly consider the changes in thinking on the concept of participatory development in respect of the villagers or communities or group action/form. The participation, therefore, related to the participation of the poor people in communities. Today, participation may be at different levels. While participation at the individual level is an old form or conventional form, participatory development has assumed as an institutional model of development. In the new concept of participatory development, the process of participation may exist at different levels and in different forms such as the village society/community organizations, panchayats, non-governmental organisations, cooperative institutions etc. Thus, the structure of participatory development consists of various compositions encompassing various forms of institutions and organisations. Thus, participatory development will start from the grass-roots level in the process of development and it is at the "bottom of the pyramid". At the top, the state seems to be far away from the people. But, the state assumes different role to create conditions for participation of the people in the development process. Thus, in this new concept, the participation of individuals may be viewed in the form of institutions, groups, class, etc. And, it is at the people's sector level. But the participatory development cannot be a homogenous concept as it compromises various forms of organisations and institutions. Again, in the participatory system, the people can take their own decisions for development. This does not mean that the people should be away from the government. In this new participatory system of development, the state needs to recognise all the participatory institutions and extend necessary support for promoting the participatory model of development. We may now consider the conditions or requirements for a new system of participatory development. In this new system, the participatory development is basically concerned with the participation of the poor in the development process. In the development programmes of the country, there is also the emphasis on the participation and empowerment of the poor people. But it is difficult to expect participation of the poor and the unemployed youths in the development process without institutional and infrastructural support of the government. Therefore, it is necessary to strengthen the bottom of the "pyramid" i.e. the people at the grass - roots level. This calls for launching large scale programmes for providing appropriate training for the general mass of the poor and the educated unemployed youths in other to enable them to participate in the development process at the people's sector. In this new process of the development, there is also the need for involving participatory institutions in an organised form. The people should have decision - making power in various fields of development with necessary support of government. Appropriate rules and regulations need to be enforced by the government in order to promote new participatory development institutions in less developed states like Manipur. However, it may be noted that the collective action cannot replace the whole system of unorganised participation of the private individuals in the private sector. The new paradigm shift in development suggests that there is still the need for institutionalising participatory model of development in which people are expected to participate in various fields of development. The poor need to be given opportunities to participate in the process of institutional changes. And this system can continue to exist with all other forms of participation in various socio - economic activities. The participation of the individuals and participatory development in the form of institutions can simultaneously co-exist both in the rural and urban areas. But the ultimate objectives of development are the same i.e. provision of basic needs of life, eradication of poverty and unemployment, reduction in economic inequality etc. along with the higher rate of economic growth. The poor and the unemployed cannot participate in any form unless they are given the opportunities for participation. In the new form of participatory development model, the general mass of the poor need to be encouraged to act as partners of development rather than being "the target groups" or passive recipients of the benefits of growth and development. However, the government needs to play active role in creating conducive atmosphere for evolving a participatory regime of development in states like Manipur. While the several ongoing programmes of rural development and urban poor, which are equally necessary call for through examination to plug the loopholes of the various programmes, there is also the need for placing greater emphasis on participation and empowerment of the poor in various programmes of development relating to health, literacy and education, environment, etc. in the development process. In fact, there is the view that it is only when the government launches massive programmes for eradication of poverty and unemployment and general economic development, people will find opportunities for participation in development both at the individual and the institutional or organisational level. In this participatory system, there should be conditions for empowerment of the poor to enable them to participate in an organised from. As already noted, it is difficult to evolve a general theory of participatory development. Some have argued that people should refuse the vested interest of the bureaucrats and professionals. This theory of people's participation refuses to accept the authority. This strand of thinking believes in the logic of "control from below" and "people should control their own" (Streeten: 2004). But the poor can organise themselves for participation in development and educate themselves to support or co-operate the projects that meet the felt needs of the people. In the new participatory model of development, there should not be missing links between the people and the government in formulating and implementing the various development projects or schemes like irrigation projects, power projects etc. The state-led participatory system of development needs to create a congenial atmosphere for initiating and accelerating the process of development in which the people need to cooperate. It is, therefore, necessary to identify the areas or fields where people can participate in the development process. The basic requirements for participatory development are to strengthen the democratic institutions to promote a system of interdependence and manage the whole programmes of development at different levels. In participatory development, it is necessary to fulfil the following two conditions. First, it is necessary to follow the path to "people-centre development programmes" for eradication of poverty. Secondly, it is also necessary to evolve or set up participatory form of organizations or institutions in which people should be empowered to take decision for their own development and also for overall development of the community. The participatory model of development can also be initiated as decentralisation in planning. Therefore, in participatory system, there is also the question of devolution or sharing of power. For example, Panchayati Raj Institution is considered to be a participatory institution in which there is large scope for people's participation in rural and community development programmes. But there is still vested interest in the devolution of power. Coming to the case of Manipur, the State cannot make much headway in this model of decentralisation. Therefore, poverty and rural development still continue to be a major challenge in the whole programme of development in the State. While the devolution of power to the PRIs is constitutional, there is also the need for reorganising the planning process in Manipur with a full-fledged district level planning agency to ensure people's participation in development of the State. But an effective participatory system also calls for mobilising the people for the formation of various participatory forms of organisation for the benefits of the participants and also for the development of the community as a whole. Thus, participatory development institutions are heterogeneous in the nature of the institutions. However, participatory development model should be productive to all the members. And the participatory institutions also require necessary support of the government. For example, finance for participatory institutions like the NGOs, PRIs, etc. depends on the State and Central government. Thus, participatory development is the combination of State-action and collective action or people's action in the process of development. In participatory development, democratic control is necessary to intervene the control of the organisations or institutions by the local elites/ community elites. The elitist institutions should be checked by the government. In this model of development, there may be internal contradictions in the implementation of the various programmes of development. Therefore, there is the need for enforcing suitable rules and regulations to promote the participatory development organisations. In spite of the limitations of this model, participation in development is more beneficial than the non-participation if suitable rules are properly enforced by the government. The problem is that the non-participation in development implies more freedom for the people and their voice for development may be very high, which may affect the whole development process. There are ample evidences which reveal that the participation of the people in development absorb the whole tensions in the society. But the participation should be democratic and non-exploitative. The stages of political economy of development in different countries reveal that the system of exploitation leads to the emergence of non - exploitative system in which there is ample scope for people's participation in development. As already noted, this process is found in the Marxian analysis of the various stages of development. Also, in market economy, there is ample scope for participation of the people in development. That is to say, "market" which opens more freedom to the people provides ample scope for organising different labour classes. Even in market economy, there are vast areas like education, health, pollution control, protection of environment, irrigation, construction of village roads bridges, flood control and other income generating activities where collective action is necessary for participatory development. This strategy may be followed in the case of poverty alleviation and rural development programmes in Manipur. In advanced countries like European Union, collective action or group action is formed to protect the worker's rights and there is even legal support to it. The institution of participatory system of development is even more relevant to LDCs. This is also true in small developing economies like Manipur, where there are vast potential resources like land, water, forests etc. Social network or relationship within communities should be widened to facilitate participatory development. But, the government intervention is also necessary to provide power of participation or capacity building for the poor. The willingness for participation should also be created. And the cost of participation should be lower than the returns from participation. In the present context of Manipur, dual role of participation of the people can be introduced for facilitating the process of participatory development. At the times of natural calamities like floods, droughts, etc., collective action is necessary because the efforts of collective action can generate public goods which can be enjoyed by all whether they have participated or not. As Paul Streeten (2004:4). has clearly pointed out that "at least people often like public and participatory action, if they can muster time". Thus, public action or state action is necessary to facilitate collective action at different times and in different fields. Another role of the actors/participative members is that they should be given opportunities for participation in the income generating activities in the process of participatory development. This requires identification and formulating viable schemes/projects. These schemes or project may be in the primary sector, secondary sector and even in tertiary sector or services sector. In this model, the state action is also necessary for institutionalising the process of participatory development. Those who are outside the participatory system of development should also be given gainful employment opportunities for participation in any productive economic activity. Thus, participation is now redefined at different levels (collective action or group action and the individual action). These two types of participation can co-exist and they are mutually reinforcing or supporting in the development process. For instance, members of the reputed NGOs are from the community. In this way, there is the scope for involvement of the individuals in the participatory institutions. And the participatory institutions can be engaged in different fields of development. It is observed that there are many self-help projects in different parts of the world. Thus, in participatory development, people are the architects of their own development. But the "felt needs" of the individuals should not be the "wrong needs". And the social needs or the preferences should be created in formulating the strategy for strong government -community cooperation. Today, the presence of the government should be the sine-qua-non of the whole structure of participatory development. Again, there may arise undesirable social elements/practices in the participatory development system. Some people may be engaged in undesirable activities or malpractices in their activities for earning. Thus, there should be certain limit or strict control over the rights of the individuals involved in the participatory organisations. Several studies have also revealed that the problem of free-riders should be checked in the process of collective action which creates public goods. Today, the matrix of participatory development is very complex. It is necessary to identify the nature of participation. There may be a number of activities or policy decisions which may not be left to the participatory organisations. For example, the policy instruments of the government and macroeconomics decisions exclusively reserved for the government cannot be left to the participatory or organisations. Participatory system should be socially and culturally acceptable. Thus, the paradigm shift in participatory development is to encourage the participants in favour of democracy. But we cannot have a wholesale/total "participatory democracy" in which there will be no role of the government. This means to say that in the name of decentralisation, everything cannot be left to the people or the non-state institutions (i.e. institutions which are not under the government) and other participatory organisations. Public action or state action is necessary for promoting the process of participatory development. The activities of the participatory development organisations or institutions should be bottom-up movement from the grass-roots level, which needs to be complemented/supported by the public action or the government action of top-down approach. However, it is difficult to give standard prescription for participatory development which may vary from stage to stage. As the economy progresses, higher from of participatory development will be required. While there is limit to the rights of the people, the highly authoritarian regime/control should also be avoided. There are now a large number of documentations which reject the policy of centralisers or centralised state/nation. Real decentralisation means devolution of power to the people. The only precondition in this model is that all the participatory, autonomous and other non-state institutions require support from a strong government in the institutional framework of control from above or top-down control. Again there are instances of many strong private organisations which undermine the power of the state. Ultimately, these organisations were dissolved. As Streeten (2004:12) has rightly concluded, "It is a healthy balance between markets, governments and civil society and between national and global institutions that is needed". In the case of Manipur also, there is the need for strong government support for promoting participatory development with a view to providing opportunities of participation of the people in the whole development process. In the light of the above theoretical and empirical background of the participatory process of development, we shall now make an attempt to chart out a new strategy for promoting the process of participatory development in Manipur.

New Strategy for Participatory Development in Manipur: A Paradigm Shift

Collective Actions as Participatory Institutions

We may begin with the significance of collective action in

promoting participatory development in Manipur. From the foregoing discussions, it is clear that participatory development relates to people's participation in development in various forms. The nature of people's participation in development may be in the form of collective action or group action. It may also be in the process of decentralisation in planning at the grass-roots level. Collective actions are necessary for poverty alleviation and community development. There are limitations of the individuals who cannot address the problem of poverty without the support of the internal and external development agencies. But in the land based economy of the rural and hill areas of Manipur, there are vast common resources which can be pooled and mobilised by the villagers for the eradication of poverty and accelerating the process of development. The attempt for collective action cannot be effective due to lack of skills, finance, leadership, management etc. Thus, the lack of capacity building is a serious set back in promoting participatory development in Manipur. In such a situation, the government needs to extend necessary institutional and financial support to the people who can mobilise themselves for collective action or group action. Therefore, all forms of participatory development institutions like the village level organisations, NGOs, cooperative, panchayats, local bodies and other participatory institutions should be encouraged and strengthened in initiating and implementing the various programmes of development in Manipur. It may be noted that there are success stories in many parts of the country for participatory development without the support of the government. In spite of these experiences, panchayats can play a crucial role in promoting the participatory process of development in the State.

PRIs : Role and Defects

We may now examine the special role of PRIs in promoting participatory developments system. It is well known that PRIs provide for direct participation of the people in decision-making process. Thus, the merits of the PRIs need no elaboration here. However, the devolution of power to the panchayats is still trady in Manipur. Therefore, people cannot really participate in decision - making and decentralised planning process in the State. It is high time that there should be active involvement of the people in rural development programmes through strengthening the PRIs in Manipur. But, people's participation through PRIs may not be effective in the rural areas of Manipur, where a large number of people are caught in the "various circle of poverty". Therefore, there is the need for empowerment of the rural poor in other to provide them opportunities to participate in decision-making process for rural development. Here, people's participation may be interpreted in two aspects.

(i) First, people may participate in the election process for decentralised development or the local area development.

(ii) Secondly, there is the need for initiatives and involvement of the people in the development projects. This approach to participatory development cannot be left to the people themselves. Therefore, there is the need for empowerment of the rural poor in other to provide them opportunities to participate in decision-making process for rural development. This process also requires empowering the people to identify their own problems in the communities and grapple with them. Thus, people's participation in such a decentralised model of development can combine to fulfil the features of both bottom-up and top-down approach to development in Manipur. This approach clearly suggests that the State-led model of participatory development, which opens vast opportunities for people's participation in development needs to be strengthened in Manipur. However, there is the need for proper coordination between PRIs and planning agency at the district level. To resolve the conflict in the administrative structure and planning process, there is the need for decentralisation of planning process at the appropriate levels (i.e. block and district level) with a full-fledged state Planning Commission at the top level to supervise the planning exercises at all levels.

(iii) There should be proper coordination between the State Planning Commission and the present State Planning

Department. At the district level, there is the need for strengthening the District Planning Machinery to coordinate and evaluate all rural development programmes in the State.

Linkage between the Government and NGOs

The current thinking on participatory development suggests that the rural poor should not be excluded from the implementation of a large number of rural development programmes. Thus, the non-governmental organisations can play a vital role in promoting participatory development programmes in Manipur. There should be proper linkages between the NGOs and the government with a view to promoting an efficient system of participatory development in the State. In Manipur, we find that there are many NGOs working in various fields such as health, education, environments etc. It is observed that these NGOs continue to face a lot of problems such as lack of adequate finance, managerial skills and other trained and skilled manpower, lack of knowledge for project planning etc. Lack of proper rules and regulations also pose a serious problem of the organisations. There are also internal contradictions in the sharing of power in the management system. There are a large number of unqualified staffs and their salaries are quite irregular and low. Those in the management work on honorary capacity. This has created disincentives in the organisation. There are also evidences of the failures of the NGOs when the funding agencies have withdrawn funds from these NGOs. Thus, there are many non-viable NGOs in Manipur. The compositions of the participatory organisations are varied in the state. In recent years, there has been emergence of SHGs in Manipur as an outcome of national policy. They get the facilities of micro-finance from the banks through NABARD. These development NGOs are engaged in micro enterprises for the production of varieties of goods including the silk shari and other items for women, agro-based and forest-based products. There are also farmers' associations working at the grass- roots level. But these organisations are not alternative to other NGOs. On the other hand, they are the state-led smaller participatory institutions for poverty eradication and generation of income among the poor women living in the rural and urban areas of the State. They work both in the rural and urban areas and also in the hill districts. In spite of the vast potential for people's participation in these self-development groups, the institutional bases of these smaller participatory institutions are generally weak. The reality is that they are the organizations of some households for the formation of SHGs among the women. To avoid wastage of resources (bank loans), there is the need for constant supervision and monitoring of activities done by these SHGs. Also, they should be reorganised and strengthened as participatory development institutions. It is interesting to note that DICs are now assigned the tasks for strengthening the SHGs in different districts in Manipur. To keep proper coordination among the NGOs, panchayats and other State development agencies, there is the need for reorganising the planning system in Manipur by setting up full fledged District Planning Agencies in all the districts in the State.

Community Participation

From the above discussions, it is clear that in promoting participatory development, community participation in development is absolutely necessary. As already noted, in a land-based economy like Manipur, there are a large number of potential natural resources like land, water, forests etc. owned by the community in the form of common property resources (CPRs). A special feature of these resources is that the ownership rights of these resources are not given to the individuals. Some CPRs cannot be privatised as they belong to the state while other resources like land, forests, etc. in the hill areas of Manipur are managed by the community. This indicates that there is vast scope for people's participation in the management of CPRs in Manipur. There are still virtues of co-operation in the management and utilisation of CPRs for the common good. Our model is that the people should be empowered to take their own decisions in the process of participatory development in order to generate income in various productive activities/sectors. Here, the concept of co-operation relates to various forms of group action or collective action. Participatory institutions like the PRIs, NGOs and cooperative institutions and other community-based institutions/organisations need to be strengthened. What is necessary at the present stage of development is that in such participatory approach to development, there is the need for support of the State in terms of necessary infrastructures, technical and managerial training, finances etc. In the hill areas, the authoritarian regime in the management of community resources in the tribal communities should be reformed by introducing new land reform programmes. In the present context of national economic liberalisation and reform programmes, it is highly necessary to initiate various State-level reforms or measures in other to promote participatory institutions for development in Manipur. Therefore, it is highly essential that the ownership of land should be given to the people in the hill areas of Manipur in other to give them incentive for participation in development. Therefore, participatory development calls for reforms in legal, social, economic and planning system in order to accelerate the development process of Manipur. This underlines the significance of the institutional and administrative reforms with a view to facilitating decentralised planning system in the State. Decentralisation of planning process will help in promoting participatory development institutions and eradicate poverty in all the districts in Manipur. It is interesting to note that there is strong opinion for the preference of land ownership in a typical hill district (i.e. Churachandpur district) in Manipur. Thus, decentralisation of planning process will go a long way in bringing about changes in the social and institutional rigidity in the development process of Manipur. This will also open vast opportunities for people's participation in the State. Voluntary organisations can participate in development as an institutional mechanism of participatory development only when the planning process is decentralised at the district and block village level. Therefore, the strategy for participatory development planning should be within the framework of policy-mix of bottom-up and top-down approaches with a view to providing vast opportunities for people's participation in development. Participatory organisations can be emerged and developed at the grass-roots level, community level only when the government plays a leading role in the development process.

Decentralisation in Planning: Critical Issue

In Manipur, there is the need for decentralisation in the planning process in other to promote participatory development planning process at the grass-roots level. It is well known that national planning is highly centralised and situation at the state level is still worse. At the state level, planning is highly official and the implementing agencies in Manipur are also very weak. Again, people's participation in the decision-making of the planning process is only in name as panchayats are not yet full empowered. There is also no effective decision for incorporating research findings and views of the experts in the plan documents before sending them to the Planning Commission (New Delhi). Since planning in the state is within the federal structure, many important decisions are taken at the Centre as a national policy for the benefits of the public or general mass of the population. Even today, the state plan is prepared as the annual state budget. The preparation of plan is just like compilation of various information from different departments and putting them together in the form of Draft Plan. There is no debate of the annual state plan in the Legislature/Assembly. In Manipur, there is a long tradition for discussion of the annual state budgets after the plan size of Manipur is fixed/finalised by the Planning Commission. But the State plan documents have not yet been discussed on the floor of assembly of Manipur. Thus, the objectives, strategies, priorities, vision and overall contents of the Plan are not fully debated. Consequently, the problems of poverty, unemployment, inter-district disparity in the level of development and other development issues still continue to exist in Manipur. There are faulty projects/schemes in terms of location, design, size, quality etc. For instance, Tipaimukh Dam Project is still controversial. To avoid the people - government conflict, large dams should be avoided for sustainable development in Manipur. There is no strong monitoring and evaluation system in the planning process in Manipur. Thus, large plan funds are refunded due to the non- completion of a number of projects and schemes. Non-utilisation of plan funds is the weakness of the implementing agencies under the State government. Ultimately, the State government is responsible for such a state of affair. Under such circumstances, it is difficult to promote participatory development system in Manipur. The concept like participatory development cannot be translated into action within the present administrative and planning process or system in Manipur. As already note, there should not be further delay in the real devolution of power to the panchayats. It is interesting to note that under the Manipur Panchayat Raj (MPR) Act 1994, the District Planning Committees have been constituted for the valley districts to consolidate the plan prepared by the Zilla Parishads, Gram Panchayats, Municipal Councils etc. It may be noted that when the DPCs fail to perform their duties, there will be the failure of the whole system of decentralised planning in Manipur. In fact, there is still weak decentralised planning system in Manipur. The Eleventh Five Year Plan (2007-12) of the country seeks to achieve the objective of decentralisation in planning. It is generally accepted that the strategy of decentralisation will provide opportunities for people's participation in development. It is also generally accepted that the strategies of planning from the First Plan up to the Tenth Plan failed to eliminate poverty and unemployment completely. There are, of course, many socio- economic forces (population pressure, market economy, technological changes, etc.) which tend to create the conditions for the widespread problem of poverty and unemployment, income inequality and other development issues. The Eleventh Plan (2007-12) recognised the sectorial shift in the focus of priorities towards "social sectors". These sectors need caring of the government. It is interesting to note that the Central government now places special role to the Panchayati Raj Institutions and the Urban Local Government in order to fulfil the objectives of planning. There is, therefore, the need for devolution of power to go further down Panchayati Raj Institutions to carry out the various programmes of rural development including health, education, employment generation, rural housing, rural drinking water, watershed management etc. In all these fields of development, there is immense scope for active involvement of the local community in the rural development programmes. It is interesting to note that the gram panchayat is instructed to select the project under the NREGS. Likewise, there are also a host of other rural development programmes which are under the panchayat system/ PRIs. There are also proposals for a wide range of reforms for urban and rural development through municipality or urban local government and panchayat. The strategy in the Eleventh Plan is the application of the logic of emphasising "bottom-up planning". To ensure decentralised planning at the national level, states are constitutionally required to set up District Planning Committees (DPCs). All the village level plans and municipal plans will be consolidated by the DPC into a district level plan which take account of the availability of funds for devolution of State Plan resources (at least 30% of plan resources) and the earmarked funds flowing from various central schemes (Planning Commission, 2006:92). In the present structure of decentralised planning, there will be different layer in the decentralisation process (i.e. three tier structure in the urban areas comprising Municipality, the ward committee and the Area Sabha and the different levels of PRIs). In fact, rural decentralised planning is essential for mobilisation of community participation or people's participation in development. While the structure of decentralised planning seems to be the quite sound, it is difficult to implement most of the rural and urban development programmes in Manipur due to the delay or less action in devolving funds to the municipality and Panchayats. Besides, the DPCs which are expected to play a crucial role in decentralised planning are not functioning effectively due to the lack of commitment in planning. There is also the need for evolving a mechanism for supervising the activities of the DPCs as the Planning Commission (2006:93) has clearly stated: "It is critical to note that effective functioning of DPCs cannot occur unless both rural and urban planning processes are well-defined". Thus, there is the need for integration of rural and urban planning in Manipur. In the present model of planning, this objective cannot be easily realised due to the weak structure of planning process in the State. As already noted, to strengthen the planning process a full-fledged State Planning Commission should be established as an apex organisation with competent experts in various fields of planning and development. The Commission should also be provided with qualified staff for improving the overall efficiency of planning process. The present Planning Department should be complementary to the said State Planning Commission with the competent experts and necessary staff who can do the task of planning exercise. This calls for immediate reorganisation of the entire planning process at the State and district levels. Planning exercises including plan formulation, implementation and supervision should not be mixed up with the separate administrative work at the district level. Necessary legal provisions, rules and regulations and the constitutional requirements need to be examined with a view to strengthening the District Planning Agency/Department. Thus, the decentralisation of planning at the district and village levels through PRIs and other participatory institutions like the NGOs, village committees etc, should be initiated under a strong administrative structure with a full-fledged District-Level Planning Agency/Department in all the districts in Manipur. To avoid conflict between the elected representative of the panchayats and the officials of the Government, there should be real devolution of power to the panchayats with necessary administrative support and efficient system of planning at the district level.

Participatory System and Poverty Alleviation Model

The foregoing discussions underline that with strong support from the government, the participatory institutions like panchayats. NGOs and other participatory organisations can play effective role in promoting participatory development in Manipur. It is necessary to give emphasis on collective action at the community level. And the household approach should not be neglected in the participatory development process. Roy Burman (1984:85 & 88) emphasised both household approach and community approach in poverty alleviation programmes. If household approach to poverty alleviation is not considered in the participatory development model, the scope for people's participation will be very limited. In the current programmes of rural development under NREGS, only limited number of working days are provided to each member of the household. Therefore, household should be treated as a small participatory institution in poverty alleviation programmes in Manipur. At a relatively higher level, there is a justification for the aggregation/integration of participatory development institutions in the community. As Roy Burman (1984:88) has again clearly stated, "In the areas where common Property resources (CPRs) constitute significant segment of the economy, poverty alleviation programmes should be both individual household oriented and collectivitz oriented". This observation underlines the significance of the institution of the participatory development for poverty eradication in Manipur. Thus, the core of people's participation in poverty alleviation lies in collective action or group action along with the action of the individual households. In our participatory model of poverty alleviation programmes, the household and collective actions constitute a vital role in promoting the process of participatory development in different sectors of the economy. The participatory development sector may be treated as household and collective-based institutions which require the necessary support of the government. This suggests that there is the need for support of government to promote the participatory institutions as they cannot be left to the "free play of market forces". Since the participatory institutions also creates public goods and the generate externalities, their activities cannot be considered as a function of the market. In the case of household approach to participatory development, the production of "private goods "is essential in the poverty alleviation programmes. In such a situation, the private interest should coincide with the social interest. Thus, the market should be the signal for the production of goods in the household sector. There is also the need for upgradation of the skills of the workers and technology in the household sector. Therefore, the government can play a vital role in promoting household-based participatory development institutions. Likewise, in group or collective action, participatory development institutions need recognition and support of the government for the common benefit.

Urban Local Bodies: Role and Defects

Today, urban local bodies like the Municipality of Municipal Corporation are considered to be democratic participatory institutions. The experience of the working of the municipality in Manipur reveals that they could not effectively render public services in the urban areas of Manipur. Now, they have become a weak body in rendering urban services in the State. In this area of decentralisation, the State government has completely failed. It is, therefore, necessary to strengthen the working of the municipality as it occupies an important place for people's participation in development.

People's Participation in the Hill Areas of Manipur

In the case of people's participation in development in the hill areas of Manipur, there are special problems of decentralisation in hill areas of the State. It may be noted that panchayats are extended to valley areas / districts while the autonomous district councils are found in the hill areas of Manipur. Thus, people's participation in development in decentralised model for the hill areas of Manipur becomes a political question. However, it may be noted that they are district level councils within a district for decentralised district administration within their functional jurisdiction. In this framework, the Deputy Commissioner as a responsible officer of the government looks after the overall administration of the district while the district councils are entrusted for initiating development activities within their jurisdiction. But, there have been no election to the Six Autonomous District Councils of Manipur since 1989. Also, there has not been devolution of power and functions to district councils/or in the district councils areas. It is true that devolution and decentralisation are essential component for people's participation in development at the district level or in backward areas. But the concept of community participation and administrative arrangement in the hill districts of the State need to be re-conceptualised in order to avoid intra-state conflicts. There is apprehension for a separate state from the political autonomy. Here, it may be noted that in the hill areas of Manipur, there are still ethnic insurgencies. Thus, the rationale of people's participation in development in the form of participatory institution may go beyond a limit. The situation in the valley areas are also quite startling. Thus, in evolving participatory form of development, the system of the creation of new institution should be compatible with the democratic government. The question should not be between the government and participation. The two should be mutually re-enforcing or complementary. As Paul Streeten has clearly pointed out, "When the revolution comes, you will eat strawberries and cream and like it". Thus, in certain cases, the creation of new political institutions or administrative units may disturb the power balance in areas where the law and order becomes serious. Therefore, there should be alternative model of participatory development in the hill areas of Manipur. In the hill areas of Manipur, all democratic institutions or development institutions should be under the State government. And all participatory organizations should also be under the state government. The village authorities in the hill areas of Manipur should be recognised as participatory institutions which also should be democratic institutions. Thus, all forms of participatory development institutions like the NGOs, SHGs and the other participatory development institutions should be encouraged in the hill areas of Manipur. To promote participatory development at the grass-roots level in the hill areas of Manipur, there is the need for participatory planning in the hill areas of the State. Micro-level planning may be a suitable model for the promotion of people's participation in the hill areas of Manipur. This requires reorganisation of the entire planning process in the State. There should also be separate and full-fledged planning agencies under a strong administrative structure. Thus, there is the need for strengthening the government and community cooperation in promoting participatory process of development in the hill areas of Manipur.

Conclusion: A New Paradigm for Decentralised Development System in Manipur

We may now set a summary of the policy implications for promoting the process of participatory development in Manipur. It may be noted that participatory development is essential for involvement of the people in decision - making and implementation for various programmes of development at the grass-roots level. There is also the need for collective action or group action for achieving common benefit in the process of participatory development. Thus, the model for participatory development calls for co-operations among the people. There are also several other studies which emphasise the significance of co-operation and harmful effects of non-cooperative behaviour. Some of the outstanding theoretical and empirical studies identified the "common problem" as a prisoner's dilemma. Thus, the best strategy of the conflict is cooperation which can avoid the zero-sum game. In participatory development, there is the need for sacrificing the household and community resources for the common or collective benefits. This calls for changing the attitude and outlook of the people towards more progressive society. It may be noted that participatory development also helps in enhancing the efficiency of governance of the State. Again, good governance requires cooperation of the people. Therefore, decision-making and planning for development needs to explore wider opportunities for people's participation in development. In this model, participatory development should create not only employment opportunities but also public goods which can be enjoyed by all. The principle of free-rider should not outweigh the benefits of externalities to be generated in the economy and society of the State. Therefore, the State-led model for participatory development can be applied to Manipur. Appropriate public action like public education, incentives, employment generation programmes for the community etc. should be taken up in order to achieve development cooperation from the people in the State. This suggests that a set of policy measures need to be formulated to create willingness of the people and favourable conditions for participatory development system in Manipur. Thus, there is the need for institutional and administrative reforms for promoting participatory development in the State. While the State-led model of participatory development is necessary to achieve people's cooperation in development, there is still the need for decentralisation of planning at district and block levels in order to build up a strong institutional base for strengthening the process of participatory development in the State. In our new strategy of participatory development, we seek to combine both the State-led model of development programmes and people's participation in development in the decentralised planning process from the bottom or grass-roots levels. This requires strengthening the district level planning agency in different districts in Manipur. In the new paradigm of participatory development, district planning can provide a lasting solution to the conflicts among the state-sponsored participatory institutions like the panchayats, NGOs and other government agencies. The presence of such district level planning machinery or agency is necessary for government institutions and participation of people in the economic development system in order to develop the productive potential in such important areas of agriculture and rural development including small and village industries and provides a number of basic-needs of life. In these broad-based areas of development, people's initiative is also necessary for decision-making. Participatory development institutions like the panchayats, NGOs etc. can be entrusted to identify and formulate the various development programmes. Also, the district planning machinery should be entrusted to become the agency or institutional system for bringing about self-sustaining economic growth and development initiated by the participatory institutions. The district plan should be a design of development for the district. And the district plan should be well-coordinated for all sectors of the district economy. High-level expertise will also be necessary for techno-economic feasibility of all projects. But the district administrators may not take interest in important aspects of the concept of project-planning and other plan schemes in the State. Thus, the district planning exercises and the district administration should be effectively coordinated by the State Government. Again, in this new system the State Planning Commission can direct the necessary guidelines to the district planning machinery for district plan formulation. And the programmes of development should be entrusted to the implementing agencies in the districts. The decisions for development at the lower levels or lower level departments should also be coordinated by the Planning Agency at the district level. And the district plan incorporating all the development needs of the district should be submitted to the State Planning Department and finally to the State Planning Commission for final disposal or approval. The State Plan thus prepared should be submitted to the Planning Commission for final approval. The district plan is a kind of sub-state plan and it is also an area-based planning for integrated area development. It needs to supplement both the national and state plans with a more detailed examination of the potential resources so that necessary investment should be made in each district to cater to the needs of each district. In short, the district level planning needs to become an important planning process in other to evolve a new participatory development system at the district level, which should be consistent with the specific needs of the people in the districts. The idea of district planning is not new in India. The idea was advocated right from the beginning of the First Five Year Plan. The report of the Balwant Rai Mehta Study Team (1958) also laid emphasis on people's participation on local level planning under the framework of the democratic decentralisation or the Panchayat Raj institution during the third plan. Again, the Administrative Reforms Commission appointed after a decade of Balwant Rai Mehta Committee's Report pointed out the shortcomings of the district planning. The Commission recommended for appropriate planning machinery for the formulation of the plans at the district level. And such plans should have clear objectives, availability of local resources etc. In 1969, the Planning Commission also issued guidelines for the formulation of district plans. These guidelines also suggested the need for decentralised planning and involvement of governments and local-self government bodies in district planning. In the subsequent plans also, steps were taken for strengthening the district level planning (Mishra, 1996). In the current Eleventh Five Year Plan (2007-12) also the Planning Commission seeks to strengthen decentralised planning system. But there is conflict of interest among various agencies or institutions involved in district level planning. In Manipur, the process of devolution of power and functions to the panchayats is still tardy. There are misconceptions that the elected representatives are fully responsible for the development of the districts. While panchayats are important democratic institutions for decentralised planning, they cannot function independently of the State Government. Again, participatory democracy at the grass-roots level/village level may be conflicting with the functionaries of the other administrative hierarchies of the State Government. Thus, there should be effective planning machinery at the district level with appropriate political authority at the apex. In several states, there are district planning committees. But the district planning committees are weak. The existing arrangement for district planning is weak in Manipur. There are also no full fledged technically qualified staff and other officials for doing all exercises of planning. To make the district planning really meaningful, there should be district Planning Board in all the districts which should comprise proper representation from the panchayats and other administrative bodies or levels of the government. In the context Manipur, a local MLA of the district under the government can be the chairman or chairperson of the district planning board with all the necessary staffs in the organisational structure of planning machinery. Proper representations in the DPB will also remove the bureaucratic hurdles in the planning process. The DPB should have the planning authority to strengthen democracy in the state. There can be lower level committees also under it to initiate planning from below. Thus, the decentralised model of planning can be an effective system for promoting a new participatory system of development in Manipur.

REFERENCES

Baruah, Joydeep and Indranee Dutta (2004): "Determinants of People's Participation in Decentralized Planning and Development", *Political Economy Journal of India*, Jan-June.

Dreźe, Jean and Amartya Sen (2008): *Development and Participation*, Oxford University Press, New Delhi.

Gadgil D.R. (1973): "District Development Planning", in Charan D Wadhva (ed) *Some problems of India's Economic Policy*, Tata McGraw, New Delhi.

Hardin, Garrett (1968): "The Tragedy of the Commons", in (reprinted 2001) Ulaganathan Sankar (ed) *Environmental Economics*, Oxford, New Delhi.

Government of India (2004): *Toward Faster and More Inclusive Growth. An approach to the 11th Five Year Plan (2007-2012)*, Planning Commission.

________: *6th Five year Plan (1980-1985)*, Planning Commission

________ (2008): *Eleventh Five Year Plan 2007-2012, Vol-II, Social Sector*, Planning Commission, Oxford University Press, New Delhi.

Govt. of Manipur, Annual *Administrative Report 2005-06*, Department of Rural Development and Panchayati Raj.

_______: *Administration Report 2004-05*. Cooperative Deptt.

_______: *Administrative Report 1994-95* , DIPR,

_______: *Annual Administrative Report 2006-07*, Department of Rural Development and Panchayati Raj.

_______: *Draft 11th Five Year Plan (2007-08) Annual Plan (2007-08)*, Planning Department.

_______: Manipur *Today, 2008*, DIPR.

_______: *Statistical Abstract Manipur 2005*, DES.

_______: *Draft 10th Five Year plan (2002-07) and Annual Plan (2002-03) Vol. I*, Planning Department.

Howes, Stephen, Ashok K. Lahiri and Nicholas Stern (2003): *State Level Reforms in India Towards More Effective Government*, Macmillan, Delhi.

Jodha, NS (1995), "Common Property Resources and the Environmental Context: Role of Biophysical versus Social Stress", *Economic and Political Weekly*, Vol. XXX No 51. Dec.23, p.3278.

Kanchan, Chopra, GK Kdekodi and M.N. Murty (1990): *Participatory Development, People and Common Property Resources*, Sage, New Delhi.

Singh, Katar (1999): *Rural Development, Principles, Policies and Management*, Sage, New Delhi.

Mishra, Sweta (1996): *Changing Pattern of District Administration*, Mittal, New Delhi.

Obaidullah Khan, AZM (1980): " Participatory development: The need for structural reform and people's organisation", in United Nations Asian and Pacific Development Institute, Bangkok, *Local Level Planning and Rural Development: Alternative Strategies*", Concept Publishing Company, New Delhi.

Olson, Mancur (1965): "The Logic of Collective Action", (reprinted 1987) *The World Bank Observer*, Vol.2. No.2.

Ostrom, Elinor (1990): "An Institutional Approach to the Study of Self-organization and Self-governance in CPR situation," in (reprinted 2001) Ulaganathan Sankar (ed), *Environmental Economics*, Oxford, New Delhi., p.140.

Dasgupta, Partha (1995): "Common Property Resources: Economic Analyics", *Economic and Political Weekly*, Vol. XL No .16. April 16-22, pp.1610-1622.

Puri, Ellora (2004): "Understanding Participation Theoretical Foundations and Practical Implications", *Economic and Political Weekly*, June 12-18. pp.2511-2517.

Roy Burman, B.K. (1984): *Towards Poverty Alleviation Programmes in Nagaland and Manipur*, Mittal, Delhi.

Singh, L. Krishnamangol (2002): "Population Growth and Common Property Resources in Manipur: A Perspective" (Paper presented to the workshop on Population, Food Production and Environment organised by College of Agriculture, Central Agricultural University on 28th July, 2002 at the premise of CAU and sponsored by ICAR, New Delhi).

Singh, L. Krishnamangol (2008): "The Matrix of Participatory Development in Manipur: Changing the Paradigm", (Paper presented to the 2 - Day National Seminar on District Level Planning Issues and Prospects organized by the Manipur Economic Association and Economics Department, Manipur University on 8-9 March, 2008 at the Manipur University Senate Hall).

Streeten, Paul (2004): "Empowerment, Participation and the Poor", *Political Economy Journal of India*, Vol.13. (July-Dec), pp.1-12.

United Nations Asian and Pacific Development Institute (1980), *Local Level Planning and Rural Development Alternative Strategies*, Concept, New Delhi.

Vimal Khawas, Vimal (2006): "The Relevance of Autonomy", *The Statesman*, Kolkata, April, p.7.

Wade, Robert (1987): "The Management of Common Poverty Resources", *The World Bank Research Observer*, Vol.2. No.2, pp.212-234

World Bank (2003): *World Development Report 2003*, Washington DC.

2

An Approach to Agricultural Development with Sustainability

Kh. Menjor Singh & Silvia Lisam

Introduction

The terms sustainability and sustainable development have been widely used to day. Sustainable development gained importance and popularity since the Cocoyoc Declaration in 1974. Its importance was further emphasized by the International Union for Conservation of Nature (IUCN) in its reports (1980, 1990) and the World Commission on Environment and Development (WCED) in its report (1987). International organizations like WWF, UNEP, FAO also have recognized sustainable development as an imperative for the mankind in present and future generations. The Earth Summit held in Rio in 1992 re-empharized the need for sustainable development at global level. Because of its increasing importance, the term has been so widely pronounced by professionals and other groups of people that it appears to be a term outside the economic jargon.

The Concept

The concept of sustainable development assumes critical importance in the interest of future generations and their needs of the fast changing society without damaging the carrying capacity of the basic inputs like land, water, forests, etc. The World Commission on Environment and Development (WCED) in its report (1987) highlighted the need to simultaneously address development and environmental imperatives. According to FAO(1987), "Sustainable development is the management and conservation of the material resource base and the orientation of technological and institutional change in such a manner as to ensure the attainment and continued satisfaction of human needs for present and future generations. Such sustainable development (in agriculture, forestry and fisheries sector) which conserves land, water, plant and animal genetic resources is environmentally non-degrading, technically appropriate, economically viable and socially acceptable".

Evidently, sustainable development is a holistic concept. Since the eighties, particularly since the publication of the report of WCED in 1987 in the name "Our Common Future", many literatures have been devoted to the study of sustainable development and measures for its attainment (Barbier, 1987; Brown, et al. 1987; Daly, 1989; Pezzy, 1989; Redclift, 1987). The main objective is to find out possible application of the concept for achieving its objective.

Due to the advocacy of many definitions by many environmentalists and economists, the concept of sustainable development is sometimes misconceived and misinterpreted among the developed and developing countries. The ongoing development processes in these countries are, therefore, still characterized by unsustainablity, manifested in the form of environmental pollution, declining productivity, ecological imbalance, etc. There is little unanimity in comprehending the concept of sustainable development. Perhaps, it is due to the reason that the term conveys different meanings to different people in different countries.

In the global context as is evident from the Rio Summit, developing countries differ from the developed countries as to their viewpoints on sustainable development. By and large, the developing countries are very much concerned to address their immediate economic problems and to eliminate poverty regardless of sustainability, whereas the developed countries emphasize mainly on combating industry related pollution and maintenance of the already attained level of economic development. Studies have shown that the developed countries consume resources at a disproportionately high rate when compared to their resource base.

In the developing countries, in the course of their development process, forest resources are more exploited, trees all around felled, grazing lands and other common property resources are encroached upon, land is damaged, and water and air are polluted. The loss to the natural endowments is not recouped and thus the ecosystem is damaged and the carrying capacity of the supporting elements like land, water, etc. is already affected. The same phenomenon is witnessed in developed countries too, though different in magnitude. In the process, we all suffer and make the life of our future generations miserable. Mollison (1991) in work "Permaculture" rightly pointed out, "There is too much of contemporary evidence of ecological disaster. Out life style has led us to the very brink of annihilation. We have expanded out right to live on the earth, yet conquerors of nature always lose. To accumulate wealth, power or land beyond one's need in a limited world is to be truly immoral, be it as an individual, an institution or a nation-state...Like war, growth at any cost is an outmoded and discredited concept". That the earth is overexploited resulting in ecological disequilibrium is evident from natural calamities like earthquakes, drought, floods, etc. that we experience from time to time.

It is because of these undesirable happenings, which occur on the earth's surface that we need a real concept of sustainable development to be comprehended by all concerned. The need of the hour is to define sustainable development very clearly and evolve the development strategy guided by the principles of ecology, economics, social and gender equity and ethics. The true concept of sustainable development shall cover the following essential elements:

1. Survival of human beings and all other forms of life on the mother earth.

2. Preservation and conservation of environment and eco-system along with maintenance of biophysical productivity.
3. Economic efficiency and growth.
4. Satisfaction of basic human needs.
5. Inter and intra generational equity.
6. Social Justice.
7. People's participation and self-reliance.
8. Stabilization of human population.
9. Promotion of values and ethics.

It would appear from the above coverage that the concept of sustainable development extends far and wide beyond economic values. Indeed, the scope of sustainable development is very wide. It covers all aspects of human life including moral and ethical values. This is because the world has experienced excessive stress on biophysical environment for short-term gain, and by and by, people of the world have realized that such excessive stress is ultimately counterproductive. This means that there is a limit to which productivity can be raised, and even the renewable resources are not perpetual unless renewed and managed prudently. They have also realized that human survival with peace can only ensured by preserving the basic resource base available on the earth. This explains why the concept of sustainable development has become more comprehensive and its scope is wider than what conventional economic theory permits. Development, in the real sense of the term, being conditional of social justice and equity, must be socially justified and equitable to become sustainable.

The Objective

Within the framework of the above aspects, conceptually sustainable development aims at achieving threefold objective, namely, bio-physical objective, economic objective and social objective. Such goals of sustainable development are to be derived from Environmental economics, partly from Marxian economics and partly from welfare economics. Admittedly, the prime objective is to bring maximum good to the maximum people, provided that both the economic and social goals are maximized with due consideration of achieving the biophysical objectives. To be precise, sustainable development advocates a development process that is bio-physically permissible, economically viable and socially acceptable. In other words, sustainable development is a process of development that should operate within a framework bounded by the bio-physical, economic and social coordinates.

The Application

Having set the framework within which the objectives or goals of sustainable development are to be attained, it is necessary to know that there are certain limits within which the development process has to be functional. These limits can be broadly classified as Bio-physical and Ethico-social limits (Daly, 1989). The biophysical limit is meant to control resource availability, resource use, economic viability and crop/biomass productivity within the prescribed limits; whereas the Ethico-social limit is supposed to impose restrictions on wasteful consumption. Besides, inter-generational equity and distributive justice in the case of present generation ought to be considered as in-built system of the development process.

Before applying the concept of sustainable development the following points need to be counted as guiding principles:

1. Sustainable development should be conceived of as a whole system and, as such, a system approach should be followed in its application.
2. Since sustainability is basically a constraint, the approach to achieve this should be interventionist.
3. Sustainable development involves production management system, and, as such, inputs should be so managed that they do not affect the bio-physical potentiality.
4. As far as possible, the basic needs of the present society must be met and in the meantime, the resource base for future generations should also be mentioned (WCED,1987).

5. As far as practicable, development for sustainability should be pursued on the basis of renewable resources.

From the above discussions, it is clear that sustainable development is to be accepted as the societal goal, and as mentioned earlier, its application requires deliberate planning which is interventionist in approach. The interventions would, however, be warranted at the biophysical front or resource use level and also at the socio-political front or policy level. This entails the necessity to process for sustainable development through application of three filters - Ecologic, Economic and Social. (By filter, we mean that type of screen through which only desirable elements can pass through.)

Ecological Filter

This means that it is possible to characterize each unit of land through landscape ecological analysis covering topography, soil type, drainage condition, state for water availability and over all environmental capacity, and classify them. Accordingly, a list of land use practices may be worked out for each of the identified landscape ecological units. Further analysis of crop ecology and plant ecology can fine tune ecological filter. To workout this ecological filter the activities suggested are Investigation Assessment and Allocation.

Application of ecological filter begins with landscape ecological analysis of the concerned area. Remote sensing and other time tested field survey methods are essential tools for this activity. Selection of the method will depend upon the scale of activity macro, regional or micro.

Economic Filter

Once a set of land use or crop is found to be ecologically viable after ecological filter, economic consideration becomes important to choose from among them. The importance of economic filter arises, because ecological filter is not usually bound by time factor, whereas economic filter is time dependent as it is subjected to technological development. Efficiency, growth and stability are prime concerns under this economic exercise. Economic filter requires calculation of net internal return, cost benefit analysis, input-output ratio, market value, etc. as methods for its functioning.

In case of agriculture, individual crops may be taken into account to begin with and subsequently, all the crops raised within an agricultural calendar year need to be counted. This economic filter or exercise also needs operations of Investigation, Assessment and Allocation.

Social Filter

Social Filter is required in the process of sustainable development, because without this filter we may not be able to measure the social acceptability of a use/project from the standpoint of equity, empowerment, cultural tradition, diversity and availability of social institutions. Functioning of social institutions vis-à-vis land use is an important index to understand working of social filter.

Adaptation to new technology by any particular social group depends, to a large extent, upon the group's capacity to culturally assimilate the change. While discussing the transformation of environment, Redclift (1987) concluded that there is a need to be more aware of the relationship linking people's understanding of the environment with their behaviour.

In case of agriculture, a sustainable land use pattern cannot be designed without considering social filter. Like economic filter, social filter is also subjected to temporal change. Investigation, Assessment and Allocation are also necessary for applying this filter.

As mentioned above, ecological filter is basically nature-determined, and therefore, it is imperative to understand the nature's law through ecosystem analysis in order to prepare guidelines for economic and social interventions. Once this exercise of applying filter is completed, three other steps of action planning, implementation and monitoring are involved in chalking out sustainable land use pattern. These three activities form part of the filtering system as a whole, but start functioning from the end point of social filter. It is here that people's participation is considered to be an integral part of the entire process of sustainable development .

The Operation

After application of the conceptual frame through the above filters, operational activities are to be determined. The operational activities to be taken up include:

1. Environmental Appraisal.
2. Cumulative Environmental Impact Analysis and Trade-off.
3. Natural Resource Accounting.

Environmental Appraisal: This is an assessment of the existing conditions based on which decision on desirable activities can be taken up. It is necessary to investigate the governing principles of production potential of each unit of land to act upon. Regressing the existing use with the potentiality, it will be possible to understand the problems, associated causes and the possible way out.

Cumulative Environmental Impact Analysis and Trade off: An analysis of the cumulative environmental impact and social effects of human activities at all spatial scales is quite necessary for systematic identification and monitoring of the cumulative negative trends in production and the trade off. As these effects will be at the regional or local scale, it will be necessary to look into those problems according to functional regions based on such ecological criteria as climate and vegetation pattern, soil types and watershed boundaries. Such identification and monitoring will ensure diversified production array. A trade-off analysis will thus be there when a choice is to be made, that is, to decide upon certain activities of production.

Natural Resource Accounting: The rationale behind this accounting is that GNP does not take into account the depletion of natural stocks like forest, soil, water quality, etc. and therefore, this accounting has to take into account the economic loss due to loss of productivity or depletion of stock.

The Intervention

The operation for sustainable development calls for intervention at policy level with property rights (common property rights & private property rights to resources), distributive justice (or social optimization) and limited unbridled consumption. Sustainable Development is essentially interventionist and proactive in nature. In the context of a welfare state, the question of political economy is very important since the scale of operation for sustainable development is an important parameter to attain sustainability.

Beyond doubt, sustainable development needs deliberate planning as well as control in all spatial scales and, as such, it calls for both macro and micro level planning and political intervention that are informed, fair and open.

Sustainable Agricultural Development

Agriculture continues to be a major source of employment and income to a vast majority of India's population thereby making a case for sustainable agricultural development. But the share of agriculture in the GDP and public investment on agriculture dwindled. The share of agriculture in GDP declined from 50 p.c. in 1950-51 to 27 p.c. in 2000-2001, with almost the same proportion of population depending on agriculture.

In recent years, even under assured irrigation, yield levels are stagnated. The situation is attributed to poor drainage, soil degradation, and indiscriminate use of chemical fertilizers and pesticides. Swaminathan (1999) warns that excessive use of chemical fertilizers and pesticides would increase the incidence of dreadful diseases like cancer through the toxic residues present in the grains and other edible parts.

The paper also throws light on the issue of sustainable agriculture in the state of Manipur. The state of Manipur lies in the extreme north eastern corner of India. It has an area of 22,327 sq. km. Agriculture is the single largest source of livelihood of about 70 per cent of the population and it is also the mainstay of the state's economy. The state can be divided into two physiographical zones - valley and hills. The valley constitutes 47 per cent out of the total agricultural area and that in the hills is 53 per cent. The valley has an average altitude of 872 metres above MSL and the climate is sub-tropical and warm in the summer season. The area is predominant by permanent agriculture and is known as 'Rice bowl of the state'. Agricultural productivity is very high in the valley in comparison with that of the hill. The method of shifting cultivation is predominant in the hilly regions of Manipur. The process involved is that an area of forest is cleared, usually or rather incompletely, the debris is burnt and the land is cultivated for a few years usually less than five. It is then allowed to revert to forest on other secondary vegetation before being cleared and used again.

The size of holdings in Manipur is declining at a faster rate. Marginal holdings below one hectare constitute 72 per cent of total holdings and 92 per cent of total holdings are below two hectares. Medium and large holdings have virtually disappeared. Local production of food grains particularly rice has not been able to meet the demand for local consumption of the fast increasing population. Every year large quantities of rice, wheat, pulses, edible oil, etc. have to be brought in from other states to supplement local production. This is the major reason for intensification of agricultural practices. Because of small size of holdings, the cultivators follow the intensive cultivation system by using high amount of chemical fertilizers, insecticides, fungicides, etc. in order to extract maximum output out of the small size holdings available to them. Many people are of the opinion that this process will undoubtedly lead to soil impoverishment which will eventually lead to hazardous effect on environment and thus, affecting the ecosystem. Therefore, limited area of cultivation is also another factor which causes unsustainable agricultural situation. Denudation and destruction of forest are the result of continuous and extensive collection of fuel wood and timber as well as shifting cultivation due to fast increasing population and grazing activities. The traditional method of shifting cultivation is hazardous because the quality of soil of the farm diminishes from first year to the subsequent years. Land degradation due to shifting cultivation also causes siltation of river bed and has been cited as the main reason of flood in the valley areas of Manipur. The increasing population pressure on land, indiscriminate cutting and burning of forests, construction of roads and houses for human habitation, etc. have greatly affected the environment. In fact, droughts, floods, excessive heat and cold are the direct outcome of depletion of natural resources, which brings about imbalances in environment. It has resulted on unsustainability in agricultural productivity in the state.

In view of the need for sustainable development including sustainable agriculture, the state should not go along the line or direction, which may threaten or undermine the future agricultural growth and development. At the same time, there is need for increasing the agricultural production and productivity in Manipur in order to meet the increasing demand of food grains for the growing population in the state. It may take a long time to introduce sustainable farming system on a large scale and the problem is to meet the growing demand of food grains of the people. Therefore, it is suggested to reconcile or resolve the trade-off or conflict between the traditional green revolution technologies and sustainable agricultural strategies in the state. It is felt that the present form of technology farming in the valley needs to be quickly transformed into ecological farming methods such as organic farming which involved the use of organic manures, use of bio-fertilizers, vermiculture, biopesticides, bio-resources etc. while in the hills, agro forestry is probably the best alternative solution. It has been the way of life since the evolution of human beings in the forest. The ill-effects of Green Revolution and resource degradation lead to environment hazards and has demanded for eco-friendly practices to ensure the never-ending production.

Growth, Trends and Gap

Agricultural growth trends during the planning era clearly present the manner in which land resources are adversely affected. In the first phase of the land development up to 1960, the agricultural growth was achieved through the expansion of area under cultivation by way of bringing the fallow lands under the plough and through deforestation (Rao, 1994). During the Green Revolution period commencing from 1965-66, water and fertilizer became crucial land-saving inputs. These resulted in depletion of ground water, excessive use of chemical fertilizers and pesticides leading to degradation of the soil and the associated evil effects. During the post-Green Revolution period, rich-poor divide is found to be widening leading to extensive co-existence of un-sustainable living standards on one hand and unacceptable poverty on the other.

The need of the hour is, therefore, to make agriculture sustainable. Sustainable agricultural development calls for several measures on several fronts. On the whole, there is a need for adopting a code of environmental ethics with a sense of personal responsibility for saving the earth.

Mollison (1991) rightly speaks about the Law of Returns which says, "Whatever we take from nature we must return as nature demands a return for every gift received". He warns that nature has extreme penalties for those who break such law and for their descendents. According to him, natural resources should be avoided in the use of natural resources. He wanted that the renewable resources be used at a rate less than their rate of regeneration. He also opined that the rate of use of exhaustible resources should depend on the rate at which they can be substituted or recouped but the substitutability has its own limitations and hence a Code of Environmental Ethics is to be honoured by individuals, institutions and governments

India has already taken to liberalization and globalisation of its economy, and multinational giants have entered the Indian soil with all attempts to salvage their home economics. In such attempts, the resources may be exploited indiscriminately without thinking for sustainable development. It is, therefore, desirable that there must be effective check on the investment pattern of these multinationals in India so as to ensure sustainability of our life-supporting resources, sustainability of small producers and sustainability of the landless poor.

In view of corporatisation policy of agriculture, care must be taken to ensure that such a policy does not deprive the entrepreneurial opportunities to the individual farmers and curtail employment opportunities on the farm front. Such a policy should also not reduce the small and marginal farmers to the level of agricultural labourers and increase market dependency for food-grains leading to reduction in food security. In short, in the corporatisation arrangement, the equity issue should not become secondary (Reddy, 2001).

The Remedy

The following measures will go a long way in making agriculture developed with sustainability:

Tackling the Poverty: Poverty is the crux of all problems. Poverty has also become the worst enemy of the environment. The small and marginal farmers, agricultural labourers including casual daily labourers, etc. are also victims of poverty. Hence, alleviation of rural poverty to the maximum extent possible is needed to attain sustainable development in agriculture. However, elimination of endemic poverty and deprivation in the rural areas in the given socio-economic system would still be hard task.

Therefore, the primary task to help eradicate poverty in the rural areas should be entitlement of these poverty stricken people to adequate food and other basic essentials of their day-to-day living. Provisions for employment opportunities should be provided to this poverty-stricken population with a view to expanding their private income. There must be public provisioning for shelter, health care and education as well as for subsidized food. It is only when they can have square meals everyday that they will be inclined to convert their energy and labour into productive work for participatory development.

While tackling the poverty, besides the social security measures like old age pension, unemployment benefits, employment guarantee schemes, etc. measures like creation of employment avenues for self-employment or wage employment should also be taken up.

Strategies to achieve sustainable crop, livestock, forestry, fishery production will succeed only when they are complemented by policies to slow down population growth and enhance the alternative employment opportunities. Other policy measures should focus attention on crucial issues such as organizing the agriculturists for community action in preserving natural resources in terms of rainwater conservation, use of bio-fertilizers, rural marketing.

Minor irrigation: Water being a basic for sustainable agriculture, priority must be given to the community based rainwater harvesting and utilization. Eco-friendly minor irrigation schemes must receive priority.

Mini watershed Programme: Mini watershed programmes may be popularized aiming at rainwater harvesting along with schemes of contour bunding and check-dams and social forestry, dry-land fanning, mixed cropping and inter cropping.

Extension services: Extension services must be provided to address the problems of use of chemical fertilizers and pesticides. A rational mix of chemical fertilizers and bio-fertilizers is recommended and this will go a long way in improving the crop yields and sustaining soil fertility as well.

Drought Management: There is a vicious circle of drought, deforestation, ecological imbalance and failure of rainfall as each of these four elements is both the cause and effect of the other. Drought works against sustainable agriculture. Therefore, effective drought management should be there and rainwater must be harvested at a wider scale.

Livestock management: Management of the livestock becomes an important component of the sustainable agricultural development. There is an urgent need for relating livestock population to the bearing capacity of available land and water. This calls for improving the quality of livestock.

Institutional management: The role of the government in the spheres of land reform, provision for irrigation, construction of social overhead capitals like rural roads and bridges, and other infrastructures, provision of micro credit and subsidies for agricultural inputs and food grain distribution besides social security measures will also go a long way in helping develop the agriculture.

Marketing: To encourage farmers to produce more, it is necessary that markets for agricultural goods are regulated with a view to bringing remunerative prices for agricultural produces.

Commercialization: Economic reforms in India and its liberalization and privatization policy imply lesser and lesser role/interference of the government in the economic activities of private individuals. However, the new challenges can be faced only if there is a common wavelength of understanding of problems and solutions among local leaders, the public at large and the agriculturists. A symphonic agricultural system where there is harmony among all the components is, therefore, the need of the hour. For each agro-ecological region, a symphonic agricultural matrix must be constructed.

In the area of management technology, particular attention will have to be paid to combining the advantage of individual initiative and group endeavour. Public instruments for promoting group cooperation in the adoption of ecologically sound land, water and pest management practices are yet to be developed. Group insurance, community extension programmes, group awards, group subsidies and similar devices need to be introduced.

The coming years will be critical years in the country's agricultural scenario. With increasing population, the per capita availability of land will be hardly 0.10 hectare. This land will have to provide the food, fibre and all other requirements of over 100 crores of people in the country and fodder and feed needs of over 50 crores of farm animals in an ecologically sustainable manner. Therefore, in the ultimate analysis, in approaching a matter of such over whelming importance and magnitude, it is imperative that we should thrash out the basic issues so that our food providers, the so-called agriculturists will be involved a little seriously in their activities without waiting for government support. It would, thus, be more appropriate to treat the optimum utilization of land and water resources as an individual rather than a national responsibility.

REFERENCES

Barbier, I.B. (1987): "Two Concepts of Sustainable Development", *Environment Conservation*, 4(2).

Brown, B.J., M.E. Hanson and R.W. Merideth Jr (1987): "Global Sustainability: Towards Definition", *Environmental Management*, 11(6).

Chattopadhay, Srikumar (2002): "Application of S.D. Concept : Some Issues", in Kalwar, S.C. (ed), *Environment Issues & Sustainable Development*, Pointer Publishers, Jaipur.

Daly, H. E. (1989): "Sustainable Development: From Concept and Theory towards Operational Principles", *Population and Development Review*, Hoover Institution Conference.

Desai, Vasant (1990): *A Study of Rural Economics*, Himalaya Pub. House, Bombay.

George, K.K, V. Sankaran Nair and Jose Jacob(eds) (1977): *Economic Development and the Quest for Alternative: Essays in honour of M.A. Oomen,* Concept Pub. Company, New Delhi.

Indira, Laishram(2005): "Towards Agricultural Sustainability in Agricultural Development of Manipur : Issues and Perspectives", Unpublished thesis, Manipur University.

Kalwar, S.C.(ed)(2002): *Environmental Issues and Sustainable Development*, Pointer Publishers, Jaipur.

Mollison, Bill (1991): *Introduction to Permaculture*, Tagari Publication.

Reghava Reddy, G & P. Subrahmanyam (eds)(2003): *Dynamics of Sustainable Rural Development*, Serial Publications, New Delhi.

Pezzy, J.(1989): *Economic Analysis of Sustainable Growth and Sustainable Development*, Working Paper No.15. Environment Department, the World Bank, Washington D.C.

Priyoranjan, Chongtham (2006): *Agricultural Development in Manipur*, Working Paper, NER Vision 2020 Manipur.

Ram Singh, Ningthoujam (2007): "Strategies for Agricultural Growth in Manipur" Seminar paper, Manipur Economics Association.

Rao, C.H. Hanumantha (1994): *Agricultural Growth, Rural Poverty and Environmental Degradation in India*, Oxford University Press, New Delhi.

Redclift, M.R.(1987): *Sustainable Development: Exploring the Contradictions*, Routledge, London.

Reddy, K.V. (2003): "Sustainable Development - The Gandhian Approach" in Reddy, G.R. and P. Subrahmanyam (eds), *Dynamics of Sustainable Rural Development*, Serial Publications, New Delhi.

Sengupta, K. and Niranjan Roy (eds) (2003): *Economic Reforms and Agricultural Development in North-East India*, Mittal Publications, New Delhi.

Sushini, Yumnam (2007): "Agricultural Sustainability: Its Issues and Challenges in the Context of Manipur", Seminar paper, Manipur Economics Association.

Swaminathan, M.S.(1996): *Sustainable Agriculture: Towards an Evergreen Revolution*, Konark Publ., Delhi.

Swaminathan, M.S. (1999): *Green Revolution: The Challenges Ahead*, The Hindu Survey of Indian Agriculture.

Tyagi, B.P.(1996): *Agricultural Economics and Rural Development*, Jai Prakash Nath & Co., Meerut.

Udhop, Loitongbam (1989): *A Brief History of Agricultural Development in Manipur (1956-1983)*, L. Saratkumar Singh & Brothers, Imphal.

World Commission on Environment and Development (WCED) (1987): *Our Common Future*, Oxford University Press.

3

Problems and Prospects of Rural Economy of Manipur

Ng. Ibotombi Singh

Introduction

Development of rural economy of an underdeveloped state like Manipur is a complex process because of its multidimensional problems. In fact, the development of rural economy of Manipur has now become an essential task of the central and state governments for inclusive and equitable growth in the state. It is also equally necessary to unlock the huge potential of the population that is presently trapped in poverty. Rural economy of the state is handicapped by large scale poverty, unemployment, under-employment and backwardness. Moreover, due to lack of knowledge and physical connectivity people in rural areas cannot take part in the development programmes initiated by the central and state governments. Therefore, development of rural economy is necessary because an overwhelming majority of people live in rural areas and, at the same time, development of rural economy is essential for the acceleration of pace of the overall economic development of the state. No development programme can succeed unless it centres around rural development of the state. In the present context of Manipur, rural development programmes are formulated by the government with the assistance of government officials and urban intelligentsia who have poor knowledge of rural economy. The aim of the present paper is to study rural economic scenario of Manipur in depth so as to suggest ways and means for a healthy rural life in the state.

Rural Population

According to 1961 census, the total population of the state was 7.80 lakhs out of which 7.12 lakhs or 91.32 percent was in rural areas (Table-1). It is also observed from the same table that though the proportion of rural population has come down moderately over the census years, there has been a considerable increase in the absolute number of people living in rural areas. It stood at 17.18 lakhs in the year 2001 constituting 74.89 percent of the total population. Since in-migration is not significant in the villages the growth of population is slower as compared to the urban areas. Density of population per sq. km. according to 2001 census was 77 in rural, while for the state it was 103. Number of female per 1000 males in rural areas declined from 1018 in 1961 to 963 in 2001, but in urban areas it increased from 985 in 1961 to 1009 in 2001.

Table 1
Distribution of population between rural and urban of Manipur during 1961-2001

Census year	*Rural*	*Urban*	*Total*
1961	712320 (91.32)	67717 (8.68)	780037 (100)
1971	931261 (86.81)	141492 (13.19)	1072753 (100)
1981	1045493 (73.58)	375460 (26.42)	1420593 (100)
1991	1331504 (72.48)	505645 (27.52)	1837149 (100)
2001	1717928 (74.89)	575968 (25.11)	2293896 (100)

Source: Different Census reports
Note: Figure of 2001 includes estimated figure of three hill Sub-Divisions of Senapati District viz. Mao-Maram, Pao-mata and Pural. Figures in parentheses indicate percentages.

Villagers are relatively more homogeneous on social and economic characteristics. Occupational and social mobility of the rural people is limited. Custom, tradition and religion play a prominent role in rural life. Poverty level is very high in rural areas, 40.03 per cent of people were below the poverty line during 1999- 2000. The people affected by poverty are mainly landless agricultural workers. Low levels of income and inequalities in the distribution of income are very apparent in rural areas and it is more critical in the rural areas of the hill districts.

The number of villages in the hill is more compared to that in the valley of Manipur. As per 2001 census total number of inhabited villages in Manipur was 2391, out of which 1901 villages were in the hill and 490 villages in the valley (Table No. 2).

Table 2
District-wise inhabited villages in Manipur

District	*1971*	*1981*	*1991*	*2001*
Senapati	404	447	517	625
Tamenglong	184	190	194	171
Churachandpur	362	428	502	546
Chandel	217	254	292	361
Ukhrul	216	221	222	198
Imphal (E)	252	220	206	204
Imphal (W)	146	125	117	134
Bishnupur	58	47	45	49
Thoubal	110	103	87	103
Total Hill	1383 (70.96)	1540 (75.68)	1727 (79.15)	1901 (79.5)
Total Valley	566 (29.04)	495 (24.32)	455 (20.85)	490 (20.5)
Total Manipur	1949	2035	2182	2391

Source: GOM(2006): *Statistical Abstract Manipur 2005*, p. 10, DES.

Note: Figures in parentheses indicate percentages.

It is also observed from the same table that 1949 villages i.e. 70.96 per cent in Manipur was in the hill in 1971 which increased to 79.50 per cent in 2001. But in the valley it is observed that number of villages declined from 29.04 per cent in 1971 to 20.50 per cent in 2001.

Occupational Structure

In rural society the predominant occupations are cultivation and agricultural labour. The number of workers engaged in non-agricultural pursuits is very small and agriculture is the mainstay of the people. Table No. 3 shows the distribution of rural workers under different sectors i.e. Agriculture or primary, Secondary or Industrial sector and Tertiary or service sector.

Table 3
Distribution of rural workers under different economic activities

Census year	*Primary*	*Secondary*	*Tertiary*	*Total*
1961	236354 (71.55)	68337 (20.68)	25660 (7.77)	330351 (100)
1971	256801 (77.05)	33693 (10.11)	42794 (12.84)	333288 (100)
1981	353556 (77.8)	47733 (10.53)	52921 (11.67)	453210 (100)
1991	430061 (77.39)	42074 (7.57)	83592 (15.04)	555727 (100)
2001	443126 (61.28)	67886 (9.39)	212075 (29.33)	723087 (100)

Source: Different Census reports
Note: Figures in parentheses indicate percentages.

It is observed from the analysis of Table No. 3 that even after the completion of 50 years of economic planning, occupational structure of the rural economy of the State has not shown any appreciable change. The backwardness of rural economy is still evident from its structural rigidity accompanied by unemployment and under employment leading to low productivity of workers and low level of living in rural areas. When rural work force increased from 330351 in 1961 to 555727 in 1991, the number of workers in non-agricultural sectors was only 22.61 per cent in 1991. This indicates that agriculture had to make room for the remaining 77.39 percent of rural work force. But this sector happens to be in a very unsatisfactory state. In spite of a large number of labour force engaged in agriculture, we are not self-sufficient in a number of agricultural products and, therefore, import almost all agricultural products, including rice, for domestic consumption. Thus, prevalence of chronic under-employment or disguised unemployment in rural sector can be ascertained in Manipur. The cause of such surplus workers and low productivity is the result of various factors. However, poor infrastructure and lack of development in industrial sector are responsible to a great extent. Thus, the crucial problem in rural areas is the lack of employment opportunities in non-farm sectors and inability of the backward agriculture to absorb workers productively.

Proper employment planning in the state, therefore, needs careful attention of the policy makers. Unless the pace of development both in agricultural and industrial sphere is accelerated it will not be possible to provide gainful employment to the increasing labour force in the rural areas. Surplus workers due to natural growth of population may not find proper place in other sectors and will have to join agriculture. Only when agro-based industries and non-farm activities are strengthened, surplus workers can be withdrawn from agriculture. It is also observed from Table No. 3 that the number of workers engaged in agriculture or primary sector during 1971 to 1991 was not less than 77.00 per cent of the total rural workers. But in 2001, all of a sudden, it was reduced to 61.28 per cent. It is an emerging trend after economic reforms in India and needs to be examined carefully why the sequence of structural change to accompany economic development is not observed.

In the process of economic growth of developed countries there has been a shift of workers from primary to secondary and then to service sector. The change was associated with economic development of these countries. For a meaningful change in occupational structure, there must be simultaneous development of all economic activities i.e. agriculture, industry and service sector. But in the case of Manipur we hardly see any progress in secondary or industrial sector. This sector could absorb only 7.57 per cent in 1991 and 9.39 per cent in 2001 of the total rural work force (Table No. 3).

It is also observed from the same table that there was a sharp increase of workers in tertiary sector which rose from 15.04 per cent in 1991 to 29.33 per cent in 2001. The transfer of workers from agriculture to service sector was not associated with the expansion of agriculture and industry which is one of the generally accepted pre-conditions for a sustained economic growth of a country or state. It is a fact that during the last few years a good number of rural youths have joined retail trade and other services. It is evident from the coming up of electronic equipment shops, wearing apparel shops, PCOs, chicken centres, pan shops etc. in rural and urban areas. Almost all items of trade are imported from other states of India or foreign countries informally.

Nature and Dimensions of Rural Unemployment

Rural unemployment is essentially seasonal in character, and it is more acute during the slack reason. In fact, there are some cultivators who have enough landholdings to keep themselves busy throughout the year. They overwork during sowing and harvesting season and call in even hired labour by giving high wages. But most of the villagers do not have adequate holdings to keep themselves busy, and they seek work wherever it is be available. In short, they are employed irregularly, inadequately and intermittently throughout the year.

Over and above there are a large number of educated unemployed youths in rural areas who are seeking jobs in other occupations because they have no place in agriculture. According to the live Register of Employment Exchange, Government of Manipur, total number of rural educated unemployed youths, of different levels of education, was 3,06,920 as on 30-09-2006 (Table No. 4). They are looking for government jobs which are very limited in number. If agriculture and industrial sectors are remunerative and more productive, unemployed youths will not wait for government jobs. No nation or country has moved from chronic economic stagnation into the take-off stage of economic growth without raising agricultural productivity. It is one of the pre-conditions which must be strengthened or established before a sustained economic growth becomes possible. It is also very important to co-ordinate agriculture and industry. The relationship between agriculture and industry should be properly established, and should not be separated in the process of development planning. They are the two wheels of an economy. It is, therefore, necessary that the people and the policy makers devote more time to consider how best agriculture and industry contribute to each other and to study the interdependence between the two sectors. In fact, the Khansari Sugar Factory which was established in 1973 at Khangabok in Thoubal District as a public sector undertaking could not function due to the lack of co-ordination between agriculture and industry in the state.

Table 4
District-wise educated unemployment in rural area of Manipur (As on 30-09-2006)

District	*Male*	*Female*	*Total*
Imphal East	29609	11513	41122
Imphal West	102874	33749	136623
Thoubal	35530	15354	50884
Bishnupur	22310	9706	32016
Churachandpur	27871	7339	35210
Chandel	8025	3040	11065
Total	2,26,219	80,701	3,06,920

Source: GOM, Directorate of Employment Exchange.
Note: Figures of Senapati, Ukhrul and Tamenglong districts were not available as on 30-09-2006.

Agriculture

After the Green Revolution was launched in India in the late 1960's, significant increase in production of foodgrain was achieved. India's food production is a success story following the Green Revolution. It has helped Indian economy in every direction of her economic progress. But its impact is not satisfactory in the case of Manipur. Productivity of workers and land could not increase as expected. Due to low productivity many workers are ready to leave agriculture if they could find an alternative job. It is also a fact that some land owners are willing to sell their paddy fields, if the price of land is attractive, and invest to some other alternative activities. Under these circumstances many plots of our paddy fields have been encroached for non-agricultural activities, viz. establishment of schools and colleges, oil pumps, brick fields, offices, etc. If this trend continues for some more time, the state will face a serious food crisis in the near future. Therefore, it should be checked by a strict land policy without any further delay.

Development of agriculture is the only means to increase purchasing power of rural mass and expand market for industrial goods. Thus, it will help to bring about the needed changes in state's economic organisation. Agricultural planning needs planning at grass root level and participation of local people for optimum output. If a planner who is from a far away place and unaware of the differences in the input requirements prescribes uniform inputs for all plots of land, actual output will fall short of its potential resulting in a heavy loss for the farmers. Policy makers, scientists and farmers should join hands and take up various measures to improve agriculture in the state. Agriculture needs adequate irrigation facilities, consolidation of small holding, better seeds, fertilizers, credit facilities, etc. Among others, irrigation has a strong bearing on development of agriculture. Importance of water harvesting and management is known to everybody but no competent person cares for it. It may be mentioned that fertilizer, tractor, pump set, HYV-seeds, etc. are ready-made inputs which are available in the market, but water is not. Deficiency of water at the time of sowing and grain formation stage is the ubiquitous factor affecting crop yields. There have been many years during which farmers could not get income equal to the amount they invested in agriculture.

Many major, medium and multi-purpose irrigation projects have been introduced in Manipur from the 4th Five Year Plan period onwards but the benefit of these projects is hardly seen. Irrigation programme which started with a small plan investment of Rs. 1.41 crores during the fourth plan was increased to the order of Rs. 20.00 crores, Rs. 40.00 crores, Rs. 74.00 crores and Rs. 125.00 crores during the 5th, 6th, 7th and 8th plan respectively. During the Ninth plan the outlay for major and medium irrigation was Rs. 220.00 crores. And the proposed outlay during the Tenth plan was Rs. 414.57 crores. Inspite of the huge investment and efforts made by the government farmers are facing acute water crisis for agriculture.

In rural areas every house has a pond as a source of water for domestic uses. It is the most traditional and by far the simplest and the cheapest source of water which can harvest and store water for many months during a year. Thus, pond water is for everything in rural life. However, in paddy fields we hardly see ponds for cultivation purposes. Farmers are simply waiting for uncertain rain water. They can not take up cultivation in time when there is late monsoon, and experience bad crops in many years. In West Bengal ponds have been effectively used as a source of water for irrigation purposes. This simple practice may be introduced in our rural areas. One of the reasons for absence of ponds in our paddy fields may be small size of holding. A poor farmer with a small area of land is not willing to spare his land for a pond. On the other hand, land owners are from different places and cannot meet together for a collective programme. It is also a fact that there are a large number of rich urban land owners who hardly visit their paddy fields because their crop share is almost compulsory. If land owners are motivated through awareness programme many ponds could be constructed with traditional knowledge and skill. Once the problem of water is resolved we can expect a bountiful harvest. Now, who will initiate the project is the question. The state government may take up awareness problem for the importance and benefit of pond water for micro irrigation. Different pockets may be identified at different places for construction of ponds and compensate the farmers who scarifice the land in the form of regular income or an attractive price of the land.

Size of Holding

Next, we may consider the pattern of the size of land holdings to get an insight in the rural economy of Manipur. The state has a very limited arable land and majority of farmers have small and marginal land holdings. The area of operational holding is about 174 thousand hectares operated by 142 thousand farmers as per the agricultural census 1995-96. And the average size of operational holdings was 1.22 hectares in 1995-96 .

Land utilisation records for the entire state are not available because the hill areas are not cadastrally surveyed. As per land utilisation statistics of 2000-2001, the reporting area is about 1,90,446 hectares, of which 26, 900 hectares of land are not available for cultivation. Fallow land covers 200 hectares and other uncultivated land excluding the fallow land covers 8055 hectare of the total reporting area (Govt. of Manipur, Economic survey, 2005-06, p. 79). Rice continues to dominate acreage of all crops accounting 68.66 per cent of the total cropped areas of the state in 2003-04 (*ibid*, p. 91). The small size of holdings and absence of diversification of cropping patterns is an indicative of the rural poverty and unemployment.

Animal Husbandry

Animal husbandry is an integral part of the rural economy. Agriculture receives inputs from livestock and in turn provides feed for livestock. The main livestock available in rural areas of Manipur are cattle, buffalo, pig, goat, dog etc. The traditional agriculture livestock farming system was self-reliant and sustained itself for thousands of years in rural Manipur. However, the system became increasingly unviable and un-sustainable because of low productivity. Rearing of pig and poultry are becoming important enterprises in rural areas. Poultry is the most efficient converter of feed into food for human consumption in the shortest possible time. Its demand in the market is also increasing due to increasing population. Thus, many rural youths have joined this sector and employed themselves. However, poultry development still relies on the feed supplied by agricultural sector of other states. As such, its development cannot be isolated from agriculture.

Horticulture

Manipur is uniquely placed with diverse agro-climatic conditions, fertile soil, sub-tropical climate with pockets of temperate zones and abundant rainfall which are favourable conditions for development of horticulture. However, horticultural activities in the state are largely confined to backyard farm activities, and are characterised by lack of technical know-how, low level of productivity, improper post harvest management and poor marketing facilities. We need to tap the potential in a scientific and systematic manner to generate a sustainable level of income and employment for rural people. It is one of the most important economic activities of the rural areas, particularly in the hill which constitutes 90 percent of the total geographical area of the state. The major horticultural crops available in the state are banana, orange, pineapple, passion fruits, ginger, turmeric, potato etc.

The Technology Mission for Integrated Development of Horticulture which was launched by the Government of Manipur from 2001-2002, under the Prime Minister special package programme will give an opportunity for the villagers to expand this sector productively. According to the survey conducted by Technology Mission 2005-2006, the total potential area for horticultural crops in the state was 2,77,064 hectares, of which 19.6 per cent was actually cultivated for horticultural crops.

Table 5

Progress of horticulture in Manipur during 2000-01 to 2005-06

Crop	*2000-01*		*2005-06*	
	Area(Ha.)	*Production(MT)*	*Area(Ha.)*	*Production(MT)*
Fruits				
Banana	1440	11520	2214	22201
Orange	930	3720	1848	14800
Pineapple	9990	69930	11872	97516
Passion Fruit	–	–	3870	42926
Vegetables				
Tomato	505	4121	1369	13792
Cabbage	1320	15840	2020	26032
Pea	1010	5818	1441	13271
Spices				
Ginger	1100	11000	1830	2930
Turmeric	320	3780	230	550

Source: GOM, Technology Mission, Annual Report, 2005-06, Department of Horticulture and Soil Conservation.

It is observed from Table No. 5 that there is a good progress for expansion of horticulture in the state. Being a low chemical fertilizer consuming state, Manipur has good opportunity to take up production of organic fruits for export and domestic consumption. With growing demand for organic products in domestic and international markets, the producers can fetch good price provided documentation and certification are properly furnished by the competent officials and scientists. Transportation and marketing bottlenecks should be removed through appropriate physical and knowledge connectivity to enable the farmers to get maximum benefit.

Floriculture, another branch of horticulture which was considered to be simple garden activity to get flowers for religious offering and home decoration, has emerged as an important agri-business enterprise.

This segment can be developed in rural areas where different species are available due to favourable climatic conditions.

Sericulture which has been in practice by way of exploiting her own indigenous flora and fauna in a traditional way is another sub-sector where many rural workers may be employed. It being an agro-based enterprise can play an important role in shaping economic destiny of the rural people. This sector can provide employment at home for the entire members of the family by way of reeling, hand spinning of cocoons and silkworm rearing. As its activities do not involve hard labour, children and old people can join conveniently. Because of its simple technology and low investment, it is suitable to a poor state like Manipur. In addition, development of sericulture will provide employment opportunity through supporting occupations like bamboo weaving for making rearing trays, manufacturing of chemicals reeling and twisting machinery, dye manufacturing, etc.

Non-Farm Rural Economic Activities

Non-agricultural activity is an important part of rural economy. This sector is very important because of forward and backward production linkages. Agriculture needs implements and inputs that can be provided by rural non-agricultural activity.

Handloom is the largest non-farm rural economic activity giving employment to a large number of rural women folk. Most of the weavers are self-employed artisans who are producing different cloths of local demand. There were 2.7 lakhs looms comprising of fly-shuttle, throw shuttle and loin-looms and 2.8 lakhs of weavers according to National Handloom Census, 1987 (Economic Survey, Manipur, p. 11, 2005-06). Some of the peculiar products which are still in demand for local use are Ningthou Phee, Lamthang Khulak, Khamen-Chatpa, Moirang Phee, Leiroom, Hijamayek etc. Each design has its own history as to how and by whom they were invented. It is a fact that these products are not available in any other part of the country or world. Being a labour intensive family occupation, many family members can participate in pre-loom and post loom activities. Thus, a large number of women weavers can be engaged in this sector even though remuneration or profit is not high.

Handicrafts industry is also another non-farm economic activity supporting rural economy of Manipur. Some of the products are embroidery, cane and bamboo, ivory, stone and wood carving, metal crafts, dolls and toys etc. Various products of Kouna (local name) has a distirct place of its own. One of the important problems associated with the craftsmen is that they are by and large poor and the methods and equipments used by them are also traditional and indigenous with low productive capacity. There is enough scope for giving regular employment if they are properly trained and the skills are properly harnessed.

Rural Administration and Development Programmes

In the rural areas of Manipur, there are two types of local administration, viz. Panchayati Raj system in the Valley and District Council in the hill. Under the Pachayati Raj system, the local self-government in Manipur is organised at two levels - the Village Panchayats and the Zila Parishads. In the hill, the District Councils Act 1971 has been enforced since 1972. From August 1973 onwards, the Act has been implemented in the hill by dividing the hill areas under six autonomous hill districts. Each district has a District Council consisting of 16 elected members and two nominated members. The Manipur Hill People's Regulation, 1947 also provided for setting up of village authorities in each village. The members are nominated and consist of a chief of the village with his council of elders. The chief is virtually a sovereign and possesses the status and power of a king. Unfortunately, rural administration in Manipur both in the hill and the valley is not properly carried out due to power conflict between the local MLAs and rural representatives.

A number of rural development programmes has been planned and carried out in India from time to time right from the inception of community development programme in 1952. Implementation of rural development programmes is a success story in many states of India. However, in Manipur many programmes could not yield desired results due to power conflict between the panchayat representatives and the local MLAs. The attitude of the bureaucracy to monopolise and usurp power is another hurdle in the process of implementation of development programmes in the state. The danger of bureaucratic dominance is always there because of its alleged holding of technical knowledge. Moreover, officials all are more routine oriented than vested with the spirit of public service.

We have a sound village structure, but lack of people's participation in the process of development is one of the factors for poor performance of any programme. Awareness, willingness and capacity are the important factors on which participation depends. Maximum efforts are needed in the socio-economic structure so as to enable the villagers to gain the capacity to participate in the process of development. Adaptive response from the villagers are very important. People's participation implies participation at all the stages viz. planning, implementation, decision making, sharing benefit, monitoring and evaluation etc. People's participation is very important because villagers know their own needs and problems better than government officials working at block, district and state levels.

The 73rd Constitutional Amendment Act, 1992 provided for empowerment of women, weaker sections, the poor and the disorganised in the society thereby paving the way for active participation of people in grass root democracy. Thus, the PRIs are the basic institutions of democracy where villagers could participate in the process of administration. The PRIs should be encouraged by the state government without interfering their functioning. PRIs should be encouraged to tap all internal resources instead of always depending upon government for funds. Above all maximum efforts should be made to elect the best candidates for Panchayat services. Concentration of political power in the hands of exclusive elite groups should be checked. This may lead to a cumulative unequal social structure resulting in the alienation of majority of villagers. Mere transfer of political power to village representatives will not solve rural problems. Villagers should be motivated to take part in the process of rural upliftment. Flow of fund in the name of employment assurance scheme, wage employment programme, etc. without proper planning will not improve rural economy. Mobilising money is not a problem, the real problem is how to structure the system. Before the funds are released it is important to find out where to work or what is to be produced. Distribution of funds to the beneficiaries without job opportunities will not serve the purpose of rural development programmes. Bharat Nirman of the UPA Government for rural infrastructure and Provision of Urban Amenities in Rural Areas (PURA) propagated by Dr. APJ Abdul Kalam, President of India, and the National Rural Employment Guarantee Act (NREGA) are the new rural development programmes which will give a big push in rural economy of the country. The state government ought to take maximum care for implementation of these programmes or else the benefit may not reach the rural people. All roadblocks in effective functional transfer to village representatives should be removed.

Conclusion

It is observed from the above discussions that backwardness of rural economy of the state is a consequence of critical factors which are basically rooted in inefficient rural administration, insufficient availability of natural and man-made resources relative to the needs of the villages, and their uneven distribution. The development of rural economy of Manipur, therefore, requires proper attention of policy makers, economists, and utilisation of more man-made resources including technology, their efficient utilisation as well as distribution in a manner that the required inputs accrue to the rural mass. This would manifest itself in making the self-employed more productive, and the creation of employment opportunities for the rural labour force including the landless rural workers. It is also observed that lack of people's participation in the process of development and rural administration is one of the hurdles of rural economic growth in the state. It is, therefore, necessary to improve awareness of the various programmes and projects introduced by the central and state governments through knowledge and physical connectivity. In such a process of rural development scenario, agriculture has to play an important role to play in the process of rural development as A.W. Lewis has rightly pointed out that "failure of peasant - agriculture to increase its productivity has probably been the chief reason of holding down the expansion of industrial sector in most of underdeveloped countries". However, it has remained a weak link in the economic structure of Manipur and the strategies for rural development in the state should focus on the overall expansion of its rural economy.

REFERENCES

Baruah, Joydeep and Indranee Dutta (2004): "Determinants of People's Participation in Decentralized Planning and Development", *Political Economy Journal of India*, Jan-June.

Gadgil, D.R. (1973): "District Development Planning", in Charan D Wadhva (ed), *Some Problems of India's Economic Policy*, Tata McGraw, New Delhi.

Government of India (2004): *Toward Faster and More Inclusive Growth. An Approach to the 11th Five Year Plan (2007-2012)*, Planning Commission.

___________(2008): *Eleventh Five Year Plan 2007-12*, Vol. III, Planning Commission, Oxford University Press.

___________, *Agricultural Statistics-at-a-Glance, 2003*, Ministry of Agriculture

Government of Manipur, *Annual Administrative Report 2006-07*, Department of Rural Development and Panchayati Raj.

___________, *Statistical Abstract - 2005*, DES.

___________, *Economic Survey, 2005-2006*, DES.

___________, *Annual Administrative Report 2005-06*, Department of Rural Development and Panchayati Raj.

___________, (2006): *Annual Report of Technology Mission 2005-06.*

Lewis, W.A.(1955): *Theory of Economic Growth*, Hencewood.

Mani, R(2006): *Watershed Planning and Employment Generation*, Mittal Publications, New Delhi.

Roy Burman, B.K. (1984): *Towards Poverty Alleviation Programmes in Nagaland and Manipur*, Mittal Publications, New Delhi.

Shukla, SP (2006): *Strategy for Integrated Development of Arunachal Pradesh*, Mittal Publications, New Delhi.

Singh, Katar (1999): *Rural Development: Principles, Policies and Management*, Sage, New Delhi.

Streeten, Paul (2004): "Empowerment, Participation and the Poor", *Political Economy Journal of India*, Vol.13., July-Dec.

Todaro, Michael P.(2001): *Economic Development*, Addison-Wesley.

Vatta, Kamal (2003): "Microfinance and Poverty alleviation", *Economic and Political Weekly*, Feb. 1-7.

4

Institutional Impediments to Development in the Hill Regions of Manipur

Ch. Priyoranjan Singh

History, culture and social norms of a society and community have been identified by institutional economists as the prime determinants of the pace of development in any economy. Institutions, social, political and economic, are the fundamental framework within which markets function in the allocation of resources and the distribution of wealth. How efficiently resources are utilized are determined by the nature of institutions of the society and how these institutions adept or change according to the needs of the times. Institutions that encourage competition and technological change are more conducive to development than those that that resist change or are rigidly defined.

However, institutions are evolved over centuries and the social norms and value systems that are attached to these institutions cannot be transformed overnight. Any quick fix attempt at social engineering to transform any institution are generally met with vehement political resistance and on the net, societies end up no better off, if not worse off. As such, to find the right and socially acceptable way in the transformation of institution or the infusion of new ones are the latest headaches of state and non state agencies in the contemporary world of globalization.

Impediments to institutional change are the greatest in conservative and tribal societies where the forces of the market are weak and where the integration to the mainland economy and society are subsistence and political in nature. And yet it is the persistence of these pockets of underdevelopment within a growing economy that poses the greatest threat to development of the economy as a whole, as the inequity and exclusion becomes a liberal playground for political turmoil and unrest.

This paper focuses on the nature of development in the tribal and hill regions of Manipur and tries to examine some of the institutional hurdles that are holding back many of the development efforts since independence. The objective of this paper is three fold. In the first place the paper seeks to highlight some core features of the socio-economic status of the tribal regions of Manipur based on macro level data. Secondly the paper seeks to unravel the social reality in a Tribal village and hoes population growth, environmental degradation and funds flows are distorting the economic base of the village.

Institutions and Social Orders

In recent times, institutional economists have made seminal contributions to our understanding of economic change and the course of human development and growth. In the neo-classical world of instrumental rationality, rational choices are made under conditions of scarcity and competition and efficient outcomes/payoffs are achieved. Under assumption of perfect information and zero transaction costs, efficient markets – both political and economic – characterize economies. However agents neither have complete information nor the unlimited mental capacities to process even the available information. Under such circumstances, the choice that the individual or decision maker makes, is a matter of perceptions that their 'mental models' generates. Douglas North thus writes "Individuals process mental models to interpret the world around them. These are part culturally derived- that is produced by the intergenerational transfer of knowledge, values and norms which vary radically among differing ethnic groups and societies. In part they are acquired through experience which is "local" to the particular environment and therefore also varies widely with different environments. Consequently there is immense variations in mental models and as a result, different perceptions of the world and the way it "works". And even the formal learning that individuals acquire frequently consists of conflicting models by which we interpret the world around us". Individuals make choices in tune with their mental models and these models can change when outcomes are not consistent with expectations.

In the real world of incomplete information and limited mental capacity and where information are held asymmetrically among transacting parties, uncertainties arise, transaction costs become positive and institutions are evolved. Institutions are formed to reduce uncertainty and transaction costs. When it is costly to transact, institutions matter. Institutional economists have extended economic theory by " incorporating ideas and ideologies into the analysis, modeling political process as a critical factor in the performance of economies as the source of the diverse performance of economies and as the explanation for inefficient markets". North contends that while efficient economic markets are exceptional, it is impossible to find efficient political markets. The polity defines and informs property rights and inefficient economic markets arise out of inefficient political markets. Once an economy is on the inefficient path that produces stagnation, change is reparted because of the nature of path dependence.

Human development and economic change have been associated with a sequence of 'social orders'. primitive societies exploit an existing resource base and then graduate to new social orders with the ability to expand the resource base. Scientific revolution and its enormous productivity potentials were realized through entrepreneurs and increasing stock of knowledge under competitive conditions. North concludes that highly productive and modern social orders could only be achieved by creating in political and economic markets the institutional conditions for impersonal exchange.

North has identified four "fundamental building blocks" for the emergence of the institutional conditions for impersonal exchange. Belief systems or the ' mental model' are according to North, the source of human creativity as well as "depravity". As such belief systems underlie the choices that humans make and the development path they experience through time and space. Secondly, though personal exchange produces cooperative behavior in small group interaction it also correspondingly generate distrust of outsiders and large group interaction. Graduation into impersonal exchange requires fundamental institutional changes to permit group interaction among individuals and groups with no personal knowledge of each other. Thirdly violence either to gain resources or to protect resources underlie structures that humans create through history. Fourthly specialization and division of labour is the source of productivity and growth. These four fundamental building blocks interact with experiences like physical environment, climate and geography to shape the features of pre-modern social orders. A shift from the physical to the human environment is a basic determinant of human conditions and social orders.

Tribal Polity and Institutions

Tribal polity in Manipur is based on the village and the land holding systems. Tribal polity of both the Kukis and the Nagas never grew beyond the village and as such the autonomous political, social and economic unit of the villages never developed into a pan tribal monolithic polity or nation. The tribal villages were termed as 'small republics' by colonial writers. Gangmumei Kamei writes that the issues of ethnicity, identity and land ownership are built into the psyche of the tribal people. Ethnicity, identity and land are intricately linked in the tribal world of Manipur. Kamei further writes that the fundamental basis of tribal polity and economy are their mode of production and the nature of ownership of the resources of the community. Thus the belief system of the tribes of Manipur and the institutional structures that these belief systems have given rise to are firmly founded on the land systems of the respective tribes.[1] The tribal concept of land includes village land, territory, forests, economy and culture. Such consciousness of land by the tribes implies land as the foundation of tribal social, cultural and economic systems. Thus Shimray writes "within the village territory and its ecosystems the values, beliefs and cultural practices are regulated by the traditional social institutions", which presumably is based on the land system of the tribes. Tribal livelihood systems are sustained by the intrinsic interface between land, polity, culture and economy.

Assuming that the tribal land system is the fundamental basis of the tribal world and that the land system largely determines tribal belief systems and therefore institutions, why the tribal areas of Manipur are slow to develop or impervious to economic change could possibly be answered by a relook at the existing reality of tribal land system in tribal Manipur. Here we are not assuming that socio-cultural, political and other economic institutions need not be taken into account independently or conjointly to understand the totality of the tribal belief systems that defines the institutional matrix of tribal society. In fact it is the inexorable changes in these institutions themselves that are giving rise to the breaking down of the tribal land system itself in contemporary times[2]. What we intend to specify by focusing on tribal land systems is merely to hammer home the fact that romanticizing the centrality of the pristine land system in the tribal world is only a convenient ploy of the tribal elite to perpetuate a mental model that only serves their interests at the expense of the common tribals of the state. But it is also true that land is central to the tribal way of life, not only in the contemporary times but also through time. As a result even though occupational structures and livelihood structures are slowly shifting away from the land base to the other sectors of the economy in a large section of tribal villages of the state, the myths surrounding land, land systems and their interface with other aspects of the tribal world are still being gainfully appropriated by the elite and political organizations and entrepreneurs.

Socioeconomic Base to Tribal Districts

Manipur has a unique physiography that has historically given rise to two contrasting cultures and economies. Contrasting patterns of population and phisiographic contours have necessarily led to contrasting settlement patterns, economic base and livelihood options. There is a fertile and well drained valley right in the middle which is inhabited by the Meities, the majority population. The valley region constitutes only ten percent of the total area of the state but 62 percent of the population is concentrated in the valley. Historically the fertile valley provided the necessary food security upon which was built a stable civilization and polity that was integrated to the global markets, specially during the colonial period. In the post-colonial period, the valley region had emerged as an open agrarian society and economy that had in place many of the institutional and structural requirements of a modern economy and polity. On the other hand the hill regions surrounding the valley constitutes 90 percent of the state's area but accounts for only 38 percent of the population and it is in these mountain terrains that the 32 tribes of the state have resided through history. The two major umbrella tribes of the Kukis and the Nagas within which the 32 sub- tribes are affiliated, had never emerged as separate polities and all remained as village level republics under the suzerainty of the valley monarchy. Each village was on its own and throughout history inter-village and inter-tribal localized warfare prevented the progressive emergence of integrated political and economic structures or markets and trading systems. Though the colonial administration had partially opened up the hill regions through the development of roads and rudimentary administrative infrastructures for the extraction of colonial surplus from the rich forests of the hills, the vast areas and villages in the region virtually remained isolated and un-integrated to the dynamised economy of the valley. No doubt the colonial revenue collection of hill house tax provided the umbilical link towards monetization and the slow penetration of manufactured goods to the villages were taking place but these had never reached the level that could have brought about the transformation of tribal institutions and socio-economic structures, conducive to the emergence of a society, economy and polity, as in the valley.

Tribal villages in the hill districts are far flung, thinly spread and sparsely populated, the density of population is barely 44 persons per square kilometer as against 631 in the valley region. In the post- colonial period the five district headquarters are the hub of tertiary sector activities and some population concentration. Other small and tiny market towns have sprung up on the national and state highways but these few towns still remain at low rudimentary levels. In fact there is no classified urban area in the hill districts of Manipur according to the Census of India 2001.[3] If urbanization is taken as an indicator of development, the tribal regions of Manipur has a far way to go.

There are 1901 villages in the five hill districts of Manipur. The average population per village is the highest at 711 persons in Ukhrul district and lowest at 327 per village in Chandel district. In other words the number of households in the biggest average sized village in the hill districts would be about 120 households and the number of households in the smallest average sized village would be about 55 households. Thus the average size of the tribal village in Manipur ranges all the way from 55 households to 120 households only. In fact there are four sub-divisions in the hills which have per village average population of below 300 persons and another six sub-divisions that have per village average population of below 400 people. In other words 10 out of 23 subdivisions in the hill districts (43 p.c.) have villages whose village sizes on an average range between 50 to 66 households only.

The point of this rough exercise in tribal village demography of Manipur is to highlight the fact that the large bulk of the tribal villages or settlement patterns are economically non-viable and lack the critical population mass that can fruitfully reap conventional development interventions or sustain them. This critical structural weakness is further compounded by the fact that these tiny villages are far flung in space as well as by tough foot communication. Most of these villages have to procure the daily necessities that they do not produce, from bigger and far away villages. The little agricultural surplus they produce has to be marketed on foot in these bigger villages or further to the towns at marginal and non-worthwhile profits. These tiny populations have led to non-growth of tertiary or industrial activities and the non emergence of markets and market cultures in the bulk of tribal villages. To design an appropriate marketing infrastructure within the structural weaknesses of the tribal and hilly regions of the Northeast is perhaps one of the core challenges of any developmental intervention.

The demographic profiles and settlement patterns of the tribal districts of Manipur have their historical roots in the nature of tribal political formations and economic organization. Tribal politico-social organizations revolve around the institutions of Chief-ship or Village Council. The Chief/Village Council/Clan control the vast areas of forest and Jhum land surrounding the village. Population pressures led to migration of clan groups beyond the vast village land boundaries to set up new villages or settlements. This historical process of land colonization of forests and Jhum land has resulted in the rapid dispersal of tiny villages with vast jurisdiction over land, all over the hilly regions of the state.

Economic organization was built around a subsistence jhum culture and extraction of forest wealth, both food and non food. Historically surplus forest products have been the basis of trade and exchange with the outside world, that is the valley population. The socio-political and economic organizations which are tightly structured, suited the pysiography and climes of the hill regions, without proper communications, without technological change, without modern aspirations and above all without democracy. Unfortunately all these potent forces of modernization was simultaneously imposed on the fragile ecology of the tribal regions without giving much heed to the critical institutional structures and subs-structures that had sustained subsistence tribal societies through centuries. Development processes have spawned a political economy in tribal areas of the state which is exclusive rather than being inclusive, which is divisive rather than integrating and which is retrograde rather than progressive.

Agrarian Base

Out of the total area under paddy cultivation in the state, 75.48 thousand hectares (43 p.c.) are in the hill districts. The yield rates of 2003 Kilograms per hectare in 2004-5 are lower than the valley yield of 2833 Kg/ hectare but higher than national yield rates. Historically however, the hills have not been able to produce sufficient food grains for its population and has been dependent on valley rice surplus. The reason is not far to seek, 41 percent of cultivation in the hills are jhum cultivation, however this proportion is misleading. The district of Senapati is entirely jhum free with about one third of agricultural land. In the rest of the other four districts the jhum proportion is 87 percent. Further the area under HYV seeds and improved seeds is only 16.8 percent, which is also almost entirely in the two districts of Senapati and Chandel. The hill districts also used only 8.4 percent of the total consumption of fertilizers in the state. This is quite obvious as traditional seeds users are hardly expected to have high levels of fertilizer consumption. Irrigation was available to only 13 percent of hill agriculture. Further no tractors are used in four districts and the district of Churachandpur has eight tractors according to the Livestock Census 2003. Power tillers which are more amenable to the hilly terrain are used in three districts though the number is barely 61. Thus one can say that tribal agriculture in Manipur is yet far away from the modernization process that India has been experiencing for over half a century.[4]

The hill districts however has a stronger livestock base than the valley. About 65 percent of the states livestock are in the hill districts. About 49 percent of poultry population is also in the hills. Meat supplies in the valley is partly met by hill surpluses. The hill districts are a main source of horticultural product, especially fruits and vegetables for the valley populations.

On the industrial front, one can only say that handloom and handicrafts are the only ones worth mentioning. The public sector cement factory in Ukhrul district is closed and many private sector poultry and fruit processing ventures have not been able to sustain themselves.

Demographic and Social Profile

The tribal districts of Manipur has been experiencing exceptionally high population growth rates after independence. The population in the hill districts have grown from 1,90,112 to 8,82,130during 1951-2001[3]. This represents a 4.64 times rise during half a century. The decennial growth rate reached as high as 50.97 percent during 1991-2001. Senapati district had the dubious distinction of a repeat census in three subdivisions as it showed a phenomenal decennial growth rate of 81.96 percent. The literacy rates in the five hill districts were 74.68 percent, 68.96 percent, 58.46 percent, 57.38 percent, and 50.47 percent respectively for the districts of Churachandpur, Ukhrul,Tamenglong, Chandel and Senapati districts. Literacy rates are therefore fairly high by tribal standards. Life expectancy range between 66 and 67 years for males and 70and 71 years for females. Infant mortality rates range between 28 in Churachandpur district and 45 in Chandel district. The state rate is 36. The low infant mortality rates, high life expectancy and high educational levels are perhaps reflected in the high population growth rate. The macro picture that emerges from the economic, social and demographic profile of the tribal districts of Manipur is one of contradictions and unrealized potentials. How does higher education and better health mix with higher poverty levels (40 pc). Why are jhuming practices still the dominant cropping practice in spite of dwindling livelihood options but rising demand for food and favorable terms of trade for agriculture. Why are heightened state investments having little effect on the productive base of the hill economy. Why are tightly structured tribal societies that are seemingly more democratic, and transparent, unable to absorb development funds and programs in a more fruitful way. In short, what are the dimensions of the emerging political economy of the tribal regions that seems to have arrested midstream, the impulses of development and growth.

Tribal Land System and Development

Tribal land systems are based on the principle of common ownership of land by the community or the village. The authority in the use and distribution of land are vested in the village chief and the village council. Tribal chiefs are either hereditary or elected and the village council assist the chief in the administration of the village. The councils are variously formed but the clan heads invariably find a place in the council. The role of the clan head is important in the village polity as tribal villages were originally formed by at least two clans. Thus socially tribal villages are more or less stratified into clans. Broadly speaking, tribal land constituted the village homestead land, forests and the jhum sites. The most crucial control over the jhum and its distribution within the village in a year rested in the village council. However after the decision of the village council, the effective distribution of land rested in the hands of the clan head within the share of the clan. This fundamental framework of the tribal land system has however changed over time and one can find any number of variations within this broad framework.[5]

The most fundamental change is the emergence of private property in land within the boundary of the tribal village, though in principle, the tribal polity and economy is assumed to be founded on common property rights. The first steps in the privatization of land was perhaps started by entrepreneurs who fanned out to the river valleys in search of more fertile land and permanent wet cultivation. As these land were not in the distributive control of the village council and a lot of private investment in labour was involved, the entrepreneurs enjoyed de-facto private property rights. The rise of wet rice cultivation in the river valleys of the tribal areas during the colonial days and more so in the post colonial period can largely be attributed to its private property effect.

Not surprisingly, private property consciousness also began to creep in into the common lands systems also. Population growth, scarcity of land and limited livelihood options have galvanized proprietorial rights even on the village common lands. Among the Nagas, land is virtually privatized and the chuck of the land is in the hands of the clan heads and the emerging Naga elites. Many villages have reported even private ownership even in village forest land. Among the Kukis, reports of the village chiefs becoming virtual Zamindars are also reported even on public platforms. Kuki chiefs selling off or tribal elites buying entire villages for political purposes are now an uncomfortable fact of tribal life in Manipur. Amidst all this, large scale landlessness is emerging in the tribal areas of the state. In other words, the tribal land system based on the concept of common property and land for all in the village has failed as the institutional framework of tribal society and polity.

A more fundamental issue however is whether tribal land system as the core institution of the tribal world is efficient and whether it has lived its time. In the ecological and moral environment of low populations, abundance of land and near isolation from the forces of the market and modern economic and administrative structures, the institution did serve its purpose, it was efficient. But in the changed and rapidly changing circumstances in the economy and society, the land system seems to be serving only the political interests and not the economic interests of the large majority of the tribes of Manipur. On the one hand where the concept of common property still exists, the familiar indiscriminate extraction of forest and other resources are leading to resource depletion and unsustainable environments. Resource creation is virtually non- existent in these areas. On the other hand the tribal elite are not allowing adaptive changes to this vital institution of tribal society. In other words the necessary transitions in the social orders of the tribes are being politically held up. The reasons are not far to seek.

Tribal villages in the state have an absolute lack of information, especially those in the interiors and away from the state and national highways. The awareness of government development programs and rapid changes in the outside world are extremely limited. Underdevelopment, food scarcity and most deprivations are levered in a political blame game without an objective assessment of the economic structures of the tribal economy and the opportunities that have not yet been adequately harnessed to their potential. Many of the myths of the pristine land system are being artificially kept alive and adaptive transition to a more progressive and efficient land and market regime are being rigidly resisted at the political level. The result is that the nature of exchange, both in the political and economic markets, still remain largely personal and the transition to impersonal exchange is being stunted. The massive siphoning off of funds for the building of interior roads, schools and health infrastructures are only one of the visible designs of the elite to maintain status quo in the tribal areas. Persistence of inefficient markets and the resultant path dependence of a subsistence economy is clearly visible in the tribal areas of the state.

The reality in a comparatively developed tribal village in the Ukhrul district reveal some interesting facts of tribal life in the state. The village of Siroy is a fairly large with 153 households and being only 15 kilometers from the district head quarters and being on the national highway the educational levels are also high at 77 percent. However only 63 percent of the head of households are cultivators and 18 percent were government employees. Eleven percent of the households were landless labourers. Landlessness is quite evident in this village. There is a lot of occupational diversification and movement away from agriculture. It was also found that out of the cultivating households over 76 percent were below subsistence farmers not able to meet their annual cereal requirements. Interestingly also about 9 percent of the cultivators were pure leasees, indicating the emergence of a land market in the village. Only one cultivator practices jhum and the rest were terrace cultivators. The chief of the village showed us the extensive barren face of the mountain range which was once the jhum land of the village. The village was highly indebted at 68 percent of households and the debts ranged from Rs 15,547 to Rs 38,142 per household. Organized money lending by 'societies' run by the elite accounted for 66 percent of the borrowings in the village. The village had a big livestock population, three small scale fisheries and horticulture. The land system in this village has no inkling of the traditional norms and the political institution of the chief was virtually defunct, having been absolutely usurped by the formal state institution of the Village Council. In fact the village had conveniently elected two chief other than the hereditary one, one for the upper and another for the lower section of the village. One can imagine the type of political economy changes that is taking place in this village where there is a great struggle for changes in the social order of this village.

Tribal polity, social orders and the property rights regimes are in a state of transition in Manipur. Until comprehensive, structured and objective studies are generated, generalizations of the institutional underpinnings of the tribal social orders will not be conclusive. However the fractured belief systems of the tribes are not yet in a position to create the conditions of impersonal exchange and efficient economic and political markets. In the mean time, violence as a means of protecting resources rather than creating resources is likely to continue for quite some time and the shifts from the physical to the human environment stands arrested.

NOTES

1. Deep rooted belief in the primacy of the tribal land systems in the matrix of tribal institutions have enabled the tribal elite to oppose the land privatization measures contained in the MLR & R Act 1960, even though the Act clearly protects tribal land alienation to non- tribals. See Gangmumei Kamei in Tribalism and the Tragedy of the Commons, Ch. Priyoranjan.

2. The political institution of the Chief and Village Council have been usurped by the formal institution of the Village Authority by the Manipur (Hill Areas) Village Authorities Act 1956. The institution of the Chief is increasingly marginalized to that of a necessary appendix. Further, Christianity and the church have virtually severed the link between the land system and religions and many social systems.

3. Hill district headquarters have been de-notified as urban areas on the pressures of the tribal elite in the expectation of cornering huge central funds for rural development.

4. Jhuming has not worked because of lack of co-operant institutional inputs and failure to be adaptive to the material, ecological and institutional needs of the tribes. See Devjayoti Roy (2006), Demystifying the Myth of Shifting Cultivation in the North East, Agronomy in the North East.

5. For the varieties of land systems , its corruption, use as a political tool and the dynamics of self destruction, see Ch. Priyoranjan Singh, Tribalism and the Tragedy of the Commons, 2009.

REFERENCES

Binodini Devi, K. (2006): *Tribal Land System in Manipur,* Akansha Publishing House, New Delhi.

Brown, R. (1873): *Statistical Account of Manipur,* Reprinted 1975, Sanskaran Prakasan, New Delhi.

Haokip, T.T. (2009): "Critically Assessing Kuki Land System in Manipur", in Singh, Ch. Priyoranjan (ed), *Tribalism and the Tragedy of the Commons,* Akansha Publishing House, New Delhi.

Kamei, Gangmumei (2009): "Ethnicity, Identity and Land in Tribal Manipur", in Singh, Ch. Priyoranjan Singh (ed), *Tribalism and the Tragedy of the Commons*, Akansha Publishing House, New Delhi.

MacCulloh (1859): *Valley of Manipur,* Reprinted 1980, Gian Publications, New Delhi.

North, Douglas (1992): "Institutions and Economic Theory", *American Economist,* Spring 1992.

Roy, Devjayoti (2006): "Demystifying the Myth of Shifting Cultivation in the North East, Agronomy in the North East", *Economic and Political Weekly,* Nov 25, 2006.

Shimray, U.A. (2009): "Land Ownership System of the Naga Community", in Singh, Ch. Priyoranjan (ed), *Tribalism and the Tragedy of the Commons*, Akansha Publications, New Delhi.

Singh, C.P. (2009): *Tribalism and the Tragedy of the Commons,* Akansha Publishing House, New Delhi.

5

Agricultural Growth in Manipur

Thokchom Biren Singh & L. Romen Singh

Introduction

Agriculture is an important sector in the economy of Manipur. It provides not only food and raw material but also employment to a large proportion of the population. Further, it contributes, though declining, about thirty percent of the state income. Understanding the importance of the sector, the state government has given high priority to this sector in its five year plans from the Green Revolution phase and, consequently, agricultural production as well as productivity has also gone up over the years. However, the sector is still plagued with many problems like lack of irrigation facilities, continuous fragmentation of land, widespread jhum cultivation, etc. where the government needs to put serious attention

Production of Food Crops

An important feature of agricultural production in the state is the high importance given to food over non-food crops. Area under cereal accounts for nearly 70 to 80 percent of the agricultural land in the state (Table 1). Cultivation of rice dominates other cereal crops and its production increased from 274.17 ('000) tonnes in 1990-01 to 389.17 ('000) tonnes in 2006-07. Rice is the staple food and is grown in hill and plain areas and it accounts for about 98 percent of total food grain production of the State in 2006-07 (Economic Survey of Manipur 20007-08). Rice occupies 82 percent of the total cultivated land area. It would be appropriate to call Manipur's agrarian economy as rice economy. Other crops are maize, wheat, pulses, other misc. crops, etc. but their production cannot be considered as significant. Unlike rice, they are grown only in selected pockets and hence their area and production estimates are not reliable (Economic Review 1984-85, p. 20). Production of the next important food crop of the state after rice, i.e. maize, is not so high as compared with that of rice and stood at 11.40 ('000) tonnes in 1990-91. Its production has more or less stagnated since then.

Table 1
Cropping pattern of Manipur

(Area in '000 hectares)

Year	*Cereals*	*Pulses*	*Oilseeds*	*Cotton*	*Sugarcane*	*Other Misc. Crops*	*Total*
1990-91	162.02 (80.08)	9.26 (4.58)	2.68 (1.32)	0.14 (0.07)	1.86 (0.92)	26.37 (13.03)	202.33 (100.00)
1999-00	161.39 (77.73)	6.80 (3.28)	2.89 (1.39)	0.05 (0.02)	0.65 (0.31)	35.86 (17.27)	207.64 (100.00)
2000-01	161.66 (77.53)	6.67 (3.20)	2.76 (1.32)	0.06 (0.03)	0.74 (0.36)	36.61 (17.56)	208.50 (100.00)
2001-02	167.63 (77.55)	6.62 (3.06)	1.00 (0.46)	0.09 (0.04)	0.65 (0.30)	40.17 (18.57)	216.16 (100.00)
2002-03	153.11 (73.58)	8.08 (3.88)	2.34 (1.13)	NA	0.32 (0.15)	44.24 (21.26)	208.09 (100.00)
2003-04	157.83 (69.40)	6.68 (2.94)	0.83 (0.36)	NA	0.33 (0.15)	61.75 (27.15)	227.42 (100.00)

Source: GOM (2008): *Statistical Abstract: Manipur 2007*, DES.
Note: the figures in the brackets represent percentages.

The increase in the production of rice in spite of a decline in the area from 162.02 ('000) hectares in 1990-91 to 157.83 ('000) hectares in 2006-07 has been made possible due to increase in its yield which rose from 1741.76 kg/hectare in 1990-91 to 2353.33 kg/hectare in 2006-07 as against an all India figure of 2084 kg/hectare. Thus, compared to the all India average yield of rice, the rice yield in the state cannot be considered low though it is still less than the figures achieved by states like Punjab and Haryana. However, the yield is uneven among the districts of Manipur with the valley districts recording much higher figures. Imphal West had the highest yield of 3045.53 kg/hectare in 2005-06 followed by Imphal East with 2915.19 kg/hectare. On the other hand, the yield was the lowest in Tamenglong district with 1319.33 kg/hectare. Increasing the yield of the hill districts from the present average kg/hectare to the state average or to the figures achieved in the valley districts will help to boost agricultural production not only for the hill districts but also for the entire state.

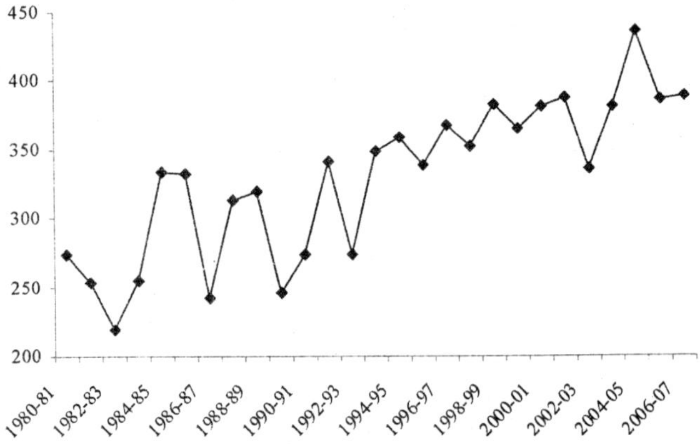

Figure 1: Rice production in Manipur
('000 tonnes)

Use of High Yielding Variety Seeds

The increase in yield has been made possible due to the adoption of new agricultural technology in terms of high yielding variety (HYV) seeds along with increased use of fertilizers and irrigation. The estimated area under HYV and improved varieties (IVs) of paddy was about 39.04 percent of the total area under paddy which gradually rose and currently stands at around 50 percent. The coverage under HYVs and IVs is much higher in the valley areas than in the hills. During 2004-05, the coverage was as high as 87.89 percent in the valley but it was only 16.82 in the hills. Thus, there is an active need for the spread of the improved varieties in the hill region to achieve higher yield.

Table 2

Use of HYVs, IVs and other local varieties of paddy

(percent)

Region	*Varieties of seeds*	*1995-96*	*1996-97*	*2002-03*	*2003-04*	*2004-05*
Hill	HYV+IV	12.07	18.65	11.98	17.99	16.82
	Others	87.93	81.35	88.02	82.01	83.18
Valley	HYV+IV	59.02	84.86	48.08	57.46	87.89
	Others	40.98	15.14	51.92	42.54	12.11
State	HYV+IV	39.04	54.11	30.93	38.19	57.47
	Others	60.96	45.89	69.07	61.81	42.53

Source: GOM(2008): *Economic Survey: Manipur 2007-08*, DES.

Use of Fertilizers

The use of fertilizers has become a necessity in the new agricultural strategy. Manipur is one of the few states which has high consumption rate of fertilizers as its consumption rate is 105 kg/ha as compared to North East average of 78 kg/ha and all India average of 90 kg/ha. Fertilizers that are commonly used are NPK or Nitrogenous, Phosphatic and Potassic. In fact, the use of NPK should be in the proportion 4:2:1 to get maximum results especially for food crops while the imbalance use may have negative effect on the soil quality. Even in the case of the all India figure, the ratio stood at 6:3:1 in 2005-06 and, thus, the imbalance is not high. But in the case of Manipur the ratio was 17:2:1. A quick interaction with some farmers and officials revealed that the relatively cheap price of nitrogenous fertilizers and lack of awareness of the benefits of phosphatic and potassic fertilizers have been the cause of the imbalance use of fertilisers.

There is uneven use of fertilizers among the districts in the state also very high percentage of fertilizer consumption in the state is in the valley districts with the hill districts accounting for a small amount. For example the consumption of Urea was as high as 23800 tonnes during 2005-06 in the valley districts while it was just 1549 tonnes in the hill districts.

Table 3
Consumption of chemical fertilizers in Manipur 2005-06

(in tonnes)

District /State	*Urea*	*DAP*	*MOP*	*SSP*	*Total*	*Percentage to total consumption*
Senapati	448	71	46	85	650	2.13
Tamenglong	208	18	10	-	236	0.77
Chandel	516	54	47	75	692	2.26
Churachandpur	183	26	10	-	219	0.72
Ukhrul	194	26	10	-	230	0.75
Hill Total	**1549**	**195**	**123**	**160**	**2027**	**6.63**
Imphal East	4580	436	220	304	5540	18.11
Imphal West	5950	505	248	350	7053	23.05
Bisnupur	3620	335	241	298	4494	14.69
Thoubal	9650	960	376	494	11480	37.52
Valley total	**23800**	**2236**	**1085**	**1446**	**28567**	**93.37**
Manipur	**25349**	**2431**	**1208**	**1606**	**30594**	**100**

Source: GOM: *Statistical Abstract: Manipur 2007*, DES.

Irrigation Facilities

Agriculture is heavily dependent on timely arrival of monsoon as irrigation facilities in the state are still poor. It receives about 2000 mm of rainfall annually which is rather not low. Irrigation, the most important input of agriculture, has received attention only after the attainment of statehood. The first major irrigation project, the Loktak Lift Irrigation (LLI) project, was taken up in the year 1973-74 and later in the Fifth Plan besides LLI, new projects comprising three medium river irrigation projects viz. Imphal Barrage, Sekmai Barrage, Khoupum Dam, and one Multi purpose project Singda Multipurpose Projects, were taken up. By the end of Ninth Plan, the irrigation potential from the completed or partially completed projects was 28,500 ha with a utilization of only 20,910 ha. Most of the major and medium irrigation projects are confined in the valley. At the end of Tenth plan, the irrigated area was 30,980 ha. i.e. 13.24% of the net agricultural land (Draft Annual Plan 2007-08). District wise irrigated and un-irrigated areas under rice from 2004-05 to 2006-07 is shown in Table 4. It is observed that the area under irrigation has been declining Out of the gross estimated area of 166.26 thousand hectares under rice, only 43.67 thousand hectares were reported to be under irrigation which accounts for 26.27 percent to the total area under paddy during 2005-2006. This means that the available irrigation facilities in the state are quite inadequate and there is an urgent need for improving irrigation facilitates not only for boosting agricultural production but also for increasing rural income and employment. It is also seen that areas under irrigation are mainly in Imphal West, Bishnupur and Thoubal districts whereas in Imphal East and the hill districts, the facilities are almost non-existent.

Table 4

District-wise estimates of irrigated area under rice

(Area in' 000 hect.)

	2004-05		*2005-06*		*2006-07*	
District /State	*Area*	*(%)*	*Area*	*(%)*	*Area*	*(%)*
1	*2*	*3*	*4*	*5*	*6*	*7*
Senapati	3.74	15.51	3.03	10.16	5.45	21.63
Tamenglong	2.05	24.06	0.86	8.98	-	-
Chandel	3.26	15.49	0.58	2.85	-	-

(Contd...)

1	*2*	*3*	*4*	*5*	*6*	*7*
Churachandpur	0.80	9.72	-	-	-	-
Ukhrul	-	-	-	-	-	-
Hill Total	**9.85**	**13.05**	**4.47**	**5.41**	**5.45**	**6.83**
Imphal East	1.49	4.93	2.66	10.33	-	-
Imphal West	10.43	45.09	14.39	75.07	0.52	2.75
Bisnupur	18.54	85.28	13.41	83.66	14.43	94.87
Thoubal	13.90	53.98	8.84	38.87	12.52	46.11
Valley total	**44.36**	**43.99**	**39.30**	**47.02**	**27.47**	**32.11**
Manipur	**54.21**	**30.75**	**43.77**	**26.33**	**32.92**	**19.91**

Source: GOM: *Statistical Abstract: Manipur 2007*, DES.
-Not available

Cultivation of Fruits and Vegetables

Cultivation of fruits like pineapple, orange, lemon, passion fruit, etc. has tremendous potential in the state because of the quality of the fruits and the suitable agro-climatic conditions in the state. Many reports of the Planning Commission have, in fact, emphasized the development of the horticulture sector in the north eastern states. Fortunately, cultivation on commercial basis has been on the increase. As per data available from the Directorate of Horticulture and Soil Conservation, Manipur, production of fruits increased from 0.03 lakh MT in 1992-93 to 2.22 lakh MT in 2003-04 while that of vegetables increased from 0.06 lakh MT to 0.57 lakh MT during the same period. More emphasis should be given on cultivation of such horticulture items in the hill areas where jhum cultivation is going on in a large scale.

Some Problems in the Agricultural Sector

The agricultural sector in the state can be said to be relatively advanced based on all India statistics. However, this sector has many problems which need to be tackled for enhancing production. Some of these points are dwelt briefly:

Imbalance in the development

The valley areas because of the very nature of the geographical features are very advanced as compared with the hill areas as was evident in terms of yield, use of HYV seeds, use of fertilizers, etc. Lagging of technical inputs and know-how, the hill areas are struggling hard to catch up with the valley in terms of both production and productivity. The Draft Annual Plan 2007-08 for agriculture has identified lack of adequate infrastructure for mobilizing development programme in the hills as major constraints during the Tenth Plan (2002-07) to the production of food grains.

Jhum cultivation

In Manipur, jhum cultivation or shifting cultivation is a method of cultivation practiced on the hill areas on a large scale. As per the data available, maximum number of families in the north east engaged in jhum cultivation is in Manipur which is not sustainable and it has started showing its negative implication on the environment. In place of jhum cultivation, some other ways of cultivation like the terrace cultivation or growing of horticultural items should be actively encouraged.

Size of the holding and unemployment in the agricultural sector

In Manipur especially in the valley districts, a growing number of unemployed labour force is turning towards the agricultural sector increasing population pressure on land. Thus, the average size of holding has gradually declined from 1.22 hectares in 1995-96 to 1.15 hectares in 2000-01. Land is becoming increasingly fragmented and the number of holdings for marginal and small farmers constituted 124 out of the total holdings of 149 in the state. A consequence of this is that about 60 percent of the population now depends on agricultural sector for employment though its contribution to the state income has dwindled to 30 p.c. Marginalization and smallness of holdings have made the farmers very hard to maintain a subsistence level and have discouraged the farmers to invest for private capital formation. Rice cultivation has become a part time job for most of the small and marginal farmers and it has become an enduring proposition rather than a commercial proposition. Now-a-days, rice cultivation is driven by push factor rather than pull factor as the farmers don't find any incentive; they are cultivating not because it is profitable or make them subsistence but because they don't want their land to remain idle.

Lack of irrigation facilities

One of the biggest problems is the lack of irrigational facilities in the state. In fact, it has been much popularized by Dandekar and Rath that one of the measures of alleviating rural unemployment and poverty in India is by increasing the availability of irrigation facilities. However, a very large proportion of agricultural land in the state is not irrigated and as a result remain uncultivated during the agricultural off season. The under utilization as well as lack of irrigation has not encouraged double and multiple cropping which would have furthered the production of rice. The irrigation system is not producing the desire result in the state. The problem is more of 'maintenance and utilization of assets'. The irrigation facility in the state focuses more on 'creation of assets' and employment generation rather than the 'maintenance, utilization and sustainability of assets'. For rice cultivation, still, the state depends on the timely arrival of monsoon. In other words, the irrigation system in the state cannot reduce, at least to some extent, the overdependence on monsoon. Deformity in irrigation not only discourages double and multiple cropping but also severely affects the use of HYVs (Hanjabam 2007).

Strategy for Agricultural Production in Manipur

There are ample prospects of increasing agricultural production in Manipur. In order to overcome socio-economic constraints confronting agricultural production, the following strategic steps may be taken up to bring about a substantial increase in crop production:

1. Identification and exploitation of agricultural land in the hills which comprises 90% of the state area but is contributing only 30% of the cropped area.

2. Checking of further reduction in the cropped area, in the valley particularly by using the land judiciously.
3. Introduction and evolution of promising crop varieties.
4. Gearing-up of irrigation projects.
5. Judicious use of arable land, due attention to soil fertility and productivity.
6. Strengthening of intensive agriculture throughout the state.
7. Extension of production technologies through demonstrations, etc.
8. Adoption of scientific cropping system and sequences.
9. Transportation and marketing facilities.
10. Restoration and preservation of agro-ecosystem.

With the coming up of more Agricultural Research Stations, in the state during the Eighth Five Year Plan, one for deep water and the other for high altitudes, coupled with the existing research institutions, specific productions technologies and crop varieties for various stress conditions it is hoped that the obstacles to the growth of agriculture in the state will be largely mitigated in future.

REFERENCES

Datt, Ruddar and KPM Sundharam (2006): *Indian Economy*, S. Chand & Co. Pvt. Ltd. New Delhi.

Government of India (2006): *Manipur State Development Report (MSDR) 2006,* Institute for Human Development, Delhi Sponsored by Planning Commission, www.manipur.nic.in 11th June, 2007, http://manipur.nic.in/planning/DraftMSDR/DefaultDraftMSDR.htm.

Government of Manipur: *Economic Review*, Directorate of Economics and Statistics (DES), Various issues.

__________, *Statistical Handbook of Manipur*, DES, Various issues.

__________, *Statistical Abstract: Manipur*, DES, Various issues.

_________, *Economic Progress 1987*, DES.

_________, *Land Utilization Survey in Manipur, 1988-89,* DES.

_________, *Annual Plan Statements 1996-97,* Planning Department.

_________, *Draft Tenth Five Year Plan Proposals 2002-2007*, Volume - II, Planning Department.

_________, *Economic Survey: Manipur 2007-08*, DES.

_________, *Draft Annual Plan, 2007-08,* Department of Agriculture.

_________, *Draft Eleventh Five Year Plan*, Planning Department.

Hanjabam, Isworchandra (2007): "Rice Economy of Manipur: Its Past and Prospects" *Alternative Perspectives,* Vol. III. Issue I, Oct-Dec.

Singh, Keisham Suresh (2008): "Agricultural Land Taxation in Manipur", Unpublished Phil. thesis submitted to Manipur University.

Singh, M. Rohinikumar (1984): "Rice in Manipur, Present Status and Future Prospects", Paper presented to seminar in Manipur Agriculture College on 21-22-1989.

Singh, N. Ram (1989): "Constraints in the Agricultural Development of Manipur", Unpublished Ph.D. thesis submitted to Manipur University.

6

Persons with Disabilities in Manipur: A Statistical Analysis

R. K. Narendra Singh, N. Sharat Singh, W. Jibol Singh & Ch.Memchanu

Introduction

The persons with disabilities are the world's largest minority with a figure of 650 million, around ten percent of the world population (UN enable, 2008). Eighty percent of them live in rural areas in developing countries. Seventy percent of them are estimated to have either limited or no access to the services they need. On an average 19 per cent of less educated people have disabilities, compared to 11 per cent among the better educated people. Twenty percent of the world's poorest people have some kind of disabilities, and they are regarded as the most disadvantaged section. Women have higher percentage with multiple disadvantages than that of her counterpart men. Persons with disabilities are sometimes treated as genderless persons. As a result, the double-discrimination suffered by women with disabilities is often neglected. So they are the most vulnerable to abuse.

According to UNICEF, thirty percent of street youths have some kind of disabilities (UN enable, 2008). Mortality among the disabled children is extremely high, around 80 per cent. Ageing, an integral part of living, is typically accompanied by gradual but progressive physiological changes with increase prevalence of acute and chronic illness. As age advances, biological and physical nature of the body is likely to deteriorate which leads to physical and sensory impairment and in turn bring about varying amount of disability.

The World Programme of Action concerning disabled persons and the United Nations Decade of Disabled Persons indicated that disability is closely linked to economic and social factors and that conditions of living in large parts of the world are so desperate that the provision of basic needs for all – food, water, shelter, health protection and education – must form the cornerstone of the national programmes (Committee on Economic, Social and Cultural Rights, CESCR, 2007). Even in advanced countries, persons with disabilities are very often denied the opportunity to enjoy the full range of economic, social and cultural rights.

Every nation needs to pay special attention for creating conditions allowing people with disabilities to live in a dignified manner and with a sense of fulfillment. Proper action must be taken up to raise awareness in society about their grievances (rights and needs), potential and contribution since the effects of disability-based discrimination have been particularly severed in exercising their economic, social and cultural rights particularly in the field of health care, education, employment, housing, transport, cultural life, and access to public places and services. In order to rehabilitate them in a dignified manner with the removal of social stigma against them, the information on the number, type of disability and grievances for every society or community is highly needed. At the same time, it is high time to take up in depth study which would highlight the magnitude and pattern of persons with disabilities with socio-economic and demographic factors. Such study would help immensely to the governments in better planning for the welfare and improvement of this minority section of people so called persons with disabilities.

Keeping this in view, an attempt is made to analyse the pattern of persons with disabilities in Manipur based on the data of Census 2001, with respect to some important socio-economic and demographic factors. The finding arrived at in the conclusion is very interesting and fascinating one.

Methodology

There is still no internationally accepted definition of the term "disability" but a person may often be referred as disabled by physical, intellectual or sensory impairment, medical conditions or mental illness (CESCR, 2007). Now-a-days the term is often used as "Persons with disabilities" rather than the older term "disabled persons". Such impairments, conditions or illnesses may be permanent or transitory in nature. Even in the history of Indian census, different definitions were adopted on the various decadal censuses since its inception in 1872. The information on disability was not deliberately counted on some censuses – 1941, 1951, 1961, 1971 and 1991. Fortunately, Census 2001 provides information on various types of disabilities under five groups viz., In seeing, In speech, In hearing, In movement and Mental.

The present analysis is strictly confined on the five major categories of disabilities as it is based on the secondary data of Census 2001 for Manipur State. There are seven parameters considered – district, sex, residence, literacy status, economic status, type of workers and type of disability. A well known morbidity formula that is prevalence rate (PR) is adopted to measure the magnitude of disabled persons or persons with disabilities over the parameters under consideration. For analysis purposes, χ^2-test is used with P-value and interpretation is made accordingly.

$$\text{PR('000) of persons with disabilities} = \frac{\text{Total no. of persons with disabilities}}{\text{Total no. of population}} \times 1000$$

Result and Discussion

District-wise variation of PR ('000) of persons with disabilities is observed (Table-1) showing Bishnupur district having the highest (16.83), followed by Thoubal (14.51), Imphal East (13.08) while the lowest (11.50) belongs to Senapati district. The unique finding is that all the valley districts except Imphal West have higher PRs than that of hill districts. It is general convention that the society or community with poor/less socio-economic and environmental amenities have more disability which is quite contradictory to the finding. Thus, in depth study is highly needed to ascertain of whether the valley district has really higher disability than the hill district. If so, it is high time to identify the causes behind it. One possible reason might be due to under reporting in hill district.

Table 1
District-wise distribution of P.R ('000) of persons with disabilities

District	*Population*	*Disabled*	*P.R. ('000)*
Senapati*	156513	1800	11.50
Tamenglong	111499	1405	12.60
Churachandpur	227905	2638	11.57
Bishnupur	208368	3506	16.83
Thoubal	364140	5285	14.51
Imphal West	444382	5385	12.12
Imphal East	394876	5164	13.08
Ukhrul	140778	1677	11.91
Chandel	118327	1516	12.81
Manipur	2166788	28376	13.10

*excludes Mao Maram, Paomata and Purul Sub-Divisions
χ^2(District) = 403.56; d.f. = 8; P < 0.001

Over all PR for Manipur is witnessed as 13.10 which is lower than the national figure of 21.30. Further, χ^2-value (403.56) with P < 0.001 shows that the district-wise variation of disability is found to be very highly significant.

Table 2
District-wise distribution of P.R. ('000) of persons with disabilities by sex

District	*Male P.R. ('000)*	*Female P.R. ('000)*
Senapati	11.78	11.21
Tamenglong	13.01	12.15
Churachandpur	12.37	10.73
Bishnupur	18.28	15.36
Thoubal	15.50	13.52
Imphal West	13.27	10.97
Imphal East	14.52	11.62
Ukhrul	12.82	10.92
Chandel	13.49	12.12
Manipur	14.11	12.06

χ^2(Dist., Male) = 242.03; d.f. = 8; P < 0.001
χ^2(Dist., Female) = 181.34; d.f. = 8; P < 0.001
χ^2(Sex) = 175.25; d.f. = 1; P < 0.001

Table-2 shows the variability of persons with disabilities in terms of PR over the nine districts of Manipur for each sex separately. Highest PR is found to exist in Bishnupur which is true in both the sexes. On the contrary, Senapati witnesses lowest PR for male (11.78) while Churachandpur has the lowest PR for female (10.73). These variations of PRs for each sex separately, over the districts are found to be very highly significant as evident by the respective values of P. Further, irrespective of districts, PR for male (14.11) is significantly higher than PR for female (12.06) as evident by χ^2(sex) = 175.25; P< 0.001.

The present finding is quite contradictory to the general convention that women have higher incidents of disability than men (UN enable, 2008). In the study of physical disability among ageing, Alan (1981) reported that women appear to be more disabled than men. This view is also supported by the findings of Kishore et al. (1997) stating that

45 per cent of the elders were males as against 55 per cent females. Even a study of disability which was conducted by Konjengbam (2004) in some urban area of Imphal West district of Manipur shows that female has higher percentage (56.41) than male (43.59 percent).

Perhaps the contradictory finding may be coupled with several factors like under reporting, lack of proper identification of disabled persons, etc. during the enumeration.

Table 3
District-wise distribution of P.R ('000) of persons with disabilities by residence

District	*Rural P.R. ('000)*	*Urban P.R.('000)*
Senapati	11.50	
Tamenglong	12.60	
Churachandpur	11.57	
Bishnupur	16.43	17.53
Thoubal	15.07	13.53
Imphal West	12.70	11.65
Imphal East	13.74	11.34
Ukhrul	11.91	
Chandel	12.41	15.57
Manipur	13.17	12.88

χ^2(Dist., Rural) = 287.09; d.f. = 8; P < 0.001
χ^2(Dist., Urban) = 189.36; d.f. = 4; P < 0.001
χ^2(Residence) = 2.71; d.f. = 1; P > 0.05

Out of the five hill districts of Manipur, only one district viz., Chandel district has urban population and therefore, the four districts have no urban population at all. Among the districts with urban population, Bishnupur has the highest PR has the highest PR (17.53) while the lowest (11.34) belongs to Imphal East. In the case of rural population, the locoest (11.50) and the highest (16.43) rates are seen in senapati and Bishnupur districts respectively. Highly significant test values suggest that there is a significant variation of disability over the districts. This is true in rural as well as in urban.

It is very interesting to note that despite a little higher PR for rural (13.17) than PR for urban (12.88), the difference is not significant even at 5 percent probability level. Thus, one can conclude that there is a uniform pattern of disability between rural and urban.

Table 4
District-wise distribution of P.R ('000) of persons with disabilities by literacy status

District	*Literate P.R. ('000)*	*Illiterate P.R. ('000)*
Senapati	8.52	14.66
Tamenglong	8.06	17.32
Churachandpur	8.67	16.12
Bishnupur	12.43	22.78
Thoubal	9.79	20.41
Imphal West	8.83	19.80
Imphal East	9.60	19.48
Ukhrul	7.90	18.50
Chandel	10.70	14.80
Manipur	9.41	18.74

χ^2(Dist., Literate) = 189.91; d.f. = 8; $P < 0.001$
χ^2(Dist., Illiterate) = 274.86; d.f. = 4; $P < 0.001$
χ^2(Literacy Status) = 3487.69; d.f. = 1; $P < 0.001$

Literate persons have significantly lower prevalence rate of disability (9.41) than that of illiterate persons (18.74). The finding is in agreement with the findings of UN enable (2008), Garg et al. (1982), Singh (1990), Kishore et al. (1997), etc. This is because of the fact that firstly literate persons are more aware about their health and its related problems. Secondly, literacy status would link with other covariates which directly or indirectly associate with disability. For instance, better education is associated with better health care, better occupation, good environment and like wise which may curtail the magnitude of disability. Further table-4 highlights that there is a variability of PRs of disabled for each literacy status over the districts (P < 0.001).

Table 5
District-wise distribution of P.R. ('000) of persons with disabilities by total workers

District	*Total workers P.R. ('000)*	*Non workers P.R. ('000)*
Senapati	10.18	12.62
Tamenglong	12.19	12.95
Churachandpur	11.00	12.02
Bishnupur	14.35	18.69
Thoubal	10.66	18.17
Imphal West	9.67	13.75
Imphal East	10.31	14.90
Ukhrul	10.15	13.49
Chandel	11.24	18.31
Manipur	10.85	14.84

χ^2(Dist., Total workers) = 146.30; d.f. = 8; P < 0.001
χ^2(Dist., Non workers) = 439.21; d.f. = 4; P < 0.001
χ^2(Workers) = 3487.69; d.f. = 1; P < 0.001
Total workers = Main + Marginal Workers

Economic status is classified here into total worker and non worker. The former consists of both main and marginal workers. The prevalence rate for total workers is found to be less than for non-workers. The difference is very highly significant at 5 percent probability level. The variation of PRs for each economic status over the districts is also very highly significant (P < 0.001).

Now Table-6 shows the district-wise variation of PR of persons with disabilities with respect to type of workers. Here, the type of workers is classified into four groups viz., Cultivators (CL), Agricultural Labourers (AL), Household Industry Workers (HHI), and workers other than the first three (Other workers). Agricultural Labourers have the highest PR (12.09), followed by cultivators (11.37), other workers (10.32) and the lowest (9.27) belongs to household industry workers. It may be concluded that type of workers has certain role towards occurrence of disability in Manipur as evident by $\chi^2 = 58.07$; $P < 0.001$.

Table 6
District-wise distribution of P.R. ('000) of persons with disabilities by type of workers

District	*CL*	*AL*	*HHI*	*Other workers*
Senapati	9.74	9.97	10.71	11.60
Tamenglong	12.61	16.89	17.10	9.35
Churachandpur	12.40	11.21	10.08	8.33
Bishnupur	14.57	17.58	10.44	14.20
Thoubal	10.89	10.32	9.41	11.09
Imphal West	10.89	11.70	8.14	9.29
Imphal East	11.71	12.43	7.75	9.91
Ukhrul	10.65	16.69	10.69	7.83
Chandel	10.13	12.32	15.60	12.55
Manipur	11.37	12.09	9.27	10.32

χ^2(Type of *workers*) = 58.07; d.f. = 3; $P < 0.001$

Further, variability of disability still persists among the districts of the State when classification is made on type of workers. This is true in each type of workers considered. Bishnupur has the highest PR in all the types of workers except HHI where Tamenglong has the highest. For the lowest PR by type of workers, Senapati accounted for both CL and AL, Imphal West for HHI and Ukhrul for other workers.

Table 7
Type of disability-wise distribution of P.C. of persons with disabilities

Type of disability	*Disabled*	*P.C.*
In Seeing	11,713	42.27
In Speech	2,769	9.75
In Hearing	2,994	10.55
In Movement	6,177	21.76
Mental	4,723	16.64
Total	28,376	

$\chi^2 = 4034.36$; d.f. = 4; $P < 0.001$

Among the five types of disability, considered, 'in seeing' has the highest percentage (42.27) of disability 'in movement' (21.76 percent), 'mental' (16.64 percent), in hearing (10.55) and in speech (9.75 percent). The present finding is in agreement with the finding of Audinarayana et al. (2002) where visual disability had the highest (29.5 percent) followed by hearing disability (12.5 percent) and walking disability (12.5 percent). Further, test value suggests that the variation of percentage of disability over the five types is found to be highly significant ($P < 0.001$) and one can, therefore, safely conclude that the State witnesses different magnitudes of various types of disability.

Conclusion

Persons with disabilities are an integral part of our society which no body can deny. Disabilities may be by birth, by accident or by human process of life. People may be disabled by physical, intellectual or sensory impairment, medical conditions or mental illness. Such impairments, conditions or illnesses may be permanent or transitory in nature. As disability is closely linked to economic and social factors of the society, it is high time to ascertain the direct or the indirect prognostic factors which have significant causal link with the persons with disabilities for future course of action of their welfare. On this perspective, the findings arrived at in the present study highlight that the magnitude of disability in Manipur is lower than the national figure. The magnitude is varied amongst the nine districts of the State with valley districts have higher than hill districts except Imphal West. At the same time, male has higher rate of disability than that of his female counterpart. Literacy status has certain link with disabled as literate person has lower rate than illiterate person. Economic status has also significant contribution towards disabled as non- workers have higher rate than total workers and the rate varies over the type of workers. Strong variation of prevalence rate of disability is observed among the type of disability as in seeing persists highest as against lowest by in speech. On the contrary, there is no variation of disability pattern between rural and urban in the State.

Some contradictory findings are coming up against the general convention that valley as well as male have higher prevalence rate than that of their corresponding counterparts-hill and female respectively. Thus, in depth study is highly needed to identify the unusual prognostic factors behind it. Of course, the finding so far arrived is very fascinating and useful particularly to the health planners and executors for their future planning towards the welfare of this most unfortunate minority section of our society.

[This is a reviewed article presented and debated on "Data Dissemination Workshop" organized by Office of the Director of Census Operations, Government of India held on 20 March 2008 at State Guest House, Sanjenthong, Imphal.]

REFERENCES

Alan, M. J. and G.B.Laurence (1981): "The Framingham Disability study II: Physical disability among the ageing", *American Journal of Public Health*, vol. 71, pp. 1211-1215.

Audinarayana, N. and J. Sheela (2002): "Physical disability among the elderly in Tamil Nadu: Patterns, differentials and determinants", *Health and Population: Perspective and Pssues,* vol. 25, no. 1, pp. 26-37.

Directorate of Census Operations, Manipur (2001): *Disabled Population in Manipur, 2001 Census.*

Directorate of Census Operations, Manipur (2004): *Census of India 2001: Primary Census Abstract, Series-15.*

Garg, B. S., S.C. Gupta, V.N. Mishra and R.B. Singh (1982): "A medical-social study of aged in urban area", *Indian Medical Gazette,* vol. 16, pp. 90-95.

Kishore, S. and B.S. Garg (1997: "Socio-medical problems of aged population in a rural area of Wardha district", *Indian Journal of Public Health,* vol. XXXXI, no. 2, pp. 43-48.

Konjengbam, S.(2004): "A study of disability in the activities of daily living among the elders 60 years and above in an urban community", MD thesis, Manipur University.

Persons with disabilities, *CESCR General Comment 5,* viewed April 2007, <http:// nhrc.nic.in/publications/ Disability/ ANNEXURE 6.HTML/>.

Registrar General and Census Commissioner, India (2008): "*History of Indian Census*", viewed March 2008, http://www.censusindia.gov.in/ Data_Products/Library/Indian perceptive link/History lin>.

Singh, C. A. (1990): "Study of health status of aged among rural population of Meerut", MD thesis, Meerut University.

United Nations enable (2008): *Rights and Dignity of Persons with Disabilities,* viewed March 2008, <http:// www.who.int/disabilities/ en>.

7

Demographic Transition in Manipur

W. Kumar Singh

Introduction

Manipur lies in the north-east corner of the country which had a population of 22,93,896 in 2001 census. The exponential growth rate of population declined by 0.35 percent from 2.57 percent in 1981-91 to 2.22 percent in 1991-2001. During the same period, the growth rate declined by 0.19 percent from 2.14 percent to 1.95 percent in the country. In other words, despite the decline, the growth rate in the state was faster than that in the country by 0.8 percent in 1991-2001. This implies the family welfare or planning programme in the state has to be intensified to achieve the growth rate of the country. The growth rate of population is the combined effect of fertility, mortality and migration. Among these factors fertility is generally regarded as a robust factor.

According to sample registration system birth rate declined from 2.7 percent in 1981 to 2.0 percent in 1991 and further to 1.8 percent in 2001. There was not much difference in the decline in both rural and urban areas. The rate declined by 0.61 percent and 0.17 percent in rural area during 1980s and 1990s. In urban area the corresponding declines were 0.64 percent and 0.21 percent respectively.

With this perspective the present study attempts to highlight interesting demographic development that has unfolded during the last three decades. Section two discusses the size and diversity of population in the state. Section three examines the determinants of population growth. The final section presents the momentum of population growth.

Size and Diversity of Population

Growth Rate

Growth rate as measured by exponential growth rate which is compounding continuously i.e. "a constant rate of change is applied at every infinitesimal of time" Shryock et al (1980:379) revealed clearly that the state has experienced a declining trend (Table - 1). The growth rate declined from 2.81 percent in 1971-81 to 2.57 percent in 1981-91 and further to 2.22 percent in 1991-2001. In valley area too the growth rate declined from 2.49 percent to 2.44 percent and further to 1.74 percent in the corresponding periods. Whereas the rate in hill areas declined from 3.45 percent in 1971-81 to 2.81 percent in 1981-91 and then it increased to 3.03 percent in 1991-01. These pictures reveal the evidence of a dismal failure of family planning programme in the hill areas assuming other things remain the same. But such assumptions are wrong in some places as witnessed by abnormal growth rate. For example in some villages - Paomata, Purul and Chakpikarong the growth rates were more than 100 percent for which re-enumeration was attempted (Singh 2006: 1473). Among the hills districts, the highest growth occurred in Chandel district and followed by Senapati. In Chandel the rate declined from 3.77 percent in 1971-81 to 2.30 percent in 1981-91 and then it increased to 5.11 percent in 1991-2001. In similar manner, the rate in Senapati declined from 4.00 percent to 2.93 percent and then it increased to 3.08 percent in the corresponding periods. Among the valley districts, Thoubal district experienced the slowest decline in the growth rate which implies the requirement for further intensification of family planning programme.

Table 1
Growth rate of population by Districts in Manipur

Region/District	*Exponential Growth Rate*		
	1971-81	*1981-91*	*1991-01*
Hill.	3.45	2.81	3.03
Senapati	4.00	2.93	3.08
Tamenglong	3.25	3.26	2.56
Churachandpur	3.18	2.68	2.57
Chandel	3.77	2.30	5.11
Ukhrul	2.87	2.76	2.53
Valley	2.49	2.44	1.74
Imphal east.	*	*	*
Imphal West.	2.47	2.46	1.65
Bisenpur	2.65	2.47	1.42
Thoubal	2.43	2.37	2.14
Manipur	2.81	2.57	2.22
India	2.20	2.14	1.95

* Imphal East figures are clubbed into Imphal West.
Source: (Basic Data) Census of India, Various volumes.

Doubling of Population

In spite of the state experiencing a decline in growth rate it, the added 52 persons every hour during 1991-2001. If the present growth rates persist, the present population of India will double in 35 years (Sept., 2036) and the state in 31.2 years (May, 2032). Within the state, the hill population will double in 22.9 years (Jan., 2023) and the valley in 39.8 years (Oct., 2040).

Sex Ratio

India has experienced deficit of female since 1901 while the state shared such deficit since only 1971. Before 1971 census, from 1901 census to 1961 census, the state experienced deficit of male instead to females (Table - 2). The sex ratio declined continuously from 1065 in 1931 to 958 in 1991 and then it rose to 974 in 2001 census. Despite the decline in sex ratio in the state, the ratio is still higher than the all India figure. In India the average sex ratio for the period from 1901 to 2001 was 945 while that in Manipur was 1015. Similarly, the average ratio in India for the period 1971-2001 was 931 which was much lower than 971 of Manipur in the corresponding period. The declining sex ratio may be due to the following factors: (1) migration, (2) female selective termination of pregnancy, (3) sex ratio at birth, (4) sex ratio at death and (5) progressive undercounts of women and double or multiple counting of males.

Table 2
Sex ratio in India and Manipur

Census year	*Sex Ratio in India*	*Rate of change in p.c.*	*Sex Ratio in the Manipur*	*Rate of change in p.c.*
1901	972		1037	
1911	964	-0.82	1029	-0.77
1921	955	- 0.93	1041	+1.77
1931	950	-0.52	1065	+2.31
1941	945	-0.53	1055	-0.94
1951	946	+0.11	1036	-1.80
1961	941	-0.53	1015	-2.03
1971	930	-1.17	980	-3.45
1081	934	+0.43	971	-0.92
1991	927	-0.75	958	-1.34
2001	933	+0.65	974	+1.67
AV(1971-2001)	931		971	
AV(1901-2001)	945		1015	

Source: (Basic Data) Census of India, various volumes.

Migration may be national or international. International migration migrition is the difference between emigrant and immigrant while in the case of internal migration it is the difference between out-migrants and in-migrants. Reliable data on net migration is very scanty and as such estimated values are often used. Another reason for estimating net migration is that "the available method does not permit making adequate estimate of immigration or emigrations separately" (Shryock et al 1980:594). The same applies in the case of the state too. Intercensal Component Method or Residual Method may be employed to estimate net migrants. This method may be defined as:

I-E = (Pt – Po) - (B – D)

where

I	=	Number of Immigrants (in-migrants in internal migration).
E	=	Number of Emigrants (out-migrants in internal migration).
Pt - Po	=	Change in population during (t – o).
B - D	=	Natural increase in population.

In the absence of reliable fertility and mortality data, the present paper uses crude birth rate and death rate of respective census years supplied by Sample Registration System Bulletin, Office of the Registrar General, India. Since sex wise data on birth rate was not available, total birth rate and total death rate are used[1]. The percentage of female migrants to the total migrants differs from country to country and differ according to inter state, intra-state, rural to urban, urban to rural, urban to urban, rural to rural migrants. Among the migration stream of female (rural to rural, rural to urban, urban to rural, urban to urban and urban to rural), migration from rural to rural is the highest. And the percentage of intra-state female migration is higher than that in the inter-state (UNO 1994: 21 - 25; Kundu 1986: 2004-2008). "Female migrants have grown faster than the male migrants in all the streams during 1961 - 81. This has resulted in an increase in the sex ratio, defined as females per thousand of male populations. The increase seems to be positively related with the distance of migration - the highest increase occurring in the case of interstate migration (from 861 to 1090, growth of 27 percent) while for the intra-district migrants the increase (from 3041 to 3244, a growth of 7 percent) is the least" (Kundu 1986: 2006). UN studies also revealed that in many countries (for example, India in 1971 and 1981, Philippines in 1965, Republic of Korea in 1970 and 1975, Brazil in 1970, Honduras in 1983) the percentage of female migrants to total migrants was higher than that of male.

Table 3

The Estimates of sex ratio of net in-migrants

Census year	*Net in-migrants*	*Net in-migrants is percent to total population*	*Sex Ratio excluding net in-migrants*	*Sex Ratio including net in-migrants*
1971	264395	2.46	0.981	980
1981	319781	2.25	0.969	971
1991	389190	2.12	0.953	958
2001	426697	1.86	0.973	974

Source: (Basic Data) Census of India, various volumes.

The higher female migrants is due to marriage factor[2] in which women move from one house to another house, sometimes involving a long distance crossing rural or urban areas, districts and sometimes states and nations. In the present case, the estimate ignores intra-district and intra-state migration. The estimates take into account only inter-state and inter-country migration. For estimating sex ratio (excluding net migration) the average percentage of female migration into the state is calculated from the study of Devi (2009:434) which shows male and female migrants into Manipur in 1961-2001. The average figure obtained is 49.44 and by applying this figure, sex ratio is calculated. Sex ratio excluding net migrants was lower in all censuses presented in the Table - 3 except 1971 in which sex-ratio excluding net migrants was 981 while the ratio including net inmigrants was

980. The table also reveals net migration does not affect sex-ratio significantly except in 1991.

Table 4
District-wise sex ratio in Manipur (1961-2001)

District	*1961*	*1971*	*1981*	*1991*	*2001*
Manipur North (Senapati)*	1002	950	929	942	935
Manipur West (Tamenglong)	1061	1016	975	935	922
Manipur South (Churachandpur)	1006	976	929	931	944
Tengnoupal (Chandel)	1008	975	935	913	981
Manipur Central **	1013	985	991	976	997
Manipur East (Ukhrul)	1033	969	917	884	858
State	1015	980	971	958	974

*Excludes 3 Sub-Divisions of Senapati District viz. Mao-Maram, Paomata & Purul.
**For sake of comparison central district includes all four valley district - Imphal West, Imphal East, Thoubal and Bisenpur.
Source: (Basic Data) Census of India, various volumes.

Table - 4 reveals that sex-ratio declined continuously in all districts since 1961 in Manipur West and Manipur East districts. In other districts too, the ratio has been witnessing a decline with fluctuations but could not reach the ratio in 1961. The ratio was lowest in Senapati and highest in Tamenglong in 1961. By examining all the determining factors except migration, Singh (199-200:100) rightly concludes – "The available secondary data pertaining to SR and related variables show the root cause of the declining SR in the state is not the status of women rather is sex-ratio at birth which might be supplemented by underenumeration of female and counting of male population more than once..."

Determinants of Population Growth

Migration

Population growth is generally determined by the interaction between birth, death and net migration. Net migration as noted above constitutes about 2 percent of the population over three decades (1971-2001). The absolute figure of net migration increased from 2,64,395 in 1971 to 4,26,697 in 2001 (i.e. during 30 years, net migration in the state nearly doubled). The figures indicate that the number of migrants entering the state, majority of them for searching of job, far exceeds out-migrants from the state particularly to other states of India. Most of the out-migrants from the states are for pursuing higher studies in different streams. In-migrants contribute their labour force in the state. Usually almost all work performed by them can be performed by native labourers. If the people of the state improve their work culture and work ethics, the increase in the number of in-migrants will decline and this will help to solve the problem of unemployment in the state.

Trends of Mortality

With the development of health sciences, increase in health facilities provided by governments and increased awareness of health and hygiene by the people, the death rate declined from 7 per thousand in 1980-89 to 6 in 1990-99 and further to 5 in 2000-07 (Table – 5). Similar declined was observed in the case of rural areas while in the case of urban areas, the rate increased from 5.5 to 6.0 and subsequently declined to 5.0 in the corresponding periods. The decline in the rural areas is particularly due to better information and awareness provided through printing and electronic media, improvement in the literacy and educational level and better transport and communication. These factors enable people of rural area to enjoy the health facility available in the urban areas.

Infant mortality rate (IMR) in the state ranked fourth lowest among the NE states in NFHS-I which rose to first in both NFHS-II and NFHS-III (Table - 6). IMR declined from 42 in 1992-93 (NFHS-I) to 37 in 1998-99 (NFHS-II) and further to 30 in 2005-06 (NFHS-II). The child under-five mortality in the state ranks third in NFHS-I becomes second in both NFHS-II and NFHS-III. It declined from 62 in the first health survey to 56 in the second health survey and further

Table 5
Estimated birth, death and infant mortality rates in Manipur

(Per thousand)

Item.	*Year.*									*Average.*		
	1981	*1991*	*2001*	*2002*	*2003*	*2004*	*2005*	*2006*	*2007*	*1980-89*	*1990-99*	*2000-07*
Birth Rate												
Rural	26.8	20.7	19.0	17.4	16.1	13.3	14.5	13.5	14.4	27.9	20.8	15.9
Urban	24.4	18.0	15.9	15.3	14.1	15.8	15.5	13.1	15.2	22.3	17.6	15.2
Combined	26.6	20.1	18.2	16.8	15.5	13.9	14.7	13.4	14.6	27.1	20.0	15.7
Death Rate												
Rural	6.8	5.4	4.8	4.2	4.9	4.3	4.0	4.4	4.2	6.9	5.7	4.9
Urban	4.5	5.7	6.1	5.8	4.4	4.4	4.4	4.6	4.9	5.5	6.0	5.0
Combined	6.6	5.4	5.1	4.6	4.8	4.3	4.1	4.5	4.4	6.6	5.7	5.0

Source: Sample Registration System Bulletin, Registrar General of India, various issues.

Table 6

Infant, child and under five mortality for the five year period preceding survey by State, India (1992-93, 1998-99, 2005-06)

State	*NFHS-I*			*NFHS-II*			*NFHS-III*		
	$_1q_0$	$_4q_1$	$_5q_0$	$_1q_0$	$_4q_1$	$_5q_0$	$_1q_0$	$_4q_1$	$_5q_0$
A.P.	40.00	33.3	72.0	63.1	37.	98.1	60.7	28.8	87.7
Assam	88.7	58.7	142.2	69.5	21.4	89.5	66.1	20.2	85.0
Manipur	42.4	20.2	61.7	37.0	19.9	56.1	29.7	12.6	41.9
Meghalaya	64.2	24.3	86.9	89.0	36.2	122.0	44.6	27.1	70.5
Mizoram	14.6	14.9	29.3	37.0	18.4	54.7	34.1	19.5	52.9
Nagaland	17.2	3.6	20.7	42.1	22.7	63.8	38.3	27.5	64.7
Sikkim	-	-	-	-	-	-	33.7	6.7	40.1
Tripura	75.8	31.2	104.6	43.9	28.4	71.0	51.5	8.2	59.2
India	78.5	33.4	109.3	67.6	29.3	94.3	57.0	18.4	74.3

1. National Family Health Survey , India 1992-93.
2. National Family Health Survey, India, 1998-99
3. National Family Health Survey, India 2005-06.

to 42 in the third. In all the three surveys, IMR in the state was much lower than those in India. IMR rates in India were 79, 68 and 57 in corresponding surveys while the respective rates in the state were 42, 37 and 30. This picture clearly reaffirms the improvement in the health conditions of the state.

Trends of Fertility

Average birth rate per thousand in the state declined from 27 in 1980-1989 to 20 in 1990-99 and further to 16 in 2000-07 (Table – 5). The decline in the rate was faster in rural areas than that in urban areas. In rural areas, the rate declined from 28 to 21 and further to 16 while in the urban areas, the rate decline from 22 to 18 and further to 15 in the corresponding periods. In view of smaller sample size, reliability of these figures are questionable when compared with the data of NFHS. The NFHS data shows that the rate increased from 24.4 in NFHS-I to 25.8 in NFHS-II and consequently declined to 25 in NFHS-III. The corresponding rates in rural areas were 25.5, 27.8 and 26.8 while those in urban areas were NC (not computed), 21.4 and 21.6.

Table 7
Total fertility in NE states

State	*NFHS-I*	*NFHS-II*	*NFHS-III*
Arunachal Pradesh	4.25	2.52	3.03
Assam	3.53	2.34	2.42
Manipur	2.76	3.04	2.83
Meghalaya	3.73	4.57	3.80
Mizoram	2.30	2.89	2.86
Nagaland	3.26	3.77	3.74
Sikkim	N.A.	2.75	2.02
Tripura	2.67	1.87	2.22
India	3.39	2.85	2.68

Source: Same as Table No.6

Total fertility in the state was third lowest in NE region in NFHS-I while it was third highest in NFHS-II (Table - 7). In the national context, it was sixth lowest in NFHS-I whereas, it was the seventh highest among the 25 states of the country in the second survey. The TFR in the state (2.76) in NFHS-I was lower by 0.63 points than that in India (3.39). On the contrary, in NFHS-II, the TFR in the state (3.04) was higher by 0.19 points than that in country (2.85). As mentioned earlier, such drastic change in the state can not be explained by the almost all known major determinants of fertility (Singh, 2006). Noting this likely overestimation of TFR in NFHS-II, the comparision of the first and third NFHS reveals over the period of 13 years (1992-93 to 2005-06) the fertility in the state remain almost unchanged (2.8). In the third survey, the figure in the state (2.83) was higher by 0.15 point than that in the country (2.68). The comparision of fertility rates in the state with those in country clearly indicates that inefficiency of family planning programme in the state.

Determinants of Fertility Decline

The present study briefly examines determinants of fertility. Several studies have shown the variations in fertility is explained by the level of literacy, status of women, per capita income, etc. With the change in the social life, the valuation of children has been changed and children have become more of a burden and less of an asset. The neoclassical theory of fertility (Becker 1960, Mincer 1963, Schultz 1973 etc.) has revealed that the decline in fertility is due to parent's income and their preference for children relative to other consumption goods. The increase in standard of living has raised the costs of rearing of child and providing education which induce parents to have lower fertility. Chicago - Columbia School (Becker 1960, Willis 1973) explained the change of fertility with the rise of per capita income in terms of preference for quality rather than quantity of children. It implies that income elasticity for number of childrens is negative, other things remain the same.

Unlike Chicago - Columbia School which emphasized the demand side, Easterlin (1975), Easterlin, Pollack and Watcher (1980) stressed the interactive process of demand for and the supply of birth. Supply side of fertility is influenced by fecundity, child survival rates, female age at marriage, duration of lactation and mother and child health care which are influenced again by economic factors. The equality between supply and demand is brought through the use of contraceptives and other birth controls.

Social development theory (Caldwell 1980, Krishnan 1986) explained the decline of fertility with the help of female literacy which has significant influence on the age at effective marriage) and health status as proxied by IMR. Diffusion theory (also known as ideation theory) enunciated by Cleland 1985, Retherford 1985, Cleland and Wilson 1987 explained the fertility transition through the diffusion of informations and new social norms about the birth control. The diffusion comes through social interaction and spillover effect of communication-information network. Diffusion takes place through education, mass media and extension programme of development.

After surveying literatures on fertility transition, Manson (1997: 44-45) concluded that none of the above theories provided a complete explanation for all known fertility decline. Thus, a decline in fertility may appear under various socio-economic and demographic conditions (Coale and Watkins 1986). The notable fertility decline in Kerela took place without industrialization, increase in per capita income and standard of living. The decline in the fertility was impressively influenced by female literacy rate (Krishnan 1986, Bhat and Ranjan 1990). The reduction in fertility in Andhra Pradesh was not explained by economic and social development but explained rather by the result of an effective governance of family planning programme and generous welfare measure (such as ICDS, public distribution of food) (James 1999, James and Subramanian 2003). The decline in fertility was associated with high infant mortality rate of 221 percent in Germany in 1890 and with low literacy rate of 40 percent in Bulgaria in 1922 (Knodel and Walle 1979). In the case of India, the decline occurred along with increase in female education and mother and child health (particularly reproductive and child health care, Manna 1998). Socially and economically backward states or regions had higher fertility (Shariff 1996). Though income variable significantly influenced fertility reduction in India, it was lesser important than non income factors, i.e. female education and health care (Measham et al 1999). The above discussion clearly reveals that there is no single prescription for reduction in fertility. The fertility change in the state has also to be searched in its own way.

The demand side factor – the structural change in the economy (change in social life by industrialization and urbanization), relative cost of children, the trade off between quality and quantity of children (in favour of quality), opportunity cost of women in child rearing and status of women are positively correlated with income and educational level of parents (particularly of mother). The supply side factors such as, fecundity, child survival rates, female age at marriage, mother and child health care are also positively influenced by income and educational level. The perverse relation between dependent (fertility) and independent variables found in some studies might be due to inappropriate proxy variable used. For example, per capita income proxy variable does not reflect income distribution in the economy and hence does not properly represent the income of the decision makers of fertility.

The present study, however, useds PCI as well as employment and literacy rate. Employment is more appropriate proxy for income as well as determinant for demand side and supply side factors. The increasing trend of net per capita income at constant (1999-2000) prices[3] (Table - 8) explains the fertility declines of SRS data while it can not properly explain the fertility variation of NFHS data. Table - 9 reveals that that unemployment rates of both usual status and current weekly status in rural as well as urban areas increases from 50th (1993-94) NSS round to 55th (1999-2000) round and then it declined in 61th (2004-05) round (except in urban female in respect of current weekly status). These ups and downs of unemployment rate moves coherently with fertility data of NFHS data.

Table 8
Net per capita income at constant (1999-2000) prices in Manipur

Year	*At constant (1999-2000) prices*	*Index No.*
1990-91	8778	100
1991-92	9292	105
1992-93	9520	108
1993-94	9494	108
1994-95	9059	103
1995-96	9134	104
1996-97	10304	117
1997-98	11019	126
1998-99	11517	131
1999-00	13260	151
2000-01	12157	138
2001-02	12641	144
2002-03	12319	140
2003-04	13389	153
2004-05	16482	188
2005-06(Q)	17950	204
2006-07 (A)	19625	224

Source (Basic Data):
1. Statistical Abstract, Manipur, 1998, Govt. of Manipur.
2. Economic Survey, Manipur 2002-03, Govt. of Manipur.
3. Economic Survey, Manipur 2007-08, Govt. of Manipur.

This conclusion is reinforced by self employment and regular salaried (Principal status and subsidiary status) data, despite casual labour which is the worst condition of employment does not support (Table - 10). Better employment status (self employed and regular salaried) for both of male and female in rural areas declined in 1999-

2000 then it increased in 2004-05. Similarly employment status in urban areas followed the same direction of variations.

Table 9
Unemployment rates in Manipur (1993-94 to 2004-05) per 1000 in labour force: Rural/urban

NSS Round.	*Rural*				*Urban.*			
	Male		*Female*		*Male*		*Female*	
	US	*CW*	*US*	*CW*	*US*	*CW*	*US*	*CW*
50 (1993-94)	19	12	11	7	53	48	44	27
55 (1999-00)	24	21	25	27	74	66	103	68
61 (2004-05)	20	14	12	9	53	54	82	79

Source: 1. NSSO (1996): Savekshana Vol.XX, No.1, July – Sept.
2. NSSO (2001), Report No. 458
3. NSSO (2006), Report No. 515
4. Reproduced from Singh (2009) "Nature of Unemployment in Manipur in Challenges of Economic Policy in Manipur, Vol. II."

Table 10
Status of employed in Manipur (per thousand)

Year.	*Rural (PS+S)*					
	Male			*Female.*		
	Self employed	*Regular salaried*	*Casual Labour*	*Self employed*	*Regular salaried*	*Casual Labour*
1993-94	767 (577)	169(85)	64(338)	929(586)	45 (27)	26 (387)
1999-00	762 (550)	127 (88)	111 (362)	882 (573)	42 (31)	76 (396)
2004-05	809 (581)	128 (90)	63 (329)	917 (637)	43 (37)	41 (326)

Note :Fig. in parenthesis are all India figures.
Source : Same as Table – 9.

While female literacy rate was fourth highest and third highest in NFHS-I and III, it is the second lowest in NFHS-II (Table – 11). The rate was 63 percent in 1992-93 (NFHS-I) which declined to 58.7 in 1998-99 (NFHS-II) and subsequently it increased to 7.3 in 2005-06 (NFHS-III). The variation in literacy rate is very much coherently with the variations in fertility data of NFHS. Thus, female literacy rate has a significant role in reducing fertility.

Table 11
Female literacy rate in NE States

States	*Female literacy Rate.*		
	NFHS-I	*NFHS-II*	*NFHS-III*
Arunachal Pradesh	42.1	57.0	52.7
Assam	50.7	59.1	63.0
Manipur	63.0	58.7	72.6
Meghalaya	60.2	66.8	69.5
Mizoram	88.9	89.4	94.0
Nagaland	71.8	68.3	75.2
Sikkim	-	64.4	72.3
Tripura	64.4	-	68.5
India	43.3	51.4	55.1

Source: Same as Table No.6.

Momentum of Population Growth

The doubling of population estimated in the above section of size and diversity may not be valid in view of momentum of growth built into the young age distribution of the state population. The young age distribution of female is particularly important for fertility rate or birth rate. The female population in the age group 0 – 24 in 2001 will attain 20 – 44 after 20 years in 2021. The female in 20 – 44 age groups is the main reproductive age group. The percentage of population in the above age group declined drastically from 56.71 in 1991 to 53.90 in 2001 (Table – 12). Similar decline was also revealed in both hill and valley. In the valley, the percentage declined by 3.71 from 56.26 in 1991 to 52.55 in 2001 and the corresponding figures for hill areas were 1.05, 57.55 and 56.50.

Table 12
Female population in the age groups of 0 - 24 by districts in Manipur in 1991 and 2001

(Percent)

State/District.	*Female population in the Age group 0-24.*		
	1991	*2001*	*Variation (2001-1991)*
Manipur.	56.71	53.90	-2.81
Senapati	57.61	57.49	-0.12
Tamenglong	59.30	57.27	-2.03
Churachandpur	58.08	56.16	-1.92
Chandel.	54.61	54.33	-0.28
Thoubal	57.52	55.29	-2.23
Bisenpur	54.56	53.00	-1.56
Imphal (West+East)	56.17	51.25	-4.92
Ukhrul	57.08	57.23	+0.15
Hill	57.55	56.50	-1.05
Valley	56.26	52.55	-3.71

Source: Census of India, 1991 Sseries 15, Manipur, Socio Cultural Tables, DCO, Manipur.
Census of India, 2001 CD File No. DDWC-140013 XLLS, Directorate of Census Operation (DCO), Manipur.

Among the districts, the highest decline occurred in Imphal (West + East) by 4.92 and followed by Thoubal District (2.23). Unlike other districts, marginal increase occurred in Ukhrul district (0.15). Thus, the decline in the possibility of population growth rate or birth rate is very clear in near future. The possibility of decline is more prominent in the valley districts which have the implication of necessity for intensification of family planning in the hill districts.

In spite of the desirable momentum built into the age distribution of young female of the sate, policy makers should not ignore the desirability for boosting the determinants of fertility in view of scarcity of state's resources and at the same time, the authority should aim at attaining the standard of living of advance states or at least mediocre states.

NOTES

1. While SRS data on male and female death rates are not available, sex-wise registered birth rate and death rate are available. But under registration has been very common in the underdeveloped countries particularly in the state. So registered birth and death rates are not used.
2. According to Indian Census, reason for migration includes – employment, business, education family moved, marriage, natural calamities like draught, flood etc. and other but excludes defence and similar personnel (see for example, Census of India 1991, Migration Tables, Directorate of Census Operation, Manipur, pp.13-15).
3. Net per capita state domestic product at constant (1980-81) prices for the year 1990-91 to 1993-94 has been spliced at 1993-94 prices to arrive a new series at constant (1993-94) prices. Then again this series for the year 1990-91 to 1999-2000 has been spliced at 1999-2000 to get a more new series of constant (1999-2000) price.

REFERENCES

Becker, G.S. (1960): "An Economic Analysis of Fertility" in *Demographic and Economic Change in Developed Countries*, Universities - National Bureau Conference Series No.11, Princeton University Press, Princeton.

Becker, G.S. and H.G. Lewis (1973): "On the interaction between Quantity and Quality of Children", *Journal of Political Economy*, Vol. 81, pp. 5279-88.

Bhat, Mari P.N. and S. Irudaya Rajan (1990): "Demographic Transition in Kerala Revised", *Economic and Political Weekly*, Sept. 1-8, pp. 1957-80.

Caldwell, J.C. (1980): "Mass Education as a Determinant of Timing of Fertility Decline", *Population and Development Review*, Vol. 6. No. 2, pp. 225-55.

Cleland, J. and C. Wilson. (1987): "Demand Theories of the fertility Transition: An Iconoclastic View", *Population Studies*, Vol. 41, No. 1, pp. 5-30.

Coale, A.J. and S.C. Watkins (1986): "The Decline of Fertility in Europe", Princeton University Press, Princeton.

Devi, Th. Umavati (2009): "Sex Ratio in Manipur" in Singh, E. Bijoykumar and Ksh. Jhaljit Singh (eds), *Challenges of Economic Policy in Manipur*, Vol. II, Akansha Publishing House, New Delhi.

Easterlin, R.A. (1975), "An Economic Framework of Fertility Analysis", *Studies in Family Planning*, Vol. 6, No.3, pp. 54-63.

Easterlin, R.A., R. Pollack and M. Watcher (1980): " Toward a More General Economic Model of Fertility Determination : Endogenous preferences and Natural Fertility" in R.A. Easterlin (ed), *Population and Economic Change in Developing Countries*, University of Chicago Press, Chicago.

James, K.S. (1999): " Fertility Decline in Andhra Pradesh - A Search for Alternative Hypothesis", *Economic and Political Weekly*, Feb. 20, pp.491-99.

James, K.S. and S.V. Subramanian (2003) "Towards a Demographic Transition", *Economic and Political Weekly*, Vol. 38, Nos. 12 and 13, pp. 1219-28.

Knodel, J. and E. van de Walle (1979): "Lessons from the Past Policy Implications of Historical Fertility Studies", *Population and Development review*, Vol. 5, No. 2, pp. 217-46.

Krishnan, T.N. (1976): "Demographic Transition of Kerala-Facts and Figures", *Economic and Political Weekly,* Vol. XI, No. 31-33, pp. 1203-24.

Kundu, Amitab (1979): "Migration, Urbanisation and Inter-regional Inequality: The Emerging Socio-Political Changes", *Economic and Political Weekly,* Vol. XXI, No. 46, Nov 15, pp-2005-08.

Manna, Mausumi (1998): "Factors Affecting Fertility Decline and Fertility Variation in 1990s-An Inter-state Analysis", *Economic and Political Weekly,* Dec. 19.

Manson, Karen Oppenheim (1997): "Explaining Fertility Transition", *Demography*, Vol.34, No. 4, pp. 443-54.

Measham, A.R., Krishna D. Rao, Dean.T. Jamison, Jia Wang and Alaka Singh (1999): "Reducing Infant Mortality and Fertility, 1975-1990:

Performance at All India and state Levels", *Economic and Political Weekly,* No. 22, June 4, pp.1359-67.

Mincher, Jacob (1963): "Market prices, Opportunity Costs and income Effects" in *Measurement in Economics: Studies in Mathematical Economics and Econometrics* in Memory of Yehuda Grundfield, Carl Christ et al (eds.), Stanford University Press Stanford, California.

Retherford, R.D. (1985): "A Theory of Marital Fertility Transitions", *Population Studies*, Vol. 39, No. 2, pp. 249-68.

Shariff, Abusaleh (1996): "Poverty and Fertility Differentials in Indian States: New Evidence from Cross Sectional Data", *Margin*, Vol. 29., No. 1, pp. 49-65.

Shryock, Henry S., Jacob Siegel and Associates (1980): *The Methods and Materials of Demography* , US Department of Commerce Bureau of the Census.

Singh, W. Kumar 1999-2000, "Declining Sex Ratio in Manipur - An Explanation", *The Indian Economic Journal*, Vol. 47, No. 4, pp. 96-100.

UNO (1994): "The Migration of Women: Methodological Issues in the Measurement and Analysis of Internal and International Migrations", International Research and Training Institute for the Advancement of Women, Saint Domingo, Dominican Republic.

Wolpin, K.I. (1984), "An Estimable Dynamic Stochastic Model for Fertility and Child Mortality", *Journal of Political Economy*, Vol. 92, pp. 852-74.

8

Some Aspects of Gender Equity in the Patriarchal Setup in Manipur

Th. Umavati Devi

Introduction

Governments around the world increasingly recognise that the advancement of women is a key to progress in attaining health and development goals. While the last half-century has seen articulation of major goals in women's health, education and rights, progress has been slow or uneven in many areas. Mortality inequality, natality inequality, basic facility inequality, special opportunity inequality, professional inequality, ownership inequality and household inequality are some notable aspects of inequality between man and woman. Gender inequality or disparities between men and women is still pronounced in the poorest regions and countries of the world.

Sen (2001), writing on the many faces of gender inequality says,

> "Gender inequality exists in most parts of the world, from Japan to Morocco, from Uzbekistan to the USA. However inequality between women and men can take many different forms. Indeed, gender inequality is not one homogeneous phenomenon, but a collection of disparate and interlinked problems."[1]

In all parts of the world women's advances in political representation have lagged behind gains in other areas such as education and employment. Gender based inequality is as disturbing as regional inequality. Sen (2001) further argues that it has implications for males as well. He writes,

> "Different forms of gender inequality can impose diverse adversities on the lives of men and boys, in addition to those of women and girls. In understanding the different aspects of the evil of gender inequality we have to look beyond the predicament of women and examine the problems created for men as well by the asymmetric treatment of women." [2]

Lower gender inequality goes with more progress in the fields of health and mortality reduction not only for females but also for the whole society. Social achievements in domains such as nutrition, child health and related matters are more impressive where women are better educated, more resourceful, more valued, more influential and generally more equal agents within the household and in society. The level of economic production is likely to be higher, other things being equal, in a society where women are able to engage in a diverse range of activities compared with that in a society where their life is confined to domestic life.

Being born a female affects one's life chances in all societies but the particular condition facing women vary from one society to another. Mason defines gender system as "the socially constructed expectations for male and female behaviour that are found (in variable form) in every known society. A gender system's expectations prescribe a division of labour and responsibilities between women and men and grant different rights and obligations to them".[3] Mason subdivides the gender system into gender stratification (institutionalised inequality between male and female members of society) and gender roles (the division of labour between men and women). Inequality between men and women and the division of labour between them in a particular gender system can be evaluated from the perspective of rights - social, political and reproductive. Levels of equity in such an evaluation of rights determine the level of gender equity.[4]

Most Asian countries have inherited the cultural legacy of strong son preference. Patri-locality, patri-lineage and patriarchal attitudes manifest in women and girls having subordinate position in the family, discrimination in property rights and lowly paid or unpaid jobs for women. Women's work especially household chores are treated as non-economic work. Hence women are perceived as burden. In the patriarchal setting in India today, the girl grows up in her natal family as *paraya-dhan* with least investment in her capacity development. Gopalan writes, "She suffers all deprivations; she is unwanted by families as evidenced through son preference, female foeticide and infanticide. She is victim to great deal of violence both inside the home and outside in the society."[5] In the more prosperous state of Punjab the conventional patriarchal preference of male children leads to sex selective abortions.

Table 1 shows different forms of violence at different stages of their lives women have to face.

Table 1
Gender violence throughout a woman's life

Phase	Types of violence
Prenatal	Prenatal sex selection, battering during pregnancy,
Infancy	Female infanticide, emotional and physical abuse
Childhood	Genital cutting, incest and sexual abuse, differential access to food
Adolescence	Dating and courtship violence, economically coerced sex
Reproductive	Abuse of women by intimate partners, marital rape, dowry abuse
Old age	Abuse of widows, elder abuse (which affects mostly women)

Source: Heise, L. (1994): *Violence against women: the hidden health burden*, World Bank Discussion Paper, Washington D.C.

The Report of the Committee on the Status of Women in India concluded that an increase in the neglect of female lives as an expendable asset was the only reasonable explanation for the declining sex ratio observed to persist over several decades. In India, female mortality rates are higher than the male mortality rates due to neglect of the female children, differential treatment with regard to access to life's amenities, maternal mortality, low status accorded to females, dowry deaths and the recent trend of NRTs (new reproductive technologies) for production of sons by killing and aborting the female foetuses. Dreze and Sen (2002) states,

> "(India's) pattern of female –male ratios is consistent with what is known as the character of gender relations in different parts of the country. The north western states (with particularly low female –male ratios) for instance, are notorious for highly unequal gender relations, some symptoms of which include the continued practice of female seclusion, low female labour force participation rates, a large gender gap in literacy rates, extremely restricted female property rights, strong son preference in fertility decisions, widespread neglect of female children and drastic separation of a married woman from her natal family."[6]

The declining sex ratio is a disgrace to democracy and representative government. Persistent gender inequality is a social failure and it can lead to other social failures. The concept of 'missing women' popularized by Dreze & Sen has given a new dimension to understanding and mapping of the problem. In 1986, 37 million Indian Women were estimated to be missing.

The articulation of practical needs effectively is closely associated with women's position in the society. If the status of woman is as high as that of man with high level of participation then many of the debilities from which females suffer would have been well known and tackled by themselves. Thus consolidation of women's position is equally important.

The following table shows the comparative profile between Norway, the country with highest HDI and GDI and India with rank 127 in 2003 in HDI. In the case of GDI India's rank are 98. The indices clearly show how backward India is and the enormity of the extent of catching up India has to do. Gender empowerment measures have not been estimated for India.

Table 2
Gender-related inequality

Indicators	*Norway*		*India*	
	Female	*Male*	*Female*	*Male*
Life expectancy at birth (years) 2003	81.9	76.8	65	61.8
Adult literacy rate (% ages 15 and above)	99.9	99.9	47.8	73.4
Combined gross enrolment ratio in primary, secondary and tertiary schools	106	97	56	64
Estimated earned income (ppp US $)	32,272	43,148	1569	4130
Gender related development index	0.960		0.586	
Human development index	0.963		0.602	

Source: Human Development Report 2005

GDI has frequently been criticized for failing to internalize dimensions such as safety and security, household allocation of resources, unpaid labor, and constraints imposed on mobility and on sexual and reproductive freedom by patriarchal ideology. It also fails to account for dimensions such as quality of community life, access to basic amenities and human rights. Income may rise without any improvement in the male biased dimensions like son preference, nutritional status and sex ratio. The distinction between women's practical needs and strategic needs helps to cover the tension between policies that attempt to meet women's practical needs by improving the concrete material conditions of their lives and those that seek to transform women's position in an unequal society.[7]

The Manipur Experience

Contrary to the situation in other patrilineal societies in India and abroad, Manipur presents totally a different scenario. Manipuri society is patriarchal [8]. Like any other patriarchal society we have patri-local residence i.e. after marriage a man lives in his father's house with his wife and children, sometimes, with other members of his patri-clan. A woman therefore leaves her natal home after her marriage and takes up the family name of her husband and lives with him and his parents.

The children born out of such marriages take the family name of their father. The important fact to be noted is that in Manipuri society with the patrilineal principle even if there is strong son preference, we cannot trace any sign of negative attitude towards girl child which might lead to aborting a female foetus or female infanticide Moreover, in Manipur there are no reported case of dowry deaths as well as any official record of amniocentesis tests.[9]

Apart from the secondary data obtained from official sources such as Census, National Sample Survey, National Family Health Survey and Sample Registration Scheme, primary data have been collected through a survey by using a questionnaire to probe the Manipur experience deeper. It was undertaken in the four valley districts of Manipur i.e. Imphal East, Imphal West, Bishnupur and Thoubal. Altogether 750 respondents were interviewed to elicit information on their opinion on issues listed in the questionnaire. There were 600 female and 150 male respondents.[10] Opinions regarding ill treatment, husbands' control over their wives, decision making role of the housewife, dowry, attitude toward the girl child and treatment towards their children were elicited from the respondents.

Keeping in mind the attitude towards girl child, the present study investigated the sex preference of the respondents with regard to the children they desire to have. The present study reveals that, of the total respondents 30% give male preference, 16% female preference and 54 % give equal preference. Desire to have a male or a female child by a respondent is closely associated with the birth order of the children already born. In other words, absence of a male child makes a respondent desirous of having at least a son. Similarly it is the case with a female child. In the case of a respondent having both sons and daughters they have reported that they have no preference for any particular sex and therefore they give equal preference and equal treatment to their children. There are also cases of respondents having only daughters yet they are quite satisfied for they are born to them as their children, they have no negative attitude towards the idea of having sons. They would have loved to have a son but they are really fond of their daughters who are provided with all the facilities and opportunities any male child would have had. The percentage of son preference is no doubt greater than that of daughter preference. However, these do not imply that there is any neglect of female children

The classification of sex preference shows that equal preference dominates in every age group. It is most dominant in the youngest age group i.e. below 19. In all age groups except the 'below 19' category male preference dominates female preference. The percentage of female preference declines as age rises. Male preference grows as age rises peaking at '30-39' age group. (Table 3)

Table 3

Sex preference according to the age of the respondents

Age group	*Male preference*	*Female preference*	*Equal preference*
Below 19	20	20	60
20-29	27.74	15.48	56.78
30-39	35.67	15.33	49.0
40-49	24.10	18.46	57.44
50+	28.42	13.68	57.9
Total	30	16	54

Source: Thokchom (2006), p.131.

The classification of sex preference by education shows that equal preference dominates the preference matrix followed by male preference. Equal preference has the highest share i.e. 60% among the illiterate respondents. The lowest share is found in the higher secondary/pre university category i.e. 42.11%. What the field data show is that the gap between male preference and female preference narrows down as the level of education rises. In the graduate and postgraduate category female preference dominates male preference. (Table 4)

Table 4
Sex preference by education of respondents

(per cent)

Educational status of respondents	*Number of cases*	*Male preference*	*Female preference*	*Equal preference*
Under matric	185	65 (35.14)	12 (6.48)	108(58.38)
Matriculate	105	30(28.57)	20(19.04)	55(52.39)
Higher secondary/pre university	95	35(36.84)	20(21.05)	40(42.11)
Graduate	150	35(23.34)	38(25.33)	77(51.33)
Post graduate	25	6(24)	7(28)	12(48)
Technical education	15	4(26.67)	3 (20)	8(53.33)
Illiterate	175	50(28.57)	20(11.43)	105(60)
Total	750	225(30)	120(16)	405(54)

Note: Figures in parentheses indicate percentage of row total.
Source: Thokchom (2006), p. 132.

The present study reveals that 90.66% of the total respondents give equal treatment to their children, 7.34 % give special treatment to their sons and 2% give special treatment to their daughters. (Table5). There are also women who give preferential treatment to their sons because they are the only sons. Along with the sex preference it was felt that the treatment given by the respondents to all their children would definitely reflect their attitude towards their children of both the sexes. Same is the case for special treatment to daughters who are the only daughter of their parents. Most parents i.e. 90.66% of the total respondents give equal treatment to their children, the exception being those with the only child of a particular sex, either female or male. There are special efforts to have a male child by performing puja in a traditional way or sometimes by going to the doctor as some respondents reported. But the percentage is not very high. Only 17.67 % of the total respondents are reported to have given any kind of effort, which they feel are appropriate for getting a male child.

Table 5
Equal and Preferential treatment by education of respondents

Educational status of respondents	*Number of cases*	*Equal treatment*	*Preferential Daughter*	*Treatment to Son*
Under matric	185	170(91.89)	2 (1.08)	13(7.03)
Matriculate	105	90(85.71)	2(1.90)	13(12.39)
Higher secondary/Pre-university	95	75 (78.95)	6(6.31)	14(14.74)
Graduate	150	150(100)	0	0
Post graduate	25	25(100)	0	0
Technical education	15	15(100)	0	0
Illiterate	175	155(88.57)	5(2.86)	15(8.57)
Total	750	680(90.66)	15(2)	55(7.34)

Note: Figures in parentheses indicate percentage of row total.
Source: Thokchom (2006), p- 134.

The childhood experience of the total respondents indicates that 73.33% Of the total respondents receive equal treatment. In other words percentage of differential treatment was higher in the childhood experience of the respondents than the present day. The present findings show that percentage of equal treatment is higher now than in the past. Percentage of equal treatment at present is 90.66%; percentage of equal treatment as experienced by the respondents was 73.33 %. Respondents in the age group 30-39 were found to have experienced differential treatment of comparatively higher percentage than the rest. i.e. 28.33%. Interestingly this age group of the respondents registered lowest percentage of equal preference to their children i.e. 49% (Table 6).

With regard to the differential treatment the present study reveals that the age group of the respondents in between 30 to 40 experiences the highest percentage of differential treatment in their childhood and interestingly this age group has the lowest percentage of equal treatment (85%) being given to their children. The respondents who experienced differential treatment during their childhood are more likely to give the same kind of treatment to their children also. As shown in the table 6 the percentages of differential treatment experienced by the age group 30 – 39, 50 +, 40-49, 20-29 and below 19 were 28.33, 27.37, 27.18, 22.58 and 20 respectively. If we look at the percentages of equal treatment given by these respondents to their children we find that there is a close association between personal experience of the respondents and their treatment towards their children

Table 6

Personal experience of differential treatment by age in percentage of respondents

Age	*No. of cases*	*Experienced differential treatment*	*Did not experience differential treatment*
Below 19	5	1 (20)	4(80)
20 - 29	155	35(22.58)	120(77.42)
30 - 39	300	85(28.33)	215(71.67)
40 - 49	195	53(27.18)	142(72.82)
50 +	95	26(27.37)	69(72.63)
All ages	750	200(26.67)	550(73.33)

Note: Figures in parentheses indicate percentage of row total.
Source: Thokchom (2006), p. 135.

Table 7

Equal treatment and preferential treatment towards the children by age of respondents

Age	*No. of cases*	*Equal treatment*	*Preferential treatment towards*	
			Daughter	*son*
Below 19	5	5 (100)	0	0
20 –29	155	149(96.13)	2(1.29)	4(2.58)
30-39	300	255(85)	8(2.66)	37(12.34)
40-49	195	183(93.85)	2(1.02)	10(5.13)
50 +	95	88(92.63)	3(3.16)	4(4.21)
Total	750	680(90.66)	15(2)	55(7.34)

Note: Figures in parentheses indicate percentage of row total.
Source: Thokchom (2006), p- 136.

The proportion of the total respondents giving equal treatment to all their children of either of the sexes was 90.66%. Sex preference according to age of respondents shows the dominance of equal preference. Highest percentage of female preference is found to be among those who have PG degrees and lowest percentage among those who are under matriculate. (Table 4). Similarly with regard to equal treatment being given to children, respondents with graduate, postgraduate and higher educational degrees in technical education give equal treatment to all. This indicates that besides childhood experiences of the parents, educational status of the parents are also strongly associated with equal treatment. With regard to sex preference however the presence or absence of the children of either of the sexes in the birth order of the children already born influences the desired sex preference of the parents.

In the absence of evidences enough to support ill treatment and neglect of female children so as to lead to female foeticide and female infanticide, the present study concludes that the position of our women is far better than their counterparts in other parts of India at least with regard to such evil social practices. However it would be wrong to assume that there are absolutely no cases of ill treatment of housewives by their husbands and that there are no cases of divorces. Of the total respondents 9.67 % women respondents complained against their husbands for being ill-treated. In most of the cases the husbands were found to be in the habit of drinking or using drugs or gambling. Higher percentage of women reported that they were not being ill-treated. The figures show a good stable marital relationship. 88.33% were not being ill treated in any form by their husbands. Looking at the figure of marital status of the respondents the percentage of divorcees is found to be 5, that of widow 4.33 and for the currently married women, it is 90.67. The reasons given by the divorcees for their divorce differ greatly. Of the total divorcees, 66.66% of their husbands drink, 6.66% are in the habit of gambling, 13.33% divorced because of involvement of second marriages of their husbands, the remaining 13.35 % were due to other personnel reasons which they did not reveal.

As a response to the ongoing problem associated with drinking, taking drugs and other intoxicants, many NGOs, clubs and Meira paibis are taking great interest to put an end to it. Women's involvement as a collective group is also evident by their activities outside the household domain and by their contributions to the eradication of social evils in the society.

Showing some of the patrilineal tinge, 80.67% of the total respondents reported of being under the control of their husbands and 72% of them said that they feel quite secure under such control. However 8.67% did not feel free. Mean while 13% reported that they could not be listed in the category of being under control of their husbands. Of these 13% women, 5.33% felt quite secure as they were and 7.67% however did not feel secure. Another 3.3% of the total respondents said that they enjoyed equal freedom in the family. The remaining 3% did not give their opinion on this matter.

Considering another indicator of status of women the present study reveals that all the children both male and female of the respondents are receiving formal education. Both male and female children have equal access to life's amenities. There is no room for depriving a girl child from receiving the same kind of education that a male child gets. If we look at the trend of literacy in Manipur according to 1901-2001 censuses it shows that even in the beginning of the 20th century there were women who received formal education. When 1.86 % males were literate, the literacy rate for females was 0.04. %. Till the 50s there was sharp difference with 22.93% of males being literate as against 2.73 % of females. The literacy rate rose from 1961 onwards reducing the gender gap in literacy. When a few old women were being interviewed they replied "people used to laugh at us if we go to school. I wanted to study but in our time hardly any girl child goes to school." As expressed by other women the reasons for not going to school were not because their parents were unwilling to send them but because of the fear of other people's reaction in the society. While a few said that learning English was considered to be defiling and even the male children who learnt English had to go for a bath after they came back from school. Now as per 2001 census female literacy rate in Manipur has reached 59.7%.

Conclusion

The very basis of gender equity is very much in existence in the areas covered under this study and in the mind-set of the people therein, while it is found to be absent in other patrilineal society with a higher degree of female disadvantages (such as the right to be born as a girl child , the right for a girl child to grow up as a boy child with equal access to existing facilities , dowry deaths, etc) leading to the so called "missing million women "and " dispensing with daughters"[11]. This genuine aspect of gender equity should not be ignored while we try to promote the opportunities for women in education and employment that would enhance their voice and decision making role in the family and the wider society as well. What are considered to be the social handicaps that make women completely voiceless and powerless and which are expected to be reversed in the society in other parts of India with low sex ratio (i.e. male outnumbering females due to female disadvantages) are absent in Manipur. This genuine aspect in the Manipuri culture where the girl child is so well placed unlike other patrilineal society is something which all of us should be proud of. Increasing crime rate is not only for women but also for men as well. Peace in the society can be attained only when there is peace within the self, the family and the neighbourhood. We need good and understanding parents to mould the children who would be the future pillars of society moving towards human excellence, innovative and resourceful teachers for quality education and edu-care and above all, honest and esteemed administrators who would understand the problem of the masses. How ideal we are in this regard is a question which we all need to ask ourselves for a better society.

NOTES

1. Sen (2001), p.4.
2. Sen (2001), p.6.
3. Quoted from McDonald (2000), p.427.

4. McDonald (2000), pp. 427-428.
5. Gopalan (2000), p.400.
6. Dreze & Sen (2002), p.232.
7. Kabir N. (1994)
8. Singh, R.K. Jhaljit (1965), p.13.
9. Mukherjee et al (2001), p.4073.
10. The details are available in Umavati Thokchom (2006).
11. John et al. (2009), p.16.

REFERENCES

Government of India (1975): *Towards Equality: Report of the Committee on the Status of Women in India*, Committee on the Status of Women in India, Min. of Education and Social Welfare.

Collymore, Yvette (2005): *Gender equality: New Opportunities for Moving Ahead*, Population Research Bureau.

DasGupta, M. (1987): "Selective Discrimination against Female Children in Rural Punjab, India" *Population and Development Review*, 13(1), pp.77-100.

DasGupta, M.(2005): "Explaining Asia's "Missing Women: A New Look at the Data", *Population and Development Review*, 31(3), pp. 529-535.

DasGupta, M. and P N Mari Bhat (1997): "Fertility Decline and Increased Manifestation of Sex Bias in India", *Population Studies*, 51, pp. 307-15.

Government of Manipur: *Statistical Abstract Manipur*, (several issues), Directorate of Economics and Statistics.

Dreze, J. and A. Sen (1995): *India: Economic Development and Social Opportunity*, Oxford University Press.

Dreze, J. and A.Sen (2002): *India: Development and Participation*, Oxford University Press.

Dyson, T. and M. Moore (1983): " On Kinship Structure, Female Autonomy and Demographic Behaviour in India," *Population and Development Review*, 9(1): pp. 35-60.

Fox, Robin (1967): *Kinship and Marriage; An Anthropological Perspective,* Penguin Books.

George Sabu and R.S. Dahiya (1998): "Female Foeticide in Rural Haryana", *Economic and Political Weekly*, Vol. XXXIII, No.32 Aug 8-14, pp.2191-2198.

Gopalan, Sarla (2000): *The Profile of the Empowered Woman: Vision 2020*, Planning Commission, Govt. of India.

Gupta, Jyotsna Agnihotri (2000): *New Reproductive Technologies, Women's Health and Autonomy: Freedom on Dependency*, Sage, New Delhi.

John, Mary E, Kaur, R. Palriwala and Saraswati Raju (2009): "Dispensing with Daughters: Technology, Society, Economy in North India", *Economic and Political Weekly*, Vol. XLIV No. 15, April 11-17.

Kabir, Naila (1999): "Resources, Agency, Achievement: Reflections on the Measurement of Women's Empowerment", *Development and Change,* 30(3) pp. 435-64.

Kulkarni, P.M. (1999): "Gender Preference, Contraceptive Prevalence: Evidence of Regional Variations" *Economic and Political Weekly*, Vol. XXXIV No 42and 43, Oct. 16-23.

Kulkarni, S. (1986): *Prenatal Sex Determination Tests and Female Foeticide in Bombay City - A Study*, Foundation for Research in Community Health, Mumbai.

McDonald, P.(2000): "Gender Equity in Theories of fertility Transition", *Population and Development Review,* Vol. 26, No.3.

Mari Bhatt, P.N.(2000): *Indian Demographic Scenario Vision 2020*, India Vision 2020, The Report, Planning Commission, Academic Foundation.

Mazumdar,Veena (1994): *Amniocentesis and Sex selection*, Centre for women's Development Studies, Occasional paper series no. 21, Delhi.

Miller, Barbara Diane (1989): "Changing Patterns of Juvenile Sex ratios in Rural India, 1961 to 1971", *Economic and Political Weekly*, Vol. XXIV No. 22 June 3, pp. 1229-1235.

Mukherjee, Ch., Rustagi, P. and Krishnaji, N. (2001): "Crimes against Women in India: Analysis of official statistics", *Economic and Political Weekly,* Vol. XXXVI No.43 , Oct. 27- Nov. 2.

Randeria, S. and L. Visaria (1984): "Sociology of Bride Price and Dowry", *Economic and Political Weekly*, 19(15) 14 April, pp. 648-652.

Sarkar, Bisakha de (2004): "Girl, Interrupted", *Telegraph*, Sept 19.

Sen, A. (1990): More than 100 million women are missing, New York Review of Books (Dec 20), pp 61-66.

Sen, A.(2001): "Many faces of Gender Inequality", *Frontline*, Nov. 9.

Singh, G. and Sunita Jain (1983): Opinion of Men and Women regarding Amniocentesis, College of Home Sciences, Punjab Agricultural University.

Singh, R.K. Jhalajit (1965): *A Short History of Manipur*, The O.K. Store, Imphal.

Umavati, Thokchom (2006): *An Investigation into the Dynamics of Sex Ratio in Manipur since 1951*, Unpublished Ph.D. thesis, Manipur University.

Vanaik, A.(1986): "Female Foeticide in India", Times of India June 20.

Voluntary Health Association of India(2003): *Darkness at Noon-Female Foeticide in India*, Delhi.

9

Fertility and Fertility Preference by Wealth Index in Manipur: Experiences from NFHS-3

Ksh. Anand Singh

Introduction

India is experiencing a substantial decline in the birth rate since the first round of the National Family Health Survey (NFHS-1), 1992-93. The total fertility rate (TFR) in the country had declined from 3.4 in NFHS-1 (1992-93) to 2.9 in NFHS-2 (1998-99) and further to 2.7 in the latest round of the national survey, NFHS-3 (2005-06). This decline in the total number of children per women can be explained through various socio- economic characteristics of the women. Both the educational level and occupation of women play an important role in the fertility and fertility preference pertaining to the choice of the ideal family size (Goldstein, 1972). An increase in the age at marriage of women combined with a higher level of acceptance in contraceptive use may also be considered as important determinants of fertility (Kirsty et al, 2003).

In addition to the factors mentioned above, the economic status of the family is believed to be an important factor influencing the fertility behavior (Becker, 1991; Easterlin, 1978; Johnson and Lean,

1985; Robinson, 1997). This is because in the modern concept of married couples, the cost of bringing up their wards is of primary concern to them. The economic model has, for the last 15-20 years, been the dominant model in fertility and family planning studies (Robinson, 1997). Despite its prominence as a theoretical paradigm of fertility behaviour, many studies on fertility in less developed countries or regions have not incorporated empirical studies of the effect of wealth or income on fertility.

The present study attempts to analyse the effect of wealth on the current marital fertility and fertility preferences of Manipur using data from NFHS-3 (2005-06). The state of Manipur, in the north-eastern region of India, has also witnessed a declining TFR as indicated by latest round of NFHS survey. The TFR of Manipur in NFHS-1 and NFHS-2 were 2.8 and 3.0 respectively but declined to 2.8 in NFHS-3. Further, as the economy of the family may also be interacted by the educational levels of both husband and wife in their fertility decisions and issues, it is worthwhile to consider both these characteristics simultaneously, even though one can be considered as an adjustment factor of the other.

Material and Methods

The National Family Health Surveys (NFHS) are nationwide surveys conducted with a representative sample of households throughout the country. The Ministry of Health and Family Welfare (MOHFW), Government of India initiated the NFHS surveys to provide high quality data on population and health indicators. The three NFHS surveys conducted are a major landmark in the development of a demographic and health database in India. The country's first NFHS was conducted in 1992-93 and the second was conducted in 1998-99. NFHS-1 covered a representative sample of 89,777 ever married women in the age group 13-49 while NFHS-2 covered a representative sample of 91,000 ever married women in the age group 15-49. The latest round i.e. NFHS-3 which was conducted in 2005-06 covered a representative sample of 1,24,385 women in the age group 15-49 irrespective of their maxital status.

The present study uses data from the latest round of the NFHS-3 (2005-06) in the state of Manipur. NFHS -3 collected information related to wealth and fertility from 3498 households in Manipur.

The Wealth Index

One of the background characteristics used in the NFHS-3 is an index of the economic status of households called the "wealth index". The index has been developed and tested in a large number of countries in relation to inequalities in household income, use of health services and health outcomes (Rutstein et al., 2000). It is an indicator of the level of wealth that is consistent with expenditure and income measures (Rutstein, 1999). The wealth index is constructed using household asset data and housing characteristics. The NFHS-3 wealth index is based on 33 assets and housing characteristics such as ownership of consumer items, type of dwelling, source of water, availability of electricity etc. Each household asset is assigned a weight (factor score) generated through principal component analysis and the resulting asset scores are standardized in relation to a normal distribution with a mean of zero and standard deviation of one (Gwatkin, et al. 2000). Each household is then assigned a score for each asset, and the scores are summed up for each household. The household population is divided into five equal groups of 20% each (quintiles) at the national level from 1(lowest/poorest) to 5 (highest/wealthiest). In NFHS-3, one wealth index has been developed for the whole sample and for the country as a whole. Table 1 shows the percent distribution of population by wealth index of the country and the state of Manipur. It is evident from the table that majority of the population in the state lies in the middle and fourth levels whereas very few (2.4%) of the population are in the lowest income category.

Measures of Fertility

An important objective of NFHS-3 is to provide detail information on fertility levels, differentials and trends. Most of the fertility measures presented are based on the complete birth histories collected from women aged 15-49 years. Several measures and procedures are used to obtain complete and accurate reporting of births, deaths and timings of these events. NFHS-3 provides estimates of age-specific fertility rate (ASFR) and total fertility rate (TFR) for the three years period preceding the survey. The ASFR for any specific age group is calculated by dividing the number of births to women in that age group during the three years period preceding the survey by the number of women years lived by women in that age group during the same three years period. The TFR is a summary measure based on the ASFR and indicates the number of children a woman would bear during her lifetime if she were to experience the prevailing ASFR. Another measure of fertility is the total children ever born (CEB), which is the total number of children a woman has ever born as on the date of survey. The number of children a woman has ever born is a cohort measure of fertility in the past. It provides a somewhat different picture of fertility levels, trends and differentials than do the period measures such as TFR.

Table 1

Percentage distribution of population by wealth quintiles

	Wealth quintile					
	Lowest	*Second*	*Middle*	*Fourth*	*Highest*	*Total*
India	20.0	20.0	20.0	20.0	20.0	100.0
Urban	3.0	6.4	13.8	28.9	47.9	100.0
Rural	27.7	26.1	22.8	16.0	7.4	100.0
Manipur	2.4	15.7	33.4	31.8	16.7	100.0

Source: NFHS-3(2005-06)

The greatest differentials in fertility in India are by wealth and education (NFHS-3, 2005-06). At the current fertility rates, women in the lowest wealth quintile will have two children more than the women in the highest wealth quintile. Similarly illiterate women will have two children more than those women who have attained higher educational levels. Figures 1 and 2 illustrate these differential fertilities. The present study will investigate fertility differentials in different wealth quintiles for the state of Manipur exclusively.

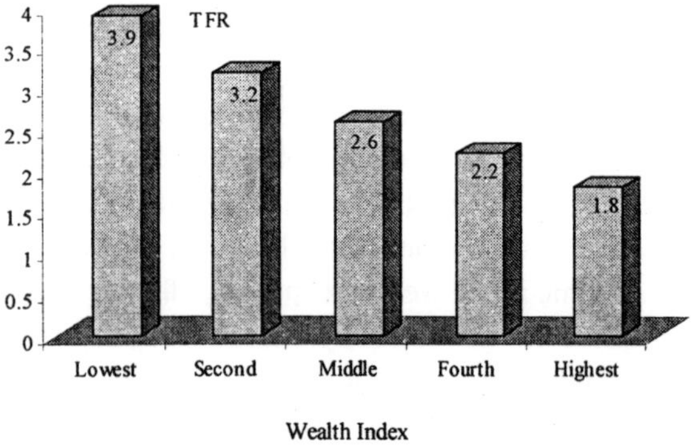

Fig 1: Differential fertility with Wealth Index

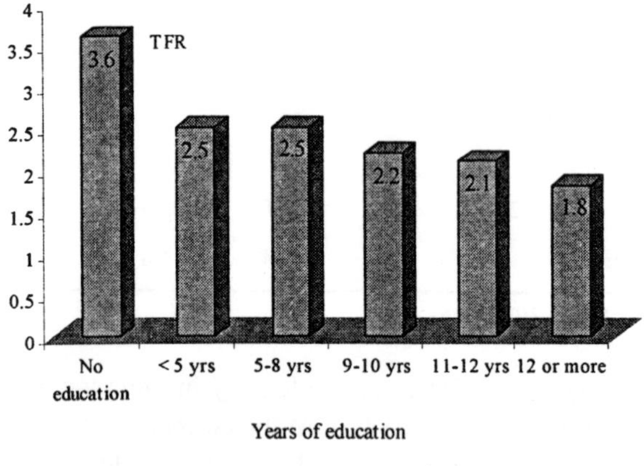

Fig 2: Differential fertility with educational level of women (India)

Educational attainment

The educational attainment of a population is an important indicator of the society's stock of human capital as well as its level of socio-economic development. Education enhances the ability of the individuals to achieve desired demographic and health goals. Educational levels of both husband and wife is believed to be a highly influencing factor to the fertility and fertility preferences of the nation as a whole. The present study includes both the educational levels of husband and wife as explanatory variables in fitting a logistic regression with fertility indicators as outcome variable. The objective is to explain fertility and fertility preferences via wealth index and educational levels. The results of analysis are presented in sections 3 and 4. Table 2 gives the percent distribution of women by age and educational levels.

Table 2

Distribution of women by age and educational level (Manipur)

Age	*No education*	*Primary*	*Secondary*	*Higher*	*Total*
15-19	54(7.2)	72(9.6)	621(82.7)	4(.5)	751(100.0)
20-24	98(11.7)	83(9.9)	538(64.3)	118(14.1)	837(100.0)
25-29	114(14.5)	80(10.2)	418(53.3)	172(21.9)	784(100.0)
30-34	135(18.8)	72(10.0)	350(48.7)	161(22.4)	718(100.0)
35-39	180(30.7)	72(12.3)	213(36.3)	122(20.8)	587(100.0)
40-44	163(36.2)	64(14.2)	146(32.4)	77(17.1)	453(100.0)
45-49	174(45.2)	53(13.8)	108(28.1)	50(13.0)	385(100.0)
Total	918(20.3)	496(11.0)	2394(53.1)	704(15.6)	4512(100.0)

(Figures within parentheses indicate % within age groups)

Association between Fertility Indicators and Wealth Index

In this section some hypotheses of association between fertility indicators and wealth index are tested using chi-squared test and the results are presented.

Association between Ideal number of children and Wealth Index

To assess women's ideal number of children, NFHS-3 asked women in the age group 15-49, the number of children they would like to have if they were given a chance to go back to the time of start of their child bearing. Table 3 gives the percent distribution of women by ideal number of children and wealth quintiles for the state of Manipur. Suspecting that the wealth of the family would certainly motivate the ideal number of children suggested by a woman, the hypothesis of no association between the two attributes is tested using a chi-squared test. The value of the test statistic is 393.94 on 16 degrees of freedom and with a p-value of 0.00, which is highly significant. The result suggests that there is a high degree of association between the wealth of the family and their ideal number of children.

Table 3
Distribution of women by ideal number children and wealth (NFHS-3, Manipur)

Wealth index	*Ideal no. of children*							*Total*
	0	*1*	*2*	*3*	*4*	*5*	*6 or more*	
Poorest	26 (1.4)	12 (2.2)	8 (1.1)	10 (1.6)	8 (2.3)	9 (4.6)	10 (4.8)	83 (1.8)
Poorer	185 (9.8)	63 (11.5)	85 (11.9)	91 (14.8)	51 (14.6)	47 (24.2)	54 (26.1)	576 (12.8)
Middle	540 (28.7)	141 (25.8)	201 (28.0)	208 (33.9)	134 (38.3)	74 (38.1)	81 (39.1)	1379 (30.6)
Richer	681 (36.1)	192 (35.1)	270 (37.7)	190 (31.0)	118 (33.7)	47 (24.2)	56 (27.1)	1554 (34.4)
Richest	452 (24.0)	139 (25.4)	153 (21.3)	114 (18.6)	39 (11.1)	17 (8.8)	6 (2.9)	920 (20.4)
Total	1884 (100.0)	547 (100.0)	717 (100.0)	613 (100.0)	350 (100.0)	194 (100.0)	207 (100.0)	4512 (100.0)

χ^2 = 393.94 on 16 degrees of freedom, p-value = 0
(Figures within parentheses indicate % within ideal number of children)

Association between Number of living children, fertility preference and Wealth Index

In order to obtain information on fertility preferences, NFHS-3 collected relevant information on fertility preferences from eligible women in the age group 15-49. Assuming that future preference will also depend on the number of living children, the percent distribution of currently married women by future fertility preference and number of living children is presented in Table 4. For currently married women 1564(34.8%) out of a total of 4491 women said that they did not want any more children and an additional 245(5.5%) women could not have another child because either the wife or the husband had been sterilized. Out of 857 women who wanted another child 367(67%) already had 1(one) child and 179(25%) already had 2(two) children. This number sharply declines as the number of living children increases. This is an indication that the ideal family size in Manipur will eventually lie between 2 and 3 and is consistent with the NFHS-3 finding of the total fertility rate in Manipur as 2.8. Out of 4491 currently married women, 1634 women reported that they never had sex.

Table 4
Distribution of women by fertility preference and number of living children (NFHS-3, Manipur)

Fertility preference	*No. of living children*							*Total*
	0	*1*	*2*	*3*	*4*	*5*	*6 or more*	
Have another	193 (10.3)	367 (67.2)	179 (25.0)	83 (13.5)	21 (6.0)	8 (4.1)	6 (2.9)	857 (19.1)
Undecided	6 (.3)	9 (1.6)	13 (1.8)	6 (1.0)	2 (.6)	3 (1.5)	-	39 (.9)
No more	22 (1.2)	144 (26.4)	444 (62.0)	421 (68.7)	241 (68.9)	133 (68.6)	159 (77.6)	1564 (34.8)
Sterilized	2 (.1)	3 (.5)	51 (7.1)	79 (12.9)	65 (18.6)	30 (15.5)	15 (7.3)	245 (5.5)
Declared infecund	10 (.5)	23 (4.2)	29 (4.1)	24 (3.9)	21 (6.0)	20 (10.3)	25 (12.2)	152 (3.4)
Never had sex	1634 (87.5)							1634 (36.4)
Total	1867 (100.0)	546 (100.0)	716 (100.0)	613 (100.0)	350 (100.0)	194 (100.0)	205 (100.0)	4491 (100.0)

(Figures within parentheses indicate % within number of living children)

The income of the family to which a woman belongs will also be an important motivating factor to the future fertility preference of the woman. Table 5 presents the percent distribution of women by fertility preference and wealth index. To statistically verify the association between the wealth index and fertility preference, the hypothesis of no association is tested using chi-square test and with a value 82.23 of the test statistic on 20 d.f. (p-value = 0), it strongly suggests that there is high degree of association between income and fertility preference.

Table 5
Distribution of women by fertility preference and wealth index

Fertility preference	*Wealth index*					*Total*
	Poorest	*Poorer*	*Middle*	*Richer*	*Richest*	
Have another	21 (25.9)	120 (21.0)	230 (16.8)	310 (20.0)	176 (19.2)	857 (19.1)
Undecided		11 (1.9)	12 (.9)	10 (.6)	6 (.7)	39 (.9)
No more	36 (44.4)	245 (42.8)	502 (36.6)	502 (32.4)	279 (30.5)	1564 (34.8)
Sterilized	1 (1.2)	25 (4.4)	80 (5.8)	91 (5.9)	48 (5.2)	245 (5.5)
Declared infecund	5 (6.2)	17 (3.0)	59 (4.3)	52 (3.4)	19 (2.1)	152 (3.4)
Never had sex	18 (22.2)	154 (26.9)	488 (35.6)	586 (37.8)	388 (42.4)	1634 (36.4)
Total	81 (100.0)	572 (100.0)	1371 (100.0)	1551 (100.0)	916 (100.0)	4491 (100.0)

$\chi^2 = 82.23$ on 20 degrees of freedom, p-value = 0.
(Figures within parentheses indicate % within Wealth index)

Total Children Ever Born

The number of children a woman has given birth as on the date of interview is a cohort measure of fertility. Since it reflects fertility in

Table 6
Percentage distribution of women by CEB

Age group	*CEB*										*Total*
	0	*1*	*2*	*3*	*4*	*5*	*6*	*7*	*8*	*9 or more*	
15-19	715 (95.2)	29 (3.9)	4 (.5)	3 (.4)	- -	- -	- -	- -	- -	- -	751 (100.0)
20-24	561 (67.0)	159 (19.0)	80 (9.6)	25 (3.0)	9 (1.1)	3 (.4)	- -	- -	- -	- -	837 (100.0)
25-29	324 (41.3)	143 (18.2)	160 (20.4)	93 (11.9)	36 (4.6)	20 (2.6)	6 (.8)	1 (.1)	1 (.1)	- -	784 (100.0)
30-34	161 (22.4)	97 (13.5)	192 (26.7)	136 (18.9)	73 (10.2)	32 (4.5)	20 (2.8)	4 (.6)	1 (.1)	2 (.3)	718 (100.0)
35-39	59 (10.1)	44 (7.5)	134 (22.8)	153 (26.1)	86 (14.7)	50 (8.5)	25 (4.3)	10 (1.7)	15 (2.6)	11 (1.9)	587 (100.0)
i40-44	29 (6.4)	27 (6.0)	69 (15.3)	101 (22.4)	95 (21.1)	53 (11.8)	36 (8.0)	15 (3.3)	12 (2.7)	13 (2.9)	450 (100.0)
45-49	23 (6.0)	19 (4.9)	43 (11.2)	59 (15.3)	79 (20.5)	60 (15.6)	42 (10.9)	25 (6.5)	15 (3.9)	20 (5.2)	385 (100.0)
Total	1872 (41.5)	518 (11.5)	682 (15.1)	570 (12.6)	378 (8.4)	218 (4.8)	129 (2.9)	55 (1.2)	44 (1.0)	46 (1.0)	4512 (100.0)

(Figures within parentheses indicate % within age group)

the past, it provides a somewhat different picture of fertility levels, trends and differentials than do period measures of fertility such as CBR and TFR. Table 6 shows the percent distribution of currently married women by children ever born (CEB) in different age groups.

The table shows that early child bearing is not so common in Manipur as compared to the whole country. Only 4.8% of currently married women aged 15-19 already had a child whereas in India this figure is 44%. For women aged 45-49, the number of children ever born is of particular interest because these women have virtually completed their childbearing span. Among all currently married women in this age group, 15.3% has reached the end of childbearing period with three children ever born and 20.5% has four children ever born. Only 6% of currently married women aged 45-49 have never given a birth which is a little higher than the all India figure of only 2% . This suggests that primary infertility is not so high in Manipur which is also the case in India.

Table 7 gives the mean number of children ever born to women aged 40-49 in different wealth quintiles. The average children ever born for these women who are at the end of their childbearing period is 4.08 in Manipur which is slightly higher than the all India figure of 4.00. For both Manipur and India, a similar pattern of a decline in the mean CEB is observed. The mean CEB declines from 4.6 in the poorest wealth quintile to 2.8 in the richest category of wealth in Manipur, whereas in India, it declines from 5.17 to 4.00 respectively. This is a first hand observation of the hypothesis of "the poorer the more CEB" and this will be statistically verified in the next section by modeling the mean CEB via the wealth index in a logistic regression model.

Table 7

Mean number of CEB in different wealth quintiles

Wealth Index	*Mean no. of CEB to women aged 40-49*	
	Manipur	*India*
Poorest	4.6	5.17
Poor	4.9	4.70
Middle	4.4	4.15
Richer	3.7	3.68
Richest	2.8	2.98
Total	4.08	4.00

The Logistic Regression Analysis

Before beginning the actual analysis, it is important to understand that the goal of an analysis using logistic regression model is the same as that of any model building technique used in statistics, which is in fact to find a reasonable relationship between an outcome variable and a set of predictor variables called covariates. What distinguishes a logistic regression model from other regressions like the multiple linear regressions is that the outcome variable in the former is binary or dichotomous. Otherwise, the approach to the analyses of both the models requires the same theoretical concepts. The advantage of using the logistic regression model is the interpretability of the estimated coefficients via the odds ratio. For detailed logistic regression modeling and odds ratio the reader is referred to David W. Hosmer and Stanley Lemeshow (2000).

For the present discussion the outcome variable will be CEB (Children ever born) for women in the age group 40-49 who are in the last stage of child bearing span. The analysis consists of 835 women in this age group. Table 8 presents the number of women in different wealth quintiles by recategorized CEB. The outcome variable is dichotomized with the value 0 for CEB less than or equal to 3 and 1 for CEB greater than 3. The rationale for choosing 3 as the cut-point is motivated by the fact that ideal family size in Manipur lies between 2 and 3. The covariate of interest which is believed to explain the outcome variable is the wealth index. However, educational levels of both the women and her partner will also be incorporated in the model so that the interpretations become less biased.

Table 8
Women by recategorized CEB

CEB	*Wealth index*					*Total*
	Poorest	*Poorer*	*Middle*	*Richer*	*Richest*	
ceb <=3	6	28	88	122	126	370
ceb > 3	12	78	158	158	59	465
Total	18	106	246	280	185	835

In Table 9, the results of fitting the logistic regression model is presented. It consists of the estimated coefficients, standard error of the estimated coefficients, Wald test and its p-values for the significance test of the coefficients and the odds ratios (OR). The covariates included in the model are written along with the reference categories. The analysis is performed using two statistical packages viz. SPSS 11.0.1(2001) and S-Plus 4.5(1996).

Results

As stated earlier, our objective in fitting a logistic regression model is to explain a fertility indicator like the CEB through the wealth of the family. Out of the 5 wealth quintiles, the first four categories are being compared with the richest category. In the last column of Table 9, the odds ratio for the poorest is 2.44. It can be interpreted that women in the poorest category of wealth quintile is 2.4 times more likely to have 4 or more children than those women in the richest wealth category. For the next wealth category (i.e. poor), the odds ratio is approximately 3 and that is women belonging to a poor family are 3 times more likely to have larger number of children than those women in the richest wealth category of Manipur. The odds ratio declines with the next higher wealth quintiles and for the rich women it is about 1.8 times higher risk of having 4 or more children as compared to the richest category women.

Regarding education of women, it is evident from Table 9 that the odds ratio for the less educated women are approximately 6, indicating that less educated women are more likely to have larger number of CEB as compared to women who have attained higher education. Finally, women who had completed secondary education are 3.9 times more likely to have larger number of children than the higher educated women. Partner's education is included in the model as an adjustment factor and no interpretation is made with this covariate.

Table 9
Results of logistic regression analysis

Covariates and categories	*Coeff.(β)*	*Std. error of β*	*Wald test*	*p-value*	*Odds Ratio exp (β)*
Wealth Index					
Poorest	0.893	0.585	2.331	0.008	2.441
Poor	1.093	0.313	12.207	0.127	2.983
Middle	0.712	0.244	8.541	0	2.039
Richer	0.596	0.223	7.163	0.003	1.814
Richest (ref.)	-	-	13.888	0.007	-
Education of women					
No education	1.746	0.293	35.535	0	5.73
Primary	1.761	0.318	30.669	0	5.818
Secondary	1.363	0.273	25.002	0	3.907
Higher (ref.)	-	-	39.4	0	-
Partner's education	0.079	0.069	1.31	0.252	1.083
Constant	-1.784	0.31	33.213	0	0.168

Conclusion

India's population has already crossed one billion mark and at the current rate of population growth, India will overtake China to become the most populous country in the world during the next few decades. Population growth and development go hand in hand and as such a rapid growth of population has its own merits and demerits. So far, India's growth of population is mostly unplanned and consequently, it leads to deeper poverty to millions of already poor population.

The objective of the present article is to find and explain a relationship between wealth and population growth through various fertility indicators in the state of Manipur. Possible comparative explanations have been made for both Manipur and India. As one suspects that the economy of a family will be a motivating factor for the eligible couples to decide on their own family size, it has been statistically verified the validity of the hypothesis of association between wealth and fertility and fertility preferences. The hypothesis of "the poorer the more CEB" has been justified using a logistic regression analysis. Another finding from the logistic model is that if a woman has higher education, she will have lesser number of CEB as compared to a woman who has a lower educational level.

REFERENCES

Becker G.S (ed) (1991): *A treatise on the family,* Harvard University Press.

Easterlin R.A.(1978): "The economics and sociology of fertility: a synthesis", in C. Tilly (ed), *Historical studies of changing fertility,* New Jersey: Princeton University Press, pp. 57 -113.

Easterlin, R.A.(ed)(1980):*Population and economic change in developing countries,* University of Chicago Press.

Goldstein, Sidney (1972): "The influence of labour force participation and education on fertility in Thailand", *Population Studies*, Vol. 26, No. 3, pp. 419-436.

Gwatkin, D.R., S. Rutstein, K. Johnson, R.P. Pande and A. Wagstaff (2000): *Socio-economic differences in health, nutrition and poverty,* HNP/ Poverty Thematic group of the World Bank, Washington D.C., The World Bank.

Hosmer, D.W. and S. Lemeshaw (2000): *Applied logistic regression,* John Wiley and Sons Inc., New York.

International Institute for Population Sciences: *National Family Health Survey, 1992-93,* Mumbai.

International Institute for Population Sciences and ORC Macro: *National Family Health Survey, 1998-99*, Mumbai.

International Institute for population Sciences: *National Family Health Survey, 2005-06*, Mumbai.

Mathsoft Inc. (1997): *S-Plus 4.5, Guide to Statistics*, Data Analysis Products Division, Washington, pp. 193 - 204.

McNay, Kirsty, Perianayagam Arokiasamy, Robert H. Cassen (2003): "Why Are uneducated women in India using contraception? A multilevel analysis", *Population Studies*, Vol. 57, No. 1, pp. 21-40.

Johnson, Nan E. and Suewen Lean (1985): "Relative income, race, and fertility" *Population Studies*, Vol. 39, No.1, pp. 99-112.

Robinson, W: "The economic theory of fertility over three decades" *Population Studies*, pp. 213 - 65.

Rutstein, S. (1999), *Wealth versus expenditure: Comparison between the DHS wealth index and household expenditures in four departments of Guatemala,* Calverton, Maryland: ORC Macro.

Rutstein, S., K. Johnson and D. Gwatkin (2000): *Poverty, health inequality, and its health and demographic effects*, Paper presented at the 2000 Annual Meeting of the Population Association of America, Los Angeles, California.

10

Civil Service Reforms in the North Eastern States:

With Special Reference to Manipur

Damodar Nepram

Introduction

The civil services in many developing countries are often too large for reasons "other than the desire to increase production of public goods and services" (Lindauer,1988:18) and they are frequently "too expensive and too insufficiently productive" (Nurnberg and Nellies, 1995:1). In India too public employment expanded rapidly and stood at 195.59 lakh persons in 1997 as against 154.84 lakhs in 1981. The enormity of the size became evident after the implementation of the Fifth Pay Commission (FPC) recommendations in the late nineties which resulted in the escalation of committed expenditures Financial Condition of the states deteriorated and an urgent need was felt to scale the size of public employment. The Planning Commission of India (2001:17) even commented that, "Surplus staff in government is a serious problem and correctives steps cannot be postponed". Downsizing of public employment has been given high priority since then by both the central and the state governments. In addition, wage restraint measures were also implemented to contain the rising salary expenditure.This chapter examines the success of the reform measures in the north eastern states of the country in general and Manipur in particular.

Definition of Public Employment

Public sector employment is generally taken to mean total employment in the government sector. For the current study, it has been taken as total employment in the government sector without those in the public sector undertakings or enterprises. Thus, public sector employment in our context is the totality of civil services which would include those in administration, teachers, health workers, etc.[1]

The Size of Public Employment the North East

A comprehensive picture of public employment in the north eastern (NE) states as on 31st March 2001 given in Table 1 shows that Assam had a total government employee size of 3.76 lakh employees, excluding central government employees, followed by that of Tripura and Manipur with 1.03 and 0.73 lakh employees respectively.[2] Mizoram had the smallest employee size with about thirty eight thousand employees. Measured as a percentage of population, state government employment size was the highest in Mizoram and the lowest in Assam. This was not surprising as a state with a larger population enjoys economies of scale in the provision of public services. However, Meghalaya was an exceptional case as the employee size was quite low, both in absolute number and as a percentage of population. Its employee size was lower than that of Manipur by as much as twenty-eight thousand even though their population figures were almost equal. For Meghalaya and Mizoram also, state employee sizes were very similar though the population of Meghalaya was 2.6 times the population of the latter. A thorough examination is necessary as to understand how the state was able to provide services with a much lower employee size.

Table 1
Public employment in the north eastern states as on 31st March 2001

(in lakhs)

State	*State govt.*	*State Quasi Govt.*	*Local Govt.*	*Central govt.*	*Central Quasi govt.*	*State (1+2+3)*	*Total (4+5+6)*
Arunachal Pradesh	0.40	NA	NA	NA	NA	NA	NA
Assam	3.07	0.58	0.13	0.77	0.77	3.76	5.3
Manipur	0.65	0.03	0.04	0.05	0.04	0.72	0.81
Meghalaya	0.37	0.08	0.03	0.16	0.08	0.48	0.72
Mizoram	0.33	0.02	0.03	0.01	0.01	0.38	0.4
Nagaland	0.62	0.03	0.00	0.07	0.02	0.65	0.74
Tripura	0.92	0.03	0.08	0.02	0.04	1.03	1.09
Total	6.32	0.77	0.31	1.08	0.96	7.02	9.06

Source: DGET (2002), *Employment Review 2002.*

The large employee size witnessed in many of the NE states can be ascribed to the policy of continuous recruitment. For example, during the period 1994-95 to 1999-00 (Table 2) the increase was by 28.87 p.c. in Meghalaya followed by Arunachal Pradesh, Nagaland and Tripura with 18.73, 17.94 and 16.32 percent respectively while it was comparatively lower in case of Assam and Manipur.[3] However, employee size began to decline beginning with Assam from 1999-00, Tripura from 2000-01 and Manipur from 2001-02 respectively. The increase in employment size for the remaining states also exhibited a declining trend. The decline or the slowdown in the growth of the employee size can be attributed to the efforts made by the states to curb the expansion of public employment as a means of checking the growth of committed expenditures. In aggregate the result was a decline (Figure 1) in the size of state government employees.[4]

Table 2
State government employee sizes

	1994-95	*1995-96*	*1996-97*	*1997-98*	*1998-99*	*1999-00*	*2000-01*	*2001-02*
Arunachal Pr.	33222	36325	37420	39222	39606	39445	40231	40322
Assam	413464	422690	430357	441590	459701	453245	447424	441634
Manipur	60682	61379	62158	62698	63605	63829	64596	64290
Meghalaya	36194	38014	39613	42830	44928	46644	47427	48776
Mizoram	NA	NA	39376	NA	42144	43443	44282	43611
Nagaland	62212	64444	64517	70888	72629	73373	73448	73476
Tripura	90300	89242	96310	96725	96673	105038	103736	101604
Total	696074	712094	769751	753953	819286	825017	821144	813713

Source: Twelfth Finance Commission Report
Statistical Handbook of Manipur 2002
Statistical Handbook of Nagaland 2004, 2006
Census of Government Employees 2001, Mizoram

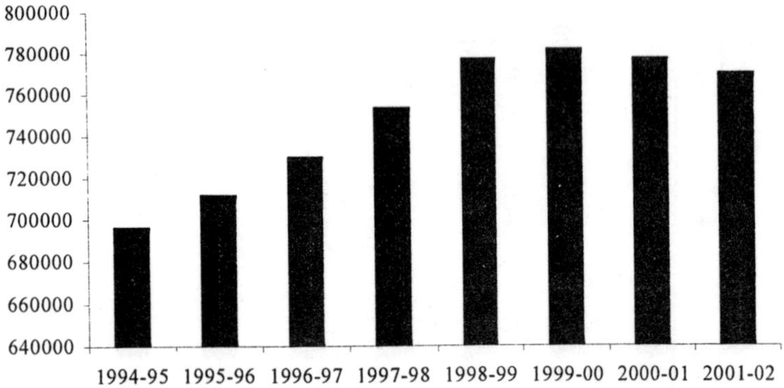

Fig. 1: State Government employees in the North East

Indications of excessive employment were evident. Measuring the right number of employee size is a difficult task but a simple manifestation of excess employment is the consumption of government budget by salaries leading to deterioration in the quality of public expenditure, thus, defeating its very purpose. Much of the revenue expenditures of the NE states were consumed by expenditures on salaries, pension and interest. It stood as high as 95.71 p.c. for Manipur in 2000-01 and 85.10 p.c. for Assam in 1999-00. Arunachal Pradesh and Mizoram were the only states which were able to sustain these expenditures to some manageable limits. On the average, for every one rupee spent on revenue expenditure the combined NE states spent 45.24 paise on salaries in 1995-96 which gradually rose to as much as 52.97 paise in 1998-99. Again for every rupee spent on revenue expenditure, the governments spent another 65.83 paise on salaries, pensions and interest in 1995-96 which rose to 78.49 paise in 1999-00.

Another manifestation of the presence of excess public employment or improper employee mix was the presence of bottom heavy employee structure along with the lack of skilled personnel. After classifying employees into four categories, it was observed that Class I and Class II employees in many states were significantly lower than Class III and Class IV employees. For example, in Nagaland the

Table 3

Proportion of committed expenditure to revenue expenditure (per cent)

	1995-96	*1996-97*	*1997-98*	*1998-99*	*1999-00*	*2000-01*	*2001-02*	*2002-03*	*2003-04(RE)*
Arunachal Pradesh	48.00	46.98	52.43	57.90	56.65	56.61	53.32	58.02	44.65
Assam	71.55	80.71	81.49	82.45	85.10	84.49	83.95	84.73	63.58
Manipur	74.41	74.10	74.88	79.88	91.90	95.71	78.84	82.47	64.15
Meghalaya	56.84	65.30	66.41	67.82	68.29	66.97	72.23	75.40	62.30
Mizoram	45.66	49.69	55.29	56.52	60.63	59.72	61.74	62.22	62.51
Nagaland	55.72	60.40	58.19	64.57	66.31	76.80	71.24	70.76	40.80
Tripura	76.41	64.31	64.48	68.59	79.11	70.29	76.18	78.60	74.31
NE	65.83	69.80	71.01	73.68	78.49	77.64	76.54	78.19	61.47

Source: GOI (2005): *Fiscal Profile of States*, www.fincomindia.nic.in,

Note: Committed expenditures include expenditures on salary, interest and pension. Salary includes expenditure on govt. employees, aid to educational institutions and local bodies.

upper two classes constituted just 8.79 p.c. of the total number of employees without taking into account the employees in education (higher and school) and police departments. Thus, an officer would be working with 11 assistants whose works are increasingly being made redundant due to computerisation and outsourcing. In Assam the upper class employees after removing employees in the education sector was 7.62 p.c. in 1999. In Tripura the number was still low at 12.36 p.c. in January 2008 after years in the reform process.

The proliferation of the number of government departments also led to the existence of large public sector employment. Among the NE states, the number varied and was as high as 71 in Mizoram.[5] Within a short span of three years, the number of departments in Nagaland rose from 53 in 1997 to 58 in 2000. It is also a known fact that the public employment size does not depend on the number of government departments alone, but also on size of the departments themselves which can be sometimes excessive. Such cases are there and to give an example, the number of government colleges in Manipur increased gradually as a result of which the teacher pupil ratio declined considerably. Three colleges were reported to be having a student strength of below 60! [6] It seems that the role of being "employer of the last resort" was being actively followed in these states where the presence of private sector capable of generating large employment was minimal.

Central Government Initiatives

The sharp deterioration in the states finances after the implementation of the Fifth Pay Commission recommendations led many of the states in the country to approach the central government for financial assistance. In turn, they were compelled to sign Memorandum of Understandings (MOUs) with the centre to bring about fiscal reforms as a condition for availing central assistance. The main aim of the reform programme was to reduce revenue deficit by introducing a number of measures aimed at compressing public expenditures, viz. downsizing, closing down of sick PSUs, power sector reforms, etc. The recommendations of the Eleventh Finance

Table 4

Composition of the employee size

State	*As on*	*Dept*	*Class I*	*Class II*	*Class III*	*Class IV*	*Total*	*Class I + II (p.c.)*	*Class III + IV(p.c.)*
Assam	1999	Police	-	-	-	-	-	-	-
		Education	878	2424	122327	11573	137202	2.41	97.59
		Others	7585	6801	127731	46752	188869	7.62	92.38
		Total	8463	9225	250058	58325	326071	5.42	94.58
Mizoram	1.4.2001	Police	125	514	6066	574	7279	8.78	91.22
		Education	767	3865	5529	1200	11361	40.77	59.23
		Others	1583	3317	11127	6817	22844	21.45	78.55
		Total	2475	7696	22722	8591	41484	24.52	75.48
Nagaland	31.3.2000	Police	224	147	8438	9365	18174	2.04	97.96
		Education	475	156	11235	2351	14217	4.44	95.56
		Others	2459	1142	22645	14736	40982	8.79	91.21
		Total	3158	1445	42318	26452	73373	6.27	93.73
Tripura	1.1.2008	Police	221	301	20823	2030	23375	2.23	97.77
		Education	232	4821	28223	4056	37332	13.54	86.46
		Others	3161	2802	26070	16197	48230	12.36	87.64
		Total	3614	7924	75116	22283	108937	10.59	89.41

Source: Government of Assam: *Statistical Handbook of Assam 1999*
Government of Mizoram: *Census of Government Employees 2001*
Government of Nagaland: *Statistical Handbook of Nagaland 2004*
Government of Tripura: *Budget at a Glance 2008-09*

Note: Education consists of Higher & Technical Education and schools only while Police does not include Jail.

Commission (EFC) which came into effect during 2000-05 also tried to incentivise federal transfers by recommending the setting up of an incentive fund. The release of money from the incentive fund was to be made available to a state in proportion to the progress made in the implementation of state specific Medium Term Fiscal Reform Programme (MTFRP). Subsequently MOUs were signed between the centre and the respective state governments in pursuance of state specific medium term fiscal reform programme.

The Twelfth Finance Commission (TFC) also offered a very attractive incentive based debt relief package to the states. In order to avail the benefits, the states had to enact fiscal responsibility legislations specifying annual targets for reducing their revenue and fiscal deficits. It was also stated that as a part of the expenditure restructuring, the ratio of salary expenditure net of interest payments and pensions to revenue expenditure should be progressively brought down to 35 p.c. which was the level prevalent before the pay rise in 1996-97. Though the FRBM Acts passed and published in the state gazettes of the region in 1995 and 1996 mentioned of reducing revenue and fiscal deficits, the mention of reducing the proportion of wage ratio was missing for some states. Further, the targets differed from one state to another.

Measures Implemented to Contain Public Expenditure of Salaries

The civil service in some African countries in the eighties were considered to be large and inefficient characterised by rapidly increasing size and declining salaries resulting in corruption, absenteeism, moonlighting, daylighting, etc. For curbing expenditures, measures widely used were conducting of census of government employees to remove the so called "ghost employees", removal of temporary workers, retrenchment, containment of wage increase, elimination of posts, etc. (see Lienert and Modi, 1997; Nurnburg and Nellis, 2001). In the North East, many of these measures, if not all, were implemented with mixed results. Some states like Manipur and Assam pursued more vigorously maybe because of the enormity of the problem faced by them while it is not so in states like Mizoram and Arunachal Pradesh.

An immediate step the state governments undertook as a part of the reform programme was the restraint on new hirings in non priority areas along with identification of redundant or excess employees and their downsizing. As a result about 30,000 posts in Assam and 14, 845 posts in Manipur were selected to be abolished. Census of government employees and creation of employee database were carried out in most of these states. Voluntary retirement scheme (VRS) has been implemented in the public sector undertakings with great success but not in the government sector. There was, of course, the odd success story with Mizoram Government successfully retrenching 10,000 drivers and selling off vehicles in a move to cut down on transportation cost (Jain, 2003). An immediate impact of these measures is the decline or stabilization in the employee sizes. A comparison of the size of state government employment in 2001 and 2005 given in Tables 1 and 5 reveals that a decline was observed in case of Manipur and Nagaland only, but when total employee size inclusive of those in quasi government and local bodies are considered, the employee size in the other states have also more or less stabilised.

In addition to downsizing, many states adopted a number of wage restraint measures which included fixing the dearness allowance constant or much lower as well as reduction in salary supplements like withdrawal of non-practicing allowance for medical professionals, reduction in medical benefits for government employees, etc. As a result, there was also a slowdown in the growth of average wage of the government employees in different states.[7] Arunachal Pradesh which witnessed a growth rate of 20.14 p.c. in the average wage in 1998-99 even had a negative growth rate in 2001-02 while in Assam it declined from 26.29 p.c. in 1999-00 to just 5.97 p.c. in 2000-01 and further to 2.42 p.c. in 2002-03. Tripura was the only state which maintained an increase in the per employee salary expenditure of more than 10 p.c. per annum during the period of reforms.

The slowdown in the growth of civil service employment and salary per employee have checked the growth of the aggregate salary expenditures of the states. Salary expenditure measured as a percentage of revenue expenditures net of interest and pension payments has gone down for all states with the exception of Tripura. The decline is fairly significant in Manipur and Assam while it is negligible in case of Nagaland. Pension reforms have been initiated in Assam and Manipur and others are expected to follow soon. If this is done, committed expenditures of the states will decline in the future. The central government has also given 100 p.c. of the sum allocated as incentive money as per the recommendations of the EFC to Manipur and Meghalaya. By and large, the reforms to contain the salary expenditure have been quite a success although a lot can still be done. In fact, it was reported in a local daily of Manipur that the state has been awarded the Prime Minister's Administrative Excellence Award 2008 for its administrative reforms and "a Central team would be arriving here very soon to study the changes in the administrative set up of the State...after the study, the Central team would make necessary recommendations to the Centre for adopting similar pattern in other States of the country".[8]

Table 5

Status of reforms aimed at containing salary and pension expenditures

State	*New pension Scheme introduced*	*Employee size as on 31st March 2005 (in lakhs)*				*Salary expenditure*	
		State Govt.	*Quasi Govt.*	*Local Govt.*	*Total*	*2000-01*	*2006-07*
Arunachal Pr.	No	0.51	NA	NA	NA	47.62	41.00
Assam	Feb-05	3.12	0.52	0.13	3.77	79.60	53.00
Manipur	Jan-05	0.62	0.03	0.04	0.69	94.12	43.00
Meghalaya	No	0.38	0.08	0.03	0.49	60.85	41.55
Mizoram	No	0.36	0.02	0.03	0.41	53.27	44.00
Nagaland	No	0.59	0.02	0.00	0.61	70.81	58.60
Tripura	No	0.93	0.03	0.09	1.05	62.12	65.53

Source: RBI: *State finances- A study of budgets of 2007-08.*DGET: *Quarterly employment review 2005.* CAG reports on state government finances (for data on salary expenditure of 2006-07.GOI (2005): *Fiscal profile of states*, www.fincomindia.nic.in (for data on salary expenditure of 2000-01).

Note: Salary expenditure is measured as a percentage of revenue expenditures net of interest and pension payments. The employee size of Arunachal Pradesh is as on Dec. 2008.[9]

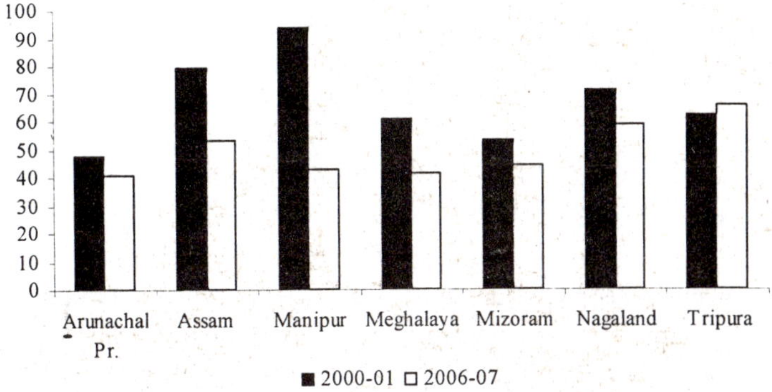

Fig. 2: Salary expenditure as a percentage of revenue expenditure

Another advantage of downsizing or hiring restraint is that the states have to spend less when the recommendations of the 6th Pay Commission recommendations come into effect. On 14th August 2008 the central government has decided to implement the 6th Pay Commission (SPC) recommendations with effect from 1st January 2006 and the additional burden of it is expected to be heavy for the NE states. However, the SPC was of the opinion that after projecting central tax devolution and own revenues in future, the states in general "would be in a position to meet the additional burden". It also mentioned that some states might have difficulty in implementing it and they should reduce expenditures, enhance revenues and postpone the implementation date. As per the estimates of Dholakia and Govil (2008) only Nagaland, Mizoram and Tripura could have some difficulties in the initial years and should be comfortable since then in meeting their FRBM obligations as a result of the implementations of the SPC recommendations.

Improving the Quality of Public Services

Wage restraint or salary compression should be taken only as a short term measure for containing expenditure as there can negative consequences of a decline in real wages. It cannot be done for long and downsizing should be the main focus instead. Periodic pay revision leading to an increase in the real wage is necessary for enhancing the performance of the civil service, though it is not the solution to the entire problem. Certain other measures need to go along with it as it was amply indicated by the experience of the last pay revision. In fact, the World Bank (2003: 38) had commented that "While the odd success story may be found, the recent wage gains generally were not compensated by any commensurate increase in the overall quantity and quality of government services". In fact, many states in India were marked with high degree of absenteeism among teachers and health workers which constituted the bulk of civil service (Table 6). Absenteeism in surprise visits to schools in Assam found as many as 34 p.c. of the teachers absent and for medical practitioners the rate was much higher.

Table 6
Absenteeism rates in public facilities in selected states

(per cent)

State	*Primary school teachers*	*Primary healthcare workers*
Andhra Pradesh	26	-
Assam	34	58
Bihar	39	58
Gujarat	15	52
Haryana	24	35
Karnataka	20	43
Kerala	23	-
Orissa	23	35
Punjab	37	-
Tamil Nadu	21	-
Uttar Pradesh	26	42
West Bengal	23	43

Source: World Development Report 2004

Although no official and systematic surveys were conducted in many of the other states, absenteeism and late coming by many employees in the government sector are often experienced and heard by many. Commenting on absenteeism in Manipur, Vunglallian (2006), thus, observed, "Absenteeism is the curse of Government schools and colleges. This is a phenomenon that exhibits itself more and more as one moves further and further from the capital of Imphal, or, in the hills, from the district headquarters. The tragedy is that the movement talked of here is not a matter of 200 or 300 km away from the centre, as it could perhaps be in a big state like UP, but in Manipur - it is a matter of a mere 5 or 10 kms!". And yet actions taken against erring employees are often unheard of. This may construe with the feeling that service providers are educated having political connections and, thus, avoid action being take against them. A question may arise about the voice of the people in times of elections and of not making absenteeism an election issue. An answer to this was given by Chaudhury *et al.* (2005) when they found, in a study consisting of a sample countries which were either democratic or have substantial elements of democracy, that absenteeism was not a major election issue and, apparently, politicians did not consider campaigning on the platform of cracking down on absent providers.

The Sixth Pay Commission Report did mention of the introduction of performance related incentive scheme (PRIS) where the stakeholders' opinion would be taken into account while assessing the performance of the service providers. With public service accountability "it is expected that attitudes and behaviours of government employees will change to public" (SPC, 2008:A-81). But this scheme talks about monetary incentives for better service delivery, but does little to address the problem of services being undelivered. It is also not known whether such schemes would be implemented by the state governments.

A partial solution to the problem of absenteeism was mentioned by the Mizoram CM in which he said efforts would be made to appoint recruits from the village/locality.[10] But an ideal solution is the involvement of stakeholders in the administration. They should be involved in the provision of public services in the local areas with powers to appoint and terminate employees. This calls for decentralizations of powers. The government should also educate the people of the necessity to complain when absenteeism and late coming are often a problem. The importance of this is clearly known from Kerala where the political awareness of the people of their right to demand and use public health care services is high. A PHC left unstaffed for a few days may lead to public protests and, as a result, primary healthcare facilities in Kerala are likely to be regularly staffed by physicians and this has helped in making healthcare services available to the poor (Mencher, 1980).

The problem of absenteeism in rural areas needs to be tackled separately from the study of absenteeism in general. Adequate incentives needs to be given or otherwise questions may arise of what does a person serving in a remote area gets in addition? In Manipur, these incentives are not there or inadequate. There is no transfer policy in the state which insures that he or she will be transferred to urban areas after staying for some years in the rural areas. In addition, government quarters in rural areas are almost non existent while roads are in bad shape. Thus, employees in rural and far flung areas get very little incentives, the only incentive being the chance to indulge in absenteeism or, in rare cases, get personal satisfaction of serving in rural areas and be a part of the nation building process.

Conclusion

The civil service reform measures being taken up is a part of the fiscal reforms being initiated by the central government and has been successful to some extent in containing the growth of civil service wage bill. But the reform programme has taken little interest in improving the quality of the public services being delivered to the people. How to award for the sincere and impose penalties on non performers are serious questions that need to be answered but never have been bothered with. There are many employees who performed much better than others and yet went unnoticed while there are many whose non performance is taken as something of common. The ultimate answer lies in two things. Firstly, the people and specially the poor who used public facilities like schools and health centres must raise their voices and, secondly, those in power must understand that good governance is really essential for the development of the country. Otherwise, one has to wait for more to witness a distinct improvement in the quality of public services.

[This paper is the product of a broader study on the finances of the north eastern states which was undertaken with funding from the UGC. However, the initial write up has been thoroughly revised and improved.]

NOTES

1. In India civil service is often taken to mean the bureaucracy. In fact, civil service can have different meanings in different countries (Schiavio Campo, et al., 1997:4-5).
2. Inclusive of quasi and local body employees. Public employment of the year 2001 was taken as make use of the 2001 census figures for estimating ratios. Reforms also accelerated afterwards.
3. There are differences in the data provided by the DGET and the TFC.
4. Excluding that of Mizoram.
5. The number of government departments was ascertained from the publications of the Directorate of Economics and Statistics of the state governments.
6. "8 Govt., 12 private colleges may face axe. Cancelling affiliation on MU's mind", *The Sangai Express*, July 10, 2008.(also available at http://e-pao.net/GP.asp/src=1..100708.jul08)
7. Estimated from average wage data given in the TFC report.
8. "Kudos for state on graft crackdown", *The Sangai Express,* October 18, 2008. The successful preparation of the list of government employees and pensioners was cited as the main reason of the state being selected.
9. "Arunachal Govt. concedes employee's pay demand", *The Assam Tribune* available at http://ne.icrindia.org/2008/12/23/arunachal-govt-

concedes-employeees%E2%80%99-pay-demand/. (accessed on 14.3.2009).

10. See the speech of Shri Zoramthanga, Chief Minister of Mizoram at the 51st Meeting of the National Development Council, June 2005.

REFERENCES

Chaudhury, Nazmul, Jeffry Hammer, Michael Kremer, Karthik Muralidharan and F. Halsey Rogers (2005): "Missing in action: Teacher and health workers absence in developing countries", *Journal of Economic Perspectives*, May 19.

Chu, Key-young, Sanjeev Gupta and others (1995): "Unproductive public expenditures: A pragmatic approach to policy research analysis", IMF Pamphlet Series No. 48.

Devarajan, Shantayanan and Shekhar Shah (2004): "Making services work for India's poor", *Economic and Political Weekly*, Feb. 28.

Dholakia, Ravindra H. and Astha Govil (2008): "Fiscal space with states and the Sixth Pay Commission", *Economic and Political Weekly*, May 10.

Government of India (2000 a): *Report of the Finance Commission 2000-2005*, June.

Government of India (2000 b): *Report of the Finance Commission on the additional terms of reference*, August.

Government of Manipur (2000): *Memorandum of Understanding entered into between Government of Manipur and Government of India on 20.6.02*, June.

Jain, Sunil (2003): "Golden handshake for 1000 Mizoram drivers". http://www.rediff.com/money/2003/jan/31spec1.htm (accessed on 12.8.2008).

Lindauer, David L. and Barbara Nunberg (1994): "Rehabilitating government pay and employment reform in Africa", The World Bank Regional and Sectoral Studies 13711.

Lienert, Ian and Jitendra Modi (1997): "A decade of civil service reform in Sub-Saharan Africa", International Monetary Fund, WP/97/179.

Mencher, Joan P. (1980): "The lessons and non-lessons of Kerala: Agricultural labourers and poverty", *Economic and Political Weekly*, Oct. Special number.

Lienert, Ian (1998): "Civil service reform in Africa: Mixed results after 10 years", *Finance & Development*, June,Vol.35, No.2.

Lindauer, David L. (1988): "Government pay and employment policies and government performance in developing economies" World Bank WPS 42.

Nag, Moni (1989): "Political awareness as a factor in accessibility of health services - A case study of rural Kerala and West Bengal", *Economic and Political Weekly*, Feb. 25.

Nepram, Damodar (2004): "Downsizing of government sector employment in Manipur", *Economic Affairs*, Oct-Dec.

Nurnberg, Barbara and John Nellies (1995): "Civil Service reform and the World Bank", The World Dank Discussion Papers, WDP 161.

Nunberg, Barbara (1994): "Experience with civil service pay and employment reform: an overview" in Lindauer, David L. and Barbara Nunberg (eds), *Rehabilitating Government Pay and Employment reform in Africa*, The World Bank Regional and Sectoral Studies 13711.

P. Beschel Jr., Robert (2003): "Civil Service reform in India: Perspectives from the World Bank's work in three states", in Howes, Stephen, Ashok K. Lahiri and Nicholas Stern (eds.), *State-level Reforms in India: Towards More Effective Government*, Macmillan, New Delhi.

Planning Commission (2001): *Approach Paper to the Tenth Five Year Plan (2002-2007).*

Reserve Bank of India: *State finances: A study of budgets*, Various issues.

Reserve Bank of India (2004): *Handbook of statistics on state government finances.*

Schivo-Campo, Salvatore, Giulio de Tommaso and Amitabha Mukherjee (1997): "Government employment and pay in global perspective: A selective synthesis of international facts, policies and experience", World Bank, WPS 1771.

Vunglallian, T(2006): Completely new education for a new Manipur-With special reference to the hills, http://www.e-pao.net/epSubPageExtractor.asp?src=education.New_Education_for_new_...(assessed on 27.10.2008).

World Bank (2003): *India: Sustaining reforms, Reducing poverty*, Oxford University Press, New Delhi.

World Bank (2004): *World Development Report 2004*, Oxford University Press.

World Bank (2005): *State level fiscal reforms in India*, Macmillan.

11

Efficiency of Resource Mobilization in Manipur

L. Debendra Singh

Introduction

Rapid economic development of a country depends *inter alia* on two factors - proper planning and mobilization of funds for financing them. A plan, whether big or small in size, can be framed and implemented only when its scheme of financing is well devised and sufficient financial resources become readily available as and when required. Availability of funds for a state means mobilization of financial resources on its own or with transfers from the centre. Too much dependence on the latter would tend to reduce financial manoeuvrability and invite interference of the centre in the affairs of the states and, hence, a state should try to mobilize own resources as much as possible. However, a state like Manipur is heavily dependent on central transfers for meeting its plan and non plan requirements. Its own tax and non tax receipts have hardly contributed ten percent of her revenue receipts. In the light of this fact, it has become necessary to examine how efficient the state is in mobilizing its resources.

Sources of funds

Central assistance

The Constitution of India defines sources of revenue for the different levels of the government. For a state, it can raise its own tax and non tax revenues and at the same time there are provisions for tax sharing with the centre as well as transfers from the latter in the form of grants and loans. Central transfers can be through three channels:

1. Statutory transfers through the Finance Commission
2. Plan transfers through the planning Commission
3. Discretionary transfers

Statutory transfers through the Finance Commission are in the form of sharing of central taxes and grants-in-aid. Apart from some grants like upgradation grants, grants for special purposes, etc. the bulk of the grants especially for the deficit states like Manipur has been in the form of gap filling grants which are for meeting the gaps that exist even after the devolution of central tax transfers in their non-plan revenue accounts. Tax sharing is formula based giving more weight on population and per capita income.

Financial resources transferred through the Planning Commission are in the form of grants and loans. The grant: loan ratio varies according to the category of the state. It is 90:10 in the case of special category states and 30:70 in the case of general category states. There were no objective criteria for allocation of plan funds among the states up to the third and the three annual plans. But in view of the demands raised by the states for an appropriate formula for transfer of resources through this channel, the entire issue was discussed on the eve of the fourth plan and Gadgil Formula was introduced. The original Gadgil formula was modified on the eve of the formulation of the sixth plan to make it more progressive for the benefit of the economically backward states and was used for the sixth and seventh five year plans. However, the tug of war among the states for central assistance continued as each state suggested a formula which best suited its interests. This led to further modification in the formula and the Gadgil formula was revised again in 1991. The XIth five year plan uses this formula as well.

Another important channel through which financial resources are coming from the centre to the states is the Discretionary Transfers. These are political-cum-bureaucratic transfers at the discretion of the central ministries. These transfers are not based on any well worked out formula and all transfers are rather ad hoc. However, under the discretionary transfers, they can exercise their powers to some extent.

As the transfers from both the Finance commission and the Planning Commission are largely formula based, we cannot expect unlimited resources from the centre. In case of the Discretionary transfers also, by its very nature, no state government can expect any assured amount from the centre. Hence, domestic resource mobilization is a must to garner maximum resources to finance development plans of a state.

Internal Sources

The internal resources of a state can be:

1. Own Tax Revenues
2. Own Non-Tax Revenues
3. Borrowings

Excessive borrowing is not considered to be a good means for resource mobilization since it involves repayment of the principal amount as well as interest. The best means is to mobilize non - debt resources which are tax and non tax revenues. Own tax revenue of a state can be grouped under the three heads:

1. Other taxes on income and expenditure which include taxes on professions, trades, callings and employment.
2. Taxes on property and capital transactions consisting of land revenue, stamps and registration fees
3. Taxes on commodities and services consisting of state excise, sales tax, taxes on vehicles, taxes on goods and passengers, taxes and duties on electricity, entertainment tax, etc.

Again, the state's own non tax revenues are collected in the form of user charges, fees and fines from the following services:

1. Fiscal services
2. Interest receipts, dividends and profits

3. General services including police, public works, jails, stationary and printing, fees from the guest houses, government hostels, etc.
4. Social services consisting of education, sports, arts and culture, medical and public health, family welfare, water supply and sanitation, labour and employment, housing, urban development, etc.
5. Economic services - crop husbandry, animal husbandry, dairy development, fisheries, forestry and wild life, power, industries, tourism, major and medium irrigation, co-operative, etc.

Present scenario of Manipur

We may now look at the resource mobilization scenario of Manipur from its own sources. It can be seen from Table 1 that the state could not mobilize enough resources on its own. The revenues raised from its own taxes fluctuated around 6 per cent of total revenue receipts while revenues from non tax sources did a little better. Both tax and non taxes combined together could contribute nearly 10 percent of the total revenue receipts in the state. On the other hand, grants and share from the central taxes were around 90 percent of the total revenue receipts indicating the high degree of the dependence of the state on central transfers.

Table 1

Composition of total revenue receipts of Manipur (Percent)

	1972-73	1975-76	1980-81	1985-86	1990-91	1995-96	2000-01	2005-06
Own tax	5.4	5.3	2.3	3.1	3.2	4	4.7	3.9
Own non-tax	8.7	6.4	27.3	4.8	5	6.6	4	3.2
Share in central taxes	8.8	8.3	6.8	24.7	29	24	15.7	14.2
Grants in-aid & contributions	77.1	80	63.6	67.4	62.8	65.4	75.6	78.7
Total	100	100	100	100	100	100	100	100

Source: Govt. of Manipur, *Finance Accounts*, Various Issues.

Efficiency of Resource Mobilization

One important area of resource mobilization is its efficiency aspect. The efficiency aspect may be defined as the maximum collection of resources given the manpower, machinery, income level and rates of tax and non-tax items. For examining the efficiency aspect of resource mobilization, it is pertinent to examine the following criteria:

1. Ratio of tax and non-tax revenues to State Domestic Product
2. The cost involved in the collection of taxes
3. The difference between the budgetary estimates and the actual revenues realised from different own tax and non-tax items

Ratio of Tax to NSDP

The concept of tax ratio or the ratio of tax collections to State Domestic Product (or GDP for a country) gives an idea of many aspects of the economy. It indicates the economic strength of a particular country or a state, taxable capacity, level of living of the people and the extent of the growth structure in tax-potentiality related sectors of the economy (Choudhury, 2001:175-76). It is also generally taken to be a proxy measure of tax effort and higher values would mean more effort of the state in mobilizing its own tax revenues. Table 2 shows that how much of the state income has been transformed into own revenue which indicates the efficiency of the state to mobilize resources from its own sources. The ratio of sales tax to the NSDP is found to be the highest followed by that of trade, callings and employment. The state could never mobilize even 2 p.c. of its state domestic product evn though the tax ratio of all states in the country was reported to be as high as 6.54 p.c. of GSDP (Govt. of India, 2005 – Annexure 7.9).

Ratio of Non - Tax Receipts to NSDP

The state can mobilize its resources from the non-tax sources also and, as a result, an examination of the contribution of different non-tax sources expressed as percentage of the state domestic product is necessary. Since non-tax receipts are collected in the form of fees and user charges, it is different from the tax receipts in the sense that the burden of the non-tax receipts falls directly on the beneficiaries of the services. Among the own non-tax sources, the contribution of economic services was found to be highest followed by that of general services (Table No.3). Another observation made is that the own non-tax to NSDP ratio has been fluctuating around 3% with the exception of 15.21% in 1980-81 because of the writing off of central loans as recommended by the Seventh Finance Commission.

Table 2
Own tax NSDP ratio of Manipur

(percent)

Item\Period	*1972-73*	*1980-81*	*1985-86*	*1990-91*	*1995-96*	*2000-01*	*2005-06*
Land Revenue	0.29	0.09	0.09	0.05	0.03	0.01	0.03
Stamps & Registration Fees	0.22	0.08	0.11	0.12	0.08	0.06	0.05
State Excise	0.09	0.16	0.30	0.30	0.11	0.04	0.06
Sales Tax	0.62	0.68	0.69	0.75	1.25	1.06	1.39
Taxes on Vehicles	0.12	0.13	0.16	0.16	0.09	0.10	0.07
Taxes on Electricity	-	0.03	0.12	0.00	0.00	0.03	0.00
Other taxes on goods & Commodities	0.17	0.10	0.22	0.10	0.07	0.02	0.00
Taxes on Profession, etc.	-	0.06*	0.13	0.19	0.31	0.33	0.23
Total tax Revenue	1.51	1.28	1.89	1.72	1.98	1.67	1.86

Source: Compiled and Computed from:
1. Govt. of Manipur: *Finance Accounts*, Various Issues.
2. Govt. of Manipur: *Statistical Abstracts*, Various Issues.
* - Relates the data for 1981-82.

Table 3
Own non-tax NSDP ratio of Manipur

(percent)

Item\Period	*1972-73*	*1980-81*	*1985-86*	*1990-91*	*1995-96*	*2000-01*	*2005-06*
Interest Receipts	0.26	0.13	0.43	0.09	0.09	0.03	0.12
Public Works	0.34	0.17	0.17	0.24	0.15	0.07	0.06
Police	0.04	0.02	0.05	0.04	0.16	0.03	0.01
General Service	0.39	14.42	0.71	0.50	1.65	0.19	0.24
Education, Sports, Art & Culture	0.12	0.06	0.07	0.07	0.12	0.07	0.02
Medical	0.08	0.01	0.005	0.06	0.03	0.009	0.005
Water supply & sanitation	0.006	0.04	0.04	0.04	0.03	0.02	0.03
Social Services	0.41	0.15	0.14	0.21	0.33	0.23	0.08
Forestry & Wild Life	0.15	0.15	0.18	0.14	0.16	0.03	0.03
Power	0.30	0.12	0.99	0.80	0.009	0.89	0.97
Economic Services	1.48	0.51	1.62	1.47	1.16	0.96	1.06
Total Own Non-Tax Revenues	2.44	15.21	2.89	2.72	3.22	1.41	1.49

Source: Same as Table No. 2.

Cost of Collection as a Measure of Efficiency of Resource Mobilisation

One important characteristic of a good tax is that the cost involved in collecting the tax should be less than the actual revenue mobilized. It is quite meaningless to spend Rs.100/- in order to collect Rs.50/-. We are better off by not trying to collect the amount. The objective of transfer of resources from the public to the government may be more effectively realised without that source. Moreover, cost of collection is associated with the effects on production (Singh, 2000). According to Dalton (1995), unnecessarily high cost of collection involves a waste of labour and materials which is equivalent to a loss of production. Other things being equal, the best tax system is that in which the cost of tax collection, in proportion to the revenue collected, is minimum. At the same time the cost of payment should be minimal on the part of the payers as well. In many cases, the tax payers are subjected to needless trouble in filing a number of forms where one would be enough. So Dalton metaphorically concludes just as a prudent man visits his dentist once a year, so a prudent and honest tax payer should pay an annual visit to his Surveyor of Taxes so that his affairs shall be kept in good order with a minimum of inconvenience".

While examining the tax effort of a state, it is necessary to examine the cost of tax collection as well. Since the revenue effort is a relative term, cost of tax collection would reveal the relative performance of states in net collection. A study by Bansal (1998) for all the States of India for the period 1967-68 to 1981-82 found that the annual growth rate of the state tax revenue was 15.93 percent and the growth rate of cost of tax collection was 11.16 percent respectively. However, the study found that the growth rate of cost of tax collection for Manipur was higher than the growth rate of state tax revenue. While the growth rate of cost of tax collection was 16.13 percent, the growth rate of the state tax collection was 15.86 percent. The study also revealed of the low tax effort of Manipur in terms of cost of tax collection for the three years average periods 1973-74 to 1975-76 and 1977-80 to 1981-82. While all States spent on the average 5.97 paise in order to collect Re. 1.00 during the three years' average period 1973-74 to 1975-76, Manipur spent 21.43 paise on the average in order to collect Rs.1.00. It became more expensive during the three years' average period 1979-80 through 1981-82. While all states spent 5.35 paise in order to collect Re.1.00, Manipur spent 29.24 paise in order to collect the same amount. This indicates that Manipur's tax effort has been becoming increasingly inefficient.

Table No. 4 shows the cost of tax collection of different own taxes of Manipur. The table reveals that highest cost is in collecting the land revenue. The cost of collecting Rs. 1 rose from Rs. 1.05 in 1972-73, to Rs.7.20 in 1990-91 and further to Rs.23.89 in 2000-01. The high cost may be due to the inefficiency of the collection machinery as well as huge expenditure on administration and proper maintenance of land records, survey and settlements, etc. A study by Singh (2008) has identified failure to maintain upto date land records and high overhead cost because of the small tax base, etc. as some of the possible reasons of poor land revenue collections resulting in high cost of collections.

Table 4
Cost of tax collection per rupee

Year	*Land Revenue*	*Stamps & Registration Fees*	*State Excise*	*Sales Tax*	*Taxes on vehicles*	*Other Taxes oncommodities and services*	*Total taxes*
1972-73	1.05	0.07	0.33	0.03	0.13	A	0.16
1980-81	2.95	0.18	0.31	0.07	0.31	0.05	0.20
1985-86	4.03	0.18	0.19	0.09	0.37	0.02	0.30
1990-91	7.20	0.13	0.17	0.08	0.48	0.04	0.32
1995-96	10.43	0.19	0.42	0.40	0.72	0.05	0.26
2000-01	23.89	0.20	0.98	0.05	0.50	0.14	0.27
2005-06	9.71	0.28	0.58	0.02	0.80	0.34	0.12

Source: Govt. of Manipur: *Finance Accounts*, Various issues
A=Rs 0.004.

State excise is another tax with high cost of collection. One important feature of this tax is that the cost of collection was declining between 1972-73 and 1990-91 but witnessed an upward movement till 2000-01. While cost per rupee of collection was Rs. 0.17 in 1990-91 it rose to Rs.0.42 in 1995-96 and further to Rs.0.98 in 2000-01(Table No.4). The factor responsible for the upward trend may be attributed to the prohibition policy in the state right from 1991. In case of sales tax, the performance is encouraging which shows improvement after 1995-96. However, overall performance of own taxes is not encouraging since their values are still very high as compared with the all states average. When we compute the cost of tax collection per rupee of Indian states, it was found that in order to collect Re. 1/- the cost were 8 paise, 6 paise and 3 paise in 1990-91, 1995-96 and 2000-01 respectively as against the 32 paise, 26 paise and 27 paise for Manipur. Hence, the efficiency of resource mobilization in the state is very low in terms of the cost of collection.

Differences between Budget Estimates and Actual Revenue as a Measure of Efficiency of Resource Mobilisation

While examining the efficiency of resource mobilization in the state, it is pertinent to examine the actual revenue realized as compared with the budget estimates. We may regard the budget estimate as the target set by the government that could be collected if it uses its administrative machinery efficiently. If the actual revenue realized is equal to or higher than the budget estimates, then it can be said that revenue is mobilized efficiently.

In case of Manipur, the actual revenue realized for many of the taxes fell short of the budget estimates barring a few years. The performance was, exceptionally, poor in the case of land revenue. The actual revenue derived from land revenue never reached the estimated target. The actual revenue declined from 62.83 % of the budget estimates in 1980-81 to 52.65% in 1990-91, and rose to 91.18 percent in 2000-01. One important thing observed is that there were fluctuations in the budget estimates and when the estimate was low, the actual revenue realized was sometimes more. For example, in case of land revenue, actual revenue realized was Rs. 43.66 lakhs as against the budget estimates of Rs.50.71 lakhs in 1995-96 which was 86.10% of the budget estimates. However, the actual revenue realised in 2000-01 was Rs. 36.47 lakhs as against the budget estimates of Rs. 40.00 lakhs or 91.18 percent of the budget estimates. Even though in most of the items the actual revenue realised fell short of the budget estimate, the overall performance seems to be improving.

In case of the non-tax items, the performance is neither satisfactory nor encouraging. In almost all the items, the actual revenue falls short of budget estimates. The worst item is found to be dividends and profits. Power sector also does not perform well. Social service does well to some extent but economic services which constitute the backbone of the economy do not perform well.

Table 5

Own tax revenue as percent of budget estimates

Year	*Land Revenue*	*Stamps & Registration Fees*	*State Excise*	*Sales Tax*	*Taxes on vehicles*	*Other Taxes oncommodities and services*	*Total taxes*
1972-73	33.17	191.61	114.20	144.42	109.80	178.83	93.84
1980-81	62.83	86.84	126.84	84.91	73.97	68.17	93.46
1985-86	96.89	127.94	89.61	150.26	101.67	107.29	133.00
1990-91	52.65	149.52	88.73	80.52	70.80	65.37	81.89
1995-96	86.10	77.41	179.01	108.19	91.32	69.92	109.44
2000-01	91.18	85.59	51.66	83.83	116.32	45.71	56.23
2005-06	164.39	99.13	83.16	101.67	69.02	10.30	99.39

Source: Computed from the Finance Accounts and Annual Financial Statements of Manipur.

Another aspect regarding the budget estimatesof both the own taxes and non taxes is that there are irregularities in setting the target. For example, in case of land revenue the budget estimates were Rs 66.50 lakhs, Rs 50.71 lakhs, Rs 40 lakhs and Rs 80 lakhs for the years 1990-91, 1995-96, 2000-01 and 2005-06. In case of state excise, the budget estimates were Rs 243.80 lakhs, Rs 88.98 lakhs Rs 240.43 lakhs and Rs 363.00 lakhs for these years. Likewise for the non tax items also we find some irregular trend in the budget estimates. Hence, we find very high ratios of actual to budget estimated figures (when the values of the latter were low) of some of the items of both the taxes and non taxes. But it cannot be considered that efficiency of resource mobilisation is high.

Table 6

Own non-taxes as per cent of budget estimates

Year	*Interest Receipt*	*Dividends& Profits*	*Public Works*	*Education, Sports, Art & Culture*	*Water Supply & Sanitation*	*Forestry & Wild Life*	*Power*	*General Services*	*Social Services*	*Economic Services*	*Total Non-Tax*
1972-73	340.21	-	226.84	82.47	-	136.83	77.92	-	-	-	-
1980-81	60.00	-	61.07	53.79	59.13	76.34	32.07	3485.76	60.66	50.16	803.64
1985-86	761.00	33.33	171.86	50.32	93.60	114.29	72.97	193.36	50.25	98.85	124.06
1990-91	133.23	00.00*	63.01	77.95	113.59	76.64	47.85	76.69	100.94	70.41	75.56
1995-96	43.31	12.50	93.38	228.51	47.24	70.93	36.07	204.76	185.42	51.58	94.09
2000-01	94.00	4.00	47.91	242.16	56.36	25.93	50.71	53.31	214.95	48.13	56.63
2005-06	279.28	3.00	69.54	50.88	61.53	105.19	58.67	180.74	63.08	61.73	74.18

Source: Same as table No. 5(a) *value is too small to enter since actual revenue was Rs. 61 only

The Pattern of Inefficiency

As almost all the indicators have indicated inefficiency in mobilising resources, it is more pertinent to examine whether the variables become more or less in-efficient over a period of time. Besides, it would be appropriate to examine whether there was a structural change[1] during the period. The structural change may be due to due to external forces or due to domestic policies of the government or a variety of reasons. The criteria appropriate for the examination of the degree of efficiency are the growth rate of the different indicators as well as their degree of acceleration or deceleration during the entire period.[2]

To examine the structural changes in the economy, the year 1991 is chosen for dividing the sample data into two time periods because in this year there was a policy shift in the economic policy of the government.[3] Moreover, in the same year, the state government also passed the Manipur Prohibition Act 1991 which came in to effect from 1st April 1991 and it has an impact on the tax source of the State. In order to confirm whether there was a structural change or not in 1991 for each variable, the Chow test is used. If the calculated F value is greater than the table value of F at 5 percent level of significance with the corresponding degrees of freedom, we say that there was a structural change.

An analysis of the own tax to NSDP ratio reveals that the economic reform had no impact on the efficiency of land revenue collections while other tax heads like sales tax, state excise, stamps & registration fees, taxes on electricity, taxes on vehicles, taxes on profession, etc., other taxes on commodities[4] and taxes on goods[5] were affected. Land revenue recorded neither acceleration nor deceleration during the period of the study which means that its inefficiency remained unchanged during the period. Stamps & Registration Fees recorded acceleration during the sub-period 1972-90 while Taxes on Goods recorded deceleration during the period. Other taxes such as Sales tax, State excise, Taxes on profession, etc., Taxes on vehicles, other taxes on commodities recorded neither acceleration nor deceleration during the period. For the sub-period 1991-2006, Taxes on profession, etc. and the other taxes on commodities recorded deceleration. Hence, the analysis shows that inefficiency is more for Taxes on profession, etc. and other taxes on commodities for the period 1991-2006 while for others it remains unchanged. But, for the sub-period 1972-90, it is found to be less inefficient for stamps & registration fees and more for taxes on goods while for other taxes they are found to be at the same level of inefficiency. In case of the own non-tax to NSDP ratio, interest receipts, education, sports, arts & culture, water supply & sanitation, power, medical and economic services were not influenced by economic reforms while others such as public works, police, forestry & wildlife, social services and general services were affected by policy changes. The non-taxes such as education, sports, arts & culture and water supply & sanitation recorded deceleration during the period 1972-2006 while the others such as interest receipt, power, medical and economic services recorded neither acceleration nor deceleration during the same period. Hence, inefficiency for the two items - education, sports, arts & culture and water supply & sanitation - were found to be more and for other items, it was found to be unchanged. The non-tax items which were influenced by the policy shift are neither accelerating nor decelerating for the sub-period 1991-2006. However, for the sub-period 1972-90, the tax head forestry & wildlife recorded deceleration while social services recorded acceleration; others recorded neither acceleration nor deceleration. Hence, the level of inefficiency as shown by the receipts under individual own tax and non-tax has exhibited a mixed pattern over items and time.

An analysis of the cost of tax collection reveals that economic reforms had no impact on the efficiency of stamps & registration fees. While other taxes like land revenue, sales tax, state excise, taxes on commodities and taxes on vehicle were affected by economic reforms. Stamps & registration fees recorded neither acceleration nor deceleration during the period of the study indicating unchanged inefficiency. Sales tax, state excise and taxes on commodities recorded deceleration during the sub-period 1972-90. Other taxes such as land revenue and taxes on vehicle recorded neither acceleration nor deceleration for the same period. For the sub-period 1991-2006, land revenue, sales tax and state excise recorded deceleration while taxes on commodities and taxes on vehicle recorded neither acceleration nor deceleration. Hence, the analysis shows that inefficiency is less for sales tax, state excise and taxes on commodities for the sub-period 1972-90 while for others, it remained unchanged. But, for the sub-period 1991-2006 it is found to be less inefficient for land revenue, sales tax and state excise while others it remained unchanged. One important finding of the analysis of the cost of tax collection is that both sale tax and state excise had shown deceleration during the entire period of the study which means there is less inefficiency for both the taxes. It is a good symptom for the state since both the taxes are important sources of state's revenue.

If we examine the ratio of actural tax collections to budget estimates, it can be said that economic reforms had its impact on the efficiency of the stamps and registration fees while land revenue, state excise, sales tax, taxes on vehicles and taxes on commodities were not affected. However, stamps and registration fees remained unchanged during the sub-period 1991-2006 even though it recorded acceleration during the sub-period 1972-90. But for the study period 1972-2006, sales tax recorded acceleration while other recorded neither acceleration nor deceleration. Hence, the analysis shows less inefficiency for sales tax whereas for other it remained unchanged during the period of the study. In case of the ratio for own non-tax items examination of some major items reveals that there was no impact of the policy shift in the economy on the items such as interest receipts, public works, education, sports, art & culture, power, forestry & wildlife, social services, economic services and general services. Besides, the growth rate of these items were found to be insignificant during the period of the study, the estimation of the acceleration or deceleration show that these items remained unchanged throughout the period 1972-2006. It means that the efficiency of collection of these items remained the same for the period of the study.

Table 7(a)
Growth rates of different items (1972-1990)

Variable	*Co-efficient*	*Growth Rate*
A. OWN TAX-NSDP RATIO		
Stamps & Registration Fees	- 0.021 (-2.56)	-2.08
State Excise	0.075 (6.41)	7.79
**Profession Tax	0.149 (11.11)	16.07
Taxes on Vehicles	0.038 (3.64)	3.87
*Land Revenue	-0.087 (-15.09)	-8.33
B. OWN NON-TAX-NSDP RATIO		
*Interest Receipts	-0.040 (-2.87)	-3.92
*Education, Sports, Arts & Culture	-0.048 (-8.05)	-4.69
*Power	0.047 (4.91)	4.81
*Medical	-0.043 (-2.91)	-34.95
C. COST OF TAX COLLECTION		
Land Revenue	0.162 (28.540	17.63
Sales Tax	0.217 (27.48)	24.25
State Excise	0.159 (23.79)	17.18
Taxes on Commodities	0.288 (12.67)	33.37
Taxes on Vehicles	0.254 (19.87)	28.92
*Stamps & Registration Fees	0.130 (45.53)	13.58
D. RATIO OF TAXES TO BUGBET ESTIMATES		
*Land Revenue	0.024 (2.96)	2.46
*State Excise	-0.011 (-2.12)	-0.65
*Taxes on Commodities	-0.044 (-4.54)	-4.34

Source: Computed from the data of the Finance Accounts and Annual Financial Statements of Manipur.
Figures within brackets are t- values
* refers to the period 1972-2006,
** refers to the period 1981-1990.

Table 7(b)
Growth Rates of Different Items (1991-2006)

Variable	*Co-Efficient*	*Growth Rate*
A. OWN TAX-NSDP RATIO		
Sales Tax	0.029 (3.74)	2.94
Stamps & Registration Fees	-0.050 (-8.86)	-4.88
Other Taxes on Commodities	-0.238 (-5.63)	-21.18
Taxes on Electricity	0.482 (3.82)	61.92
Taxes on Goods	-0.080 (-8.49)	-7.69
Taxes on Vehicles	-0.049 (-3.08)	-4.78
B. OWN NON-TAX-NSDP RATIO		
Public Works	-0.082 (-3.34)	-7.87
Police	-0.144 (-4.13)	-13.41
Forestry & Wildlife	-0.205 (-8.54)	-18.54
Social Services	-0.074 (-3.22)	-7.13
General Services	-0.144 (-2.83)	-13.41
C. COST OF TAX COLLECTION		
Land Revenue	0.098 (9.63)	10.27
Sales Tax	0.088 (9.49)	9.16
State Excise	0.094 (8.00)	9.83
Taxes on Vehicles	0.091 (11.88)	9.57

Source: Same as Table No. 7(a).
Figures within brackets are t-values.

Table 8(a)

Acceleration / Deceleration of Different Items (1972-1990)

Variable	*Co-Efficient*
A. OWN TAX-NSDP RATIO	
Stamps & Registration Fees	0.004 (2.65)
Taxes on Goods	-0.043 (6.38)
B. OWN NON-TAX-NSDP RATIO	
Forestry & Wildlife	-0.008 (-2.12)
Social Services	0.006 (2.58)
*Education, Sports, Arts & Culture	-0.001 (-2.48)
*Water Supply & Sanitation	-0.004 (-2.78)
C. COST OF TAX COLLECTION	
Sales Tax	-0.004 (-3.45)
State Excise	-0.003 (-2.50)
Taxes on Commodities	-0.012 (-3.20)
D. RATIO OF OWN TAX TO BUDGET ESTIMATES	
Stamps & Registration Fees	0.005 (2.99)
*Sales Taxes	0.001 (2.53)

* refers to the period 1972-2006.

Table 8(b)

Acceleration / Deceleration of Different Items (1991-2006)

Variable	*Co-Efficient*
A. OWN TAX-NSDP RATIO:	
Other Taxes on Commodities	-0.024 (-2.89)
Profession Tax	-0.008 (-3.13)
B. COST OF TAX COLLECTION	
Land Revenue	-0.01 (-2.86)
Sales Tax	-0.01 (-2.66)
State Excise	-0.01 (-2.10)

Source: Same as Table No. 7(a).

Conclusion

We have analysed the efficiency of the resource mobilisation efforts of the state by using three criteria, viz. (a) Ratio of tax and non-tax items to the state income, (b) Cost of collection method, and (c) Ratio of actual revenue to budget methods. It has been observed that the state is not able to mobilize its own resources efficiently. It has one of the lowest taxes: NSDP ratio in the country which needs to be carefully examined. Further, the non tax receipts always fell short of the targets set for revenue mobilisation. The study shows that the state continues to depend heavily on central transfers because of the simple fact it has not been able to mobilize its resources. The reasons for this need proper examination.

NOTES

1. By structural change, we mean that the values of the parameters of the model do not remain the same throughout the entire period.
2. For estimation of the growth rate and acceleration or deceleration of the items, we use two equations viz i) $log\ y=a+bt$ and ii) $log\ y=a+bt+ct^2$ where the co-efficient "b" of the equation $log\ y=a+bt$ is used for estimation of the growth rate and the co-efficient "c" of the equation $log\ y=a+bt+ct^2$ is used for checking the acceleration or deceleration of growth rate of the items. If the values of the co-efficient are found to be insignificant the values are considered to remain unchanged throughout the period of the study.
3. Central as well as States.
4. Other taxes on commodities– It is the taxes and duties on commodities and services which include entertainment tax, luxury tax, other receipts and share of net proceeds assigned to States.
5. Taxes on goods -It is the taxes on goods and passengers which include passenger tax, goods tax, tax on entry of goods into local areas and other receipts.

REFERENCES

Ashan, Qamar (1982): "Financing of State Plans: Innovative ways & means of Raising State's Non-Tax Revenue", *Economic Affairs*, Vol. 27. Nos. 4-6 April - June.

Bansal, R.K. (1988): *Raising Additional Resources in the States*, Atlantic Publishers and Distributors, New Delhi.

Bhatia, L. (2001): *Public Finance*, Vikash Publishing House Pvt. Ltd., New Delhi.

Bhatt, V.V.(1986): "Resource Mobilization in Developing countries: Financial Institutions and Policies", *Economic & Political Weekly*, June 21-28.

Choudhury, R.K. (2001): *Public Finance and Fiscal Policy*, Kalyani Publishers.

Dalton, H (1995): *Principles of Public Finance*, Allied Publishers.

Datt, Rudar and KPM Sundharam (2006): *Indian Economy*, S. Chand & Company Ltd., New Delhi.

Govt. of India (2005): *Report of the 12th Finance Commission.*

Govt. of Manipur, *Budget documents*.

Govt. of Manipur, *Manipur Gazette (Extraordinary)*: Various Notifications.

Govt. of Manipur: *Finance Accounts*, Various Issues.

Gujarati, Damodar.N. & Sangeetha (2007): *Basic Econometrics*, Tata McGraw Hill.

Gulati I.S. (1983): "The Budget and Resource Mobilization", *Economic and Political Weekly,* March 19.

Majumdar P.K. & RP Kataria (2002): *The Constitution of India*, Orient Publishing Company.

Rao, Hemlata (2006): *Fiscal Federalism: Issues and Policies*, New Century Publications, New Delhi.

Singh. Elangbam Bijoy Kumar (2000): *Analysis of State Taxes (1972-98),* Imphal Free Press, October 17.

Singh, Keisham Suresh (2008): "Agricultural land taxation in Manipur", An unpublished MPhil thesis submitted to Manipur University.

12

An Examination of Revenue - Expenditure Linkage: A Case Study of Manipur

Md. Samsur Jaman

Introduction

Developing countries like India or special category states like Manipur are facing dual challenges while undertaking fiscal adjustment policies. One arises from the increasing demand for public expenditures for infrastructure and social sector investment, and the other aries from the lack of capacity to raise revenue from domestic sources to finance the increased expenditure, primarily due to narrow tax base. To boost competitive capacity of the country in a rapidly globalizing world, the governments of developing countries have to invest a large portion of their revenue in building physical infrastructures. In addition, the low income developing countries also need to spend a major portion of their development expenditures in providing social services to the poor such as health, education, etc. On the other hand, as Khattry (2003: 402) pointed out, "the structural characteristics of low income countries combined with prevalence of unsophisticated tax administration limit their ability to raise taxes from domestic sources, namely income and domestic indirect taxes". Also, the existence of a large informal sector and the underground economy constrains the government's capacity for revenue growth.

The purpose of this paper is to evaluate the relationship between revenue and expenditure and its implication for managing the budget deficit. In order to do this a three variable model is formulated comprising government expenditure, revenue and NSDP. Firstly, existence of a long-run relationship among these three variables is tested by using Johansen (1991) cointegration approach. Granger causality test is applied on the corresponding Vector Error Correction Model to examine long-run causal relationship between the variables.

The goal of fiscal policy is to enhance economic growth and employment and to bring stability in economic outcome variables such as the real GDP growth rate. Under the above circumstances, the nature and objectives of fiscal policy may differ with the level of development of the countries. Long run outcome of expansionary fiscal policy depends on the nature of distribution of public resources as the same amount of public money can generate different growth pay-offs in different sectors, and the overall growth of the economy depends on the combined growth of these sectors.

Following the introduction in section one, this paper is organized as follows. Section two provides a brief discussion on fiscal reforms in Manipur and Section three discusses the dynamics of revenue and expenditure relationships. Sections four and five respectively provide a review of empirical findings of existing literature and data and methodology of the study. Section six provides the results and policy implications and finally Section seven concludes the paper.

Fiscal Reforms in Manipur

Government of Manipur initiated a fscal reform program under the behest of the guide line of central government during late 90s and till date. One of the central objectives of this reform program was to readjust government spending and to improve revenue collection.

The fiscal consolidation programs in Manipur(GOM, 2005) aim at

i) to strive to remain revenue surplus by making a balance in revenue receipt and expenditure and build up further surplus;

ii) to strive to bring down fiscal deficit to 3% of GSDP;

iii) to limit the amount of outstanding government guarantees as per the provisions of the Manipur ceiling on state government Act., 2004; and

iv) to follow a recruitment and wage policy in a manner such that the total salary bill relative to revenue expenditure excluding interest payment and pensions does not exceed 35%.

Dynamics of Revenue-Expenditure Relationships

There are four possible hypotheses regarding the relationship between revenue and expenditure. Firstly, revenue-expenditure hypothesis can arise in two distinct forms.[1] The first relationship is advocated by Friedman and his followers. According to Friedman raising taxes in an attempt to reduce deficit will also cause expenditure to rise. Therefore it will not be possible to reduce deficit by increasing taxes. The alternative version of revenue-expenditure hypothesis is popularized by Wagner and Buchanan. According to them, reducing taxes will cause expenditure to rise because of fiscal illusion of the population.

The third kind of relationship that may appear between these two variables defined as fiscal synchronization hypothesis suggests that revenue and expenditure are determined simultaneously. This argument is mainly developed by Musgrave, Meltzer and Richard. According to them, government expenditure and revenue are determined in the process of equalizing marginal benefit and marginal cost of government services by the population of the country.

Finally, there is the view that there can be no relationship between revenue and expenditure i.e. these variables are determined independent of each other. Darrat, Widavsky, Baghestani and McNown support this argument. This is a possible scenario when the government determines expenditure on the basis of requirements of the citizen and imposes taxes up to a tolerable limit to the citizen (Martin et al, 2004).

Review of Empirical Findings in the Existing Literature

Direction of causal relationship between revenue and expenditure and its implication for budget deficit has not been empirically resolved. Though over the last three decades a number of studies have been carried out in different countries to explore the issue, findings vary from country to country and also within the country.

The study of Francisco et al. (2001) by using the Preliminary Granger causality test, which is based in the notion that lagged realisations of one variable help to predict current values of another variable, offers two main results. First, the deficit is not independent of fiscal pressure or the size of the public sector. Second, there is only very weak evidence, if any, that revenues G-cause expenditures. However, these results may be biased in that they do not consider the possibility of the existence of long-run relationships among the variables involved. Once we consider this possibility and develop the causality analysis with cointegrated variables, we find clear evidence of public expenditures G-causing public revenues in the long run and also, although less clear, evidence of long-run G-causality from revenues to public expenditure. In other words, we obtain evidence of long-run bi- directional causality. Furthermore, in the short run the direction of causality seems to hold only from expenditures to public revenues in the whole sample.

The study of Barua (2005) found by examining the causal relationship between revenue and expenditure in Bangladesh that there is no causal relationship between government expenditure and revenue in the short run.

Data and Methodology

Data

Government revenue and expenditure data are collected from

various issues of Finance Accounts of Manipur and Manipur Budget at a glance, Government of Manipur. NSDP at current market price data are collected from Statistical Abstract of Manipur. NSDP deflator is used to convert the nominal data into real data. Annual data from 1972 to 2004 are taken. Real series (1972=100) of revenue, expenditure and GDP data are transformed into their logarithmic form to test causal relationships among the variables. However there is a debate whether nominal and real form of revenue and expenditure would be appropriate to test the causality between the variables. Martin et al (2004) in their study used revenue and expenditure data in real terms assuming that government takes budgetary decision by taking account of the expected level of inflation as it affects actual level of expenditure and revenue. Here we use real values of revenue and expenditure in order to eliminate the inflationary effect from revenue and expenditure.

Definitions of the variables are as follows:

LRTEM = Log of Real Government Expenditure

LRTRM = Log of Real Government Revenue

LRNSDP = Log of Real Net State Domestic Product

Methodology

Revenue (RTRM) G-cause expenditure (RTEM) if in a regression of expenditure on its own lagged values ($RTEM_{t-1}$), the inclusion of lagged values of revenue ($RTRM_{t-1}$) significantly improves the prediction of expenditure. However, existence of Granger causality from revenue to expenditure does not imply that expenditure is the result of revenue. Rather it implies that changes in revenue precede expenditure, and past and present values of revenue provide important information to forecast future values of expenditure that are not incorporated in the past values of RTEM. Granger causality form with two variables, expenditure and revenue can be expressed in following ways:

$$RTEM_t = \sum_{i=1}^{n} \alpha i RTEM_{t-1} + \sum_{j=1}^{n} \beta i RTRM_{t-1} + \varepsilon_t \qquad (1)$$

$$RTRM_t = \sum_{i=1}^{n} \chi i RTRM_{t-1} + \sum_{j=1}^{n} \delta i RTEM_{t-1} + \xi_t \qquad (2)$$

An unidirectional causality from revenue to expenditure will be found if $\sum \beta i \neq 0$ and $\sum \delta i = 0$, that is the set of estimated coefficients of lagged RTRM are significantly different from zero in RTEM equation and cluster of estimated coefficients of lagged RTEM are not significantly different from zero in RTRM equation.

Conversely, an unidirectional causality from expenditure to revenue will be found if $\Sigma\beta i \neq 0$ and $\Sigma\beta i= 0$, that is the set of estimated coefficients of lagged RTEM are significantly different from zero in RTRM equation and cluster of estimated coefficients of lagged RTRM are not significantly different from zero in RTEM equation.

There will be bidirectional causality or feedback between revenue and expenditure if both the conditions $\Sigma\beta i \neq 0$ and $\Sigma\delta i \neq 0$ simultaneously hold, that is the set of estimated coefficients of lagged RTRM and lagged RTEM are significantly different from zero in both RTEM and RTRM equation. Revenue and expenditure will be determined independently if $\Sigma\beta i =0$ and $\Sigma\delta i = 0$, that is, there is no causal link between these two variables.

Modern time series econometrics allows us to test joint significance of the coefficients of lagged terms. However, validity of the test results depends on the stationary properties of data i.e., if both revenue and expenditure series are stationary in level forms we can use Granger causality test described above. When both the series are non stationary in level forms but stationary after first differencing, that is both are integrated of order one or I(1), we can use the differenced series to test causality between the two variables. But if both the series are stationary after first differencing and cointegrated, we cannot use VAR in first differences to test the causality between the two series. If the variables are integrated of same order we can use cointegration test to check whether the variables are cointegrated or not. If the series of revenue and expenditure are cointegrated, error correction representation of cointegrated series can be estimated to examine causality between the variables.

Johansen (1991, 1995) cointegration test is used to examine cointegration between revenue and expenditure. Johansen developed a multivariate technique to evaluate the cointegration relationship among a group of variables. Johansen developed two test statistics for cointegration test, namely trace statistic $\lambda\max = -T\sum_{I=r+1}^{n}\ln(1-\lambda i)$ and maximum eigen value statistics $\lambda\max = -T\ln(1-\lambda r+1)$, where λi is defined as the estimated values of characteristics roots obtained from the estimated coefficient matrix and T is the number of included observations. If the revenue and expenditure series are cointegrated we can use error correction representation to test causality between the two series.

After including real NSDP as an additional variable, VAR in first difference with one lag of error correction term can be represented as follows:

$$\Delta LRTEM_t = \mu_1 + \sum_{i=1}^{n}\alpha_i\Delta LRTEM_{t-i} + \sum_{j=1}^{n}\beta_i\Delta LRTRM_{t-j} + \sum_{l=1}^{n}\sigma_l\Delta LRNSDP_{t-l} + \theta_1 R_{t-1} + \varepsilon \quad (3)$$

$$\Delta LRTRM_t = \mu_2 + \sum_{j=1}^{n}\chi_i\Delta LRTRM_{t-j} + \sum_{i=1}^{n}\delta_i\Delta LRTEM_{t-i} + \sum_{l=1}^{n}\phi\Delta LRNSDP_{t-l} + \theta_2 R_{t-1} + \xi_t \quad (4)$$

$$\Delta LRNSDP_t = \mu_3 + \sum_{l=1}^{n}\gamma_i\Delta LRNSDP_{t-l} + \sum_{j=1}^{n}\varphi\Delta LRTRM_{t-j} + \sum_{i=1}^{n}\eta\Delta LRTEM_{t-i} + \theta_3 R_{t-1} + \omega_t \quad (5)$$

Here R_{t-1} is the laggeded residual from the cointegrating regression, the coefficient of which represents speed of adjustment to the long-run equilibrium.

The above formulation is very useful to identify the sources of causation–we can evaluate short-run causal relationship between the variables by testing joint significance of lagged dynamic terms in each of the above equations and we can also derive information on long-run causality by testing significance of error correction terms.

In a multivariate framework Granger causality test is also called block-causality or block exogeneity test where cross equation restrictions are imposed to test causality between the variables. In this paper, we applied Granger causality test or block-exogeneity test to evaluate short-run causality between the variables. Weak exogeneity test is also conducted to evaluate whether a variable can be treated as exogenous or not, that is, whether the variable is adjusted towards long-run equilibrium or not.

Econometric Results

At the outset of the cointegration test we have to check the stationarity property of the variables. Augmented Dickey Fuller test (ADF) and Phillips–Perron (PP) tests are used to test the null hypothesis of unit root. To test formally for the presence of a unit root for each variable in the model, ADF and P-P test of the types given by equation (7) and (8) were conducted. The ADF test is conducted using the regression equation of the form:

$$\Delta W_t = a_0 + a_1 t + \rho W_{t-1} + \sum_{i=1}^{k} \lambda_i \Delta W_{t-i} + u_t \qquad (6)$$

where ΔW_t is the first difference of the series Wt, k is the lag order and t stands for time. Equation (7) is with constant and time trend.

P-P test involves computing the following OLS regression:

$$W_t = a_0 + a_1 W_{t-1} + a_2 (t - \frac{T}{2}) + u_t \qquad (7)$$

where a_0, a_1, a_2 are the conventional least squares regression coefficients. The hypotheses of unit root to be tested are H0: $a_1=1$ and H0: $a_1=1$, $a_2=0$. Akaike's Information Criterion (AIC) is used to determine the lag order of each variable under study. Mackinnon's (1991) tables provided the cumulative distribution of ADF and P-P test statistics.

Test for stationarity indicates that the null hypothesis of a unit root cannot be rejected for the levels of the variables except the variables LRTEM and LRTRM under the assumption of having constant and trend. Using differenced data, the computed ADF and P-P test suggested that the null hypothesis is rejected for the individual series at 1 or 5 percent significant level.

Table 1
Unit root test result

Test	*Trend assumption*	*Variables*	*LRTEM*	*LRTRM*	*LRNSDP*
ADF	Constant	Level	-2.02799(1)	-1.998(1)	-0.773(1)
		First diff	-5.412(1)*	-5.467(1)*	-3.9666(1)*
	Constant and trend	Level	-4.3056(1)*	-4.290(1)*	-2.084(1)
		First diff	-5.202(1)*	-5.266(10)*	-3.965(1)**
PP	Constant	Level	-2.191(3)	-2.276(3)	-1.374(3)
		First diff	-6.151(3)*	-5.803(3)*	-5.575(3)*
	Constant and trend	Level	-3.681(3)**	-3.709(3)**	-2.103(3)
		First diff	-6.466(3)*	-6.102(3)*	-5.540(3)*

Unit root test results on the basis of Augmented Dickey Fuller test (ADF) indicate that all the series are integrated of order one or I(1). The null hypothesis of unit root could not be rejected for all the three series in the log level form and clearly rejected in their first differences for both the models (constant and constant with linear trend). However, ADF test rejects the null hypothesis of unit root (for the model with constant and linear trend) only at the 5 percent level of significance for NSDP series in the log level. Though for the model with a constant and linear trend there is some doubt about the unit root property of the data in log level form, all the variables are nonetheless stationary in their first difference form. So we can use Johansen cointegration test to determine the underlying relationships among the variables.

At the start of Johansen test we have to determine the appropriate lag length for the VAR system as the test results can be sensitive to the choice of the lag length. We estimated an unrestricted VAR model in level form of the series and used Akaike Information Criterion (AIC) and Schwartz Bayesian Criterion (SBC) to choose appropriate lag length p. It is observed that it takes 2 lags to get uncorrelated and homoscedastic residual for the VAR system. The cointegration test is carried out assuming linear trend in data, and both an intercept and a trend in the cointegrating equation. Because some of the series seem to be trend stationary and a linear trend term in cointegrating space minimizes the value of AIC. Both trace statistic (Δtrace) and maximal eigenvalue (Δmax) statistics indicate that there is at least one cointegrating vector between LRTRM, LRTEM and LRNSDP. We can reject the null hypothesis of no cointegrating vector in favour of one cointegrating vector in both the cases at 5 percent level of significance. We cannot reject the null hypothesis of at most one cointegrating vector against the alternative hypothesis of two cointegrating vectors for both the Trace and Max-eigen test statistics. Therefore, there is a long-run equilibrium relationship between real government expenditure, real government revenue and real NSDP. Long-run relationships among these three variables is derived by normalizing on LRTEM, as reported in Table 3.

The estimates of normalised coefficients normalized on LRTEM are also given in the same table in under brackets. Any deviation from long-run equilibrium will be corrected by changes in government expenditure or NSDP because adjustment coefficients of these two equations are significant.

Existence of a single cointegrating vector indicates that government expenditure, government revenue and NSDP display long-run co-comovement, i.e. there is a long-run equilibrium relationship between the variables. Whenever the gap between these three variables widens above the long-run equilibrium, expenditure and NSDP will adjust to restore the equilibrium. That is, short-run adjustments are done by changes in government expenditure and NSDP to restore the long-run equilibrium.

Table 2

Johansen cointegration test result

Cointegration with unrestricted intercepts and unrestricted trends in the VAR
Cointegration LR Test Based on Maximal Eigen value of the Stochastic Matrix

List of eigen values in descending order:

0.55782 0.38875 0.11074

Null	*Alternative*	*Statistic*	*95% Critical Value*	*90% Critical Value*
r = 0	r = 1	25.2972	24.3500	22.2600
r<= 1	r = 2	15.2596	18.3300	16.2800
r<= 2	r = 3	3.6383	11.5400	9.7500

Cointegration with unrestricted intercepts and unrestricted trends in the VAR
Cointegration LR Test Based on Trace of the Stochastic Matrix

List of eigen values in descending order:

.55782 .38875 .11074

Null	*Alternative*	*Statistic*	*95% Critical Value*	*90% Critical Value*
r = 0	r = 1	44.1951	39.3300	36.2800
r<= 1	r = 2	18.8979	23.8300	21.2300
r<= 2	r = 3	3.6383	11.5400	9.7500

Table 3
Estimated cointegration equation

Vector 1					
LRTEM	11.7180	LRTRM	-11.8443	LRNSDP	91800
	(-1.0000)		(1.0108)		(-078341)

Notes: Johansen Estimation (Normalized in Brackets) under the assumption with unrestricted intercepts and unrestricted trends in the VAR

However, the existence of long-run equilibrium relationship between these three variables does not assure a balanced budget, rather the result indicates that the gap between government expenditure and government revenue will persist at a long run sustainable level. When budget deficit rises above the long run sustainable level, expenditure is reduced to maintain the deficit at a tolerable limit. It is worth mentioning that, government expenditure adjusts at a reasonable speed to the long-run equilibrium. NSDP also converges to its long-run equilibrium level through a series of partial short-run adjustments. Therefore, government expenditure must be reduced to maintain budget deficit at a long run sustainable limit. The above finding appears plausible plausible as it is not easy to raise revenue by increasing the taxes on domestic consumption and income due to various structural constraints and lack of administrative capacity to collect potential revenue in a developing country like India. On the other hand, expenditure growth is constrained by revenue shortfall and increasing cost of deficit financing. Therefore, whenever there is a tendency of rising deficit beyond its long run limit, expenditure adjusts to restore the equilibrium. Granger causality test is applied on estimated VEC, where cross equation restrictions are imposed on the lag differences in each of the equations of VEC incorporating the cointegrating vectors. If lagged values of ΔLRTEM are statistically significant in both the ΔLRTRM and ΔLRNSDP equations, we can say that LRTEM G-causes LRTRM and LRNSDP. The Granger causality test or the block exogeneity test restricts all the lag differences of LRTEM or ΔLRTEM to be equal to zero in both the ΔLRTRM and ΔLRNSDP equations. We can test these restrictions with the help of likelihood ratio test which follows chi-sq distribution. For testing long run Granger causality, θ_1, θ_2 and θ_2 from equation (3), (4) and (5) are used. If θ_1 is significantly zero, it indicates that TRM and NSDP does not long run Granger cause TEM

Table 4
Preliminary Granger Causality Tests

Null Hypothesis	*Long run test*		*Short run test (VEC)*	
	F-Statistic	*Probability*	*Ch-sq-statistic*	*Probability*
LRTRM does not G-Cause LRTEM	1.040	0.308	1.1848	0.276
LRTEM does not G-Cause LRTRM	0.380	0.537	1.5377	0.215
LRNSDP does not G-Cause LLRTEM	2.165	0.141	3.7437	0.053
LRTEM does not G-Cause LRNSDP	0.380	0.537	0.13623	0.712
LRNSDP does not G-Cause LRTRM	2.165	0.141	3.8140	0.051
LRTRM does not G-Cause LRNSDP	1.040	0.308	0.37964	0.538

Results of the Granger causality test are reported in table 4. Here it is clear from column 3 of table 4 that we cannot reject the null hypothesis that LRTRM does not short run Granger cause LRTEM which have a chi-square value of 1.18 with a probability of 0.276 in the ΔLRTEM equation reported in row one of table 4. Again the null hypothesis that LRTEM does not G-cause LRTRM cannot be rejected in the ΔLRTRM equation, which has chi-square value of 1.53 with a probability of 0.215. In both the equations, ΔLRTEM and ΔLRTRM, null hypothesis of no causal relationship from LRNSDP to LRTEM and LRNSDP to LRTRM is rejected. However, null hypothesis of no causal relationship from LRTEM to LRNSDP and LRTRM to LRNSDP cannot be rejected in ΔLRNSDP equation. The above findings indicate that there is no causal relationship between government expenditure and revenue in the long run. Granger causality test is also applied on the unrestricted VAR model for each pair of the above three variables. The column 2 of table 4 shows the calculated Chi-sq-statistic of long run G-causality for the variables. The calculated Chi-sq-statistics for both the revenue and expenditure equations also suggest that there is no causal relationship between revenue and expenditure in the long run. Therefore, we can say that government expenditure and revenue are independently determined in the short run. Budget deficit can be reduced either by reducing government expenditure or by raising revenues in the short run. When both government expenditure and taxes are raised together, rise in expenditure should be less than the rise in taxes to reduce the budget deficit.

On the other hand, in the short run, there exist uni-directional causality from NSDP to TEM and TRM. The implication is that to increase TEM and TRM, the NSDP must be boost up in the short run. Short run causality between the fiscal variable and NSDP implies that changes in expenditure policies have no affect on real NSDP growth in the short run. Further, the causal relation between the variables is studied by using the error correction terms. The results are reported in table 4 column 2. From the analysis, we noticed that there is no causality between revenue and expenditure because both the hypotheses that TRM does not G-cause TEM and its reverse cannot be rejected. But from the analysis, it is further noticed that the hypothesis that NSDP does not G-cause TRM and TEM also cannot be rejected. This indicates that NSDP, TEM and TRM have no long run Granger causal relationship.

Conclusion

The paper examines causal relationship between real expenditure and revenue for the Government of Manipur by using annual data from 1972 to 2004 period. Real NSDP is also included in the model along with these two fiscal variables. Johansen (1991) cointegration test suggests that there is a long-run equilibrium relationship between government expenditure, government revenue and NSDP. Granger causality test based on the estimated error correction terms suggests that there is no causal relationship between government expenditure and revenue in the long run. It is felt that expenditure is the key variable to reduce budget deficit because of structural constraints of the economy in raising revenue. So budget deficit should be reduced by curbing unproductive public expenditure and at the same time ensuring effective utilization of available resources such as to engender the productivity of labour and capital in the economy. If the economy achieves enhanced economic growth, it will be possible to raise revenue from domestic sources.

However, any conclusion to be derived from these results should bear in mind the limitations of the analysis, in particular the fact that this is based on past data and, consequently, the future evolution of some structural factors (for example, demographic trends) and their impact on public finances are not taken into account.

Preliminary Granger causality test offer two main results. First, the deficit is not independent of fiscal pressure or the size of the public sector. Second, we find only very weak evidence, if any, that revenues G-cause expenditures. However, these results may be biased as they do not consider the possibility of the existence of long-run relationships among the variables involved. Once we consider this possibility and develop the causality analysis with cointegrated variables, we find no evidence of public expenditures G-causing public revenues or its reverse in the long run.

NOTES

1. Martin et al (2004) discussed both the forms of the revenue-expenditure hypotheses. However, the latter one is less likely scenario due to budget constraints.

REFERENCES

Baghestani, H and R, MacNown(1994): "Do Revenues or Expenditures response to Budgetary disequilibria?", *Southern Economic Journal*, Vol. 61, No. 2, Oct. 1994, pp. 311-322.

Barro, R. J.(1988): "Government Spending in A Simple Model of Endogenous Growth", *Working Paper No. 2588*, NBER.

Barua, S (2005): "An Examination of Revenue and Expenditure Causality in Bangladesh 1974-2004", Policy Analyst Unit (PAU), Research Development Bangladesh Bank.

Cheng, B.S. (1999): "Causality between Taxes and Expenditures: Evidence from Latin American Countries", *Journal of Economics and Finance*, Vol. 23, No.2, pp. 184-192.

Darrat, A.F. (1998): "Tax and Spend, or Spend and Tax? An inquiry into the Turkish Budgetary Process", *Southern Economic Journal*, Vol. 64, No. 4, 1998, pp. 940-956.

Engle R. F and C. W. J. Granger (1987): "Co-integration and Error Correction: Representation, Estimation, and Testing", *Econometrica*, Vol. 55, No.2, 1551-1580.

Francisco, C., J. Manuel and C. Hermendez (2001): "Evaluating the Dynamics of Fiscal Policy in Spain: Pattern of interdependence and consistency of Public Expenditures and Revenues", Benco de Espana, Sevicio de Estudios, Documento de Trabazo n. 0103.

Govt. of Manipur (2005): *The Fiscal Responsibility and Budget Management Act*

Hussain, M. H. (2005): "On the Causal Relationship between Government, Expenditure and Tax Revenue in Pakistan", Economics Working Paper Archive (EconWPA), http://econwpa.wustl.edu: 80/eps/mac/papers/0509/0509014.pdf.

Johansen, S.(1991): "Estimation and Hypothesis testing of Cointegration Vectors in Gaussian Vector Autoregressive Models", *Econometrica*, Vol. 59, No. 6, pp. 1551-1580.

Johansen S., (1995): *Likelihood-based Inference in Cointegrating Vectors Autoregressive Models*, Oxford University Press.

Khattry, B. (2003): "Trade liberalization and the Fiscal Squeeze: Implications for Public Investment", *Development and Change*, 34(3), pp. 401-424.

Maghyereh, A. and O. Sweidan, (2004): "Government Expenditure and Revenues in Jordan, What Cause What? Multivariate Cointegration Analysis", Social Science Research Network Electronic Paper Collection.

M'Amanja, D., T. Lloyd, and O. Morrisey (2007): "Fiscal Aggregates, Aid and Growth in Kenya: A Vector Autoregression (VAR) Analysis", CREDIT Research Paper, University of Nottingham.

Martin, M. J., J. Krishnakumar and N. Sougel, (2004): "Application of Granger Causality Tests to Revenue and Expenditure of Swiss cantons", Cahiers du départment d' économétrie Faculté des sciences économiques et sociales Université de Genéve.

Payne, J. E., (2003): "A Survey of the International Empirical Evidence on the Tax-Spend Debate", *Public Finance Review*, Vol. 31, No. 3, pp. 302-324.

Yildirim, J., S. Sezgin and N. Ocal (2005): "Military Expenditure and Economic Growth in Middle Eastern Countries: A dynamic Panel Data Analysis", *Defence and Peace Economics*, 2005, Vol. 16(4), August, pp.283-295.

13

Water Supply in Imphal City: Demand, Supply and Sustainability

Ksh. Jhaljit Singh

"Water is fundamental for life and health. The human right to Water is indispensable for leading a healthy life in human dignity. It is a prerequisite to the realization of all other human rights".

– *United Nations 2002*

Introduction

From the global perspective, there is apparently no shortage of water as the available per capita potable water of the world is much more than an average individual's present water requirement. The above statement is hardly comforting when one is confronted with the statistic of the estimated 1.1 billion people currently without access to adequate water supply in this world. Quite evidently renewable and usable freshwater is becoming an increasingly scarce commodity for an increasing number of people. It is also quite true that many people at the regional or local level are facing or about to face critical limits of usable water.

The water stress being felt by different sections of the people over the globe may be broadly attributed to the following three features associated with water: (i) uneven availability of water (spatial as well as temporal), (ii) uneven development of water resource and (iii) uneven distribution of water.

The first feature is about the uneven endowment of water resources like rivers, springs, lake, groundwater etc. and the rainfall across the countries and regions of the world. The second feature refers to the capability of a country/region to tap its water resources. Finally, the third feature is about distribution of water amongst the people within a region/city. For example, neither all corners of a city nor all sections of a society are served equally by the water supply system of the city or the region.

Broadly, within an economy, water is required for domestic, industrial and agricultural purposes amongst which the domestic need is the smallest component. In fact, it constitutes far less than ten percent in most of the countries of the world[1]. But it is the non-fulfillment of this demand which creates most stressful conditions for the existence of human settlements. This can be gauged from the fact that there are millions (mostly women) in many regions of the world who walk miles everyday to find and carry water they and their families use and consume. Water, after all is equated to life and it is quite needless to state that the requirements of domestic use and livestock must have a first claim on available water resources in water deficient situations.

This paper shall take a holistic view of the issues relating to water supply in Imphal and its sustainability. Firstly, we shall take a look at the demand-supply situation of water in Imphal. Any deficit in supply could be met by supply enhancement programs or demand management strategies or a suitable combination of the two. In the context of Imphal, the demand management strategies have currently very limited scope as the real problem being faced is that of inadequate and erratic supply. Any attempt at this stage to restrict or squeeze the demand will amount to compromising on quality of life and health.

Manipur and its Capital Imphal

Manipur is a small hilly state of India, situated in the North-Eastern region of the country with a total land area of 22327 sq. km and a population of 2.39 million (as per 2001 census). The hill ranges occupying 90 percent of the total geographical area, completely surround an oval-shaped central valley of 2230 sq. km. Manipur receives fairly heavy rainfall. The estimated average annual rainfall for the last three decades in the hills and the central valley is respectively 1734 mm and 1238 mm.

Imphal, the capital city is situated in the central valley. Imphal, spread over an area of 135.29 sq. km comprises of (a) Imphal municipal area (33.3 sq. km) and (b) Non-municipal area (101.99 sq. km). Population of Imphal as per 2001 census is about 5.48 lakhs with gross density population of 4052 per sq. km. The average annual rainfall of Imphal is about 1210 mm(for the period 1972 to 2001) though the average annual rainfall in the last decade (i.e. 1992-2002) is just about 900 mm.[2]

The public health and engineering department (PHED), Government of Manipur deals with planning, investigation, execution and operation and maintenance for both urban and rural water supply schemes in the state.

The Water Demand-supply Situation in Imphal

The projected population of Imphal for the year 2002-03 is 5,81,267 out of which 2,19,317 are residents of municipal area. Its gross density population is 4296 per sq. km. As per the approved supply norm for Imphal of 150 litres per capita per day (lpcd) for the municipal area and 90 lpcd for the non-municipal area by Ministry of Urban Development (CPHEED), New Delhi, the current water requirement of Imphal is 65.47 million litres per day (MLD). If five percent of the municipal population is taken as a proxy for unregistered population[3] and an allowance for this additional population is accounted, then we have the projected water requirement of Imphal as 67.12 MLD.

The installed capacity of the existing water treatment plants (WTPs) under urban water supply schemes (UWSS) as on 1st April

2002 is 83.03 MLD and that under rural water supply schemes (RWSS) is about 4.32 MLD. Though the current installed capacity is 87.35 MLD, the estimated actual production is about 67.59MLD (65 MLD under UWSS & 2.59 MLD under RWSS). The main Imphal UWSSs are Kangchup (rehabilatation and new extension), Porompat (Old + New) and phase II, Canchipur, Singda, Ningthempukhri, Potsangbam Phase-I with respective installed capacities in MLD being 23.61, 15.89, 6-81, 18.16, 4.54, and 6.81. The installed capacities of Imphal RWSSs range from 30,000 to 100,000 gallons per day with average capacity being about 40,000 gallons per day. Now assuming a 30% leakage loss[4] in the distribution stage, the actual amount reaching the consumers is just about 47.31 MLD which translates to 79.88 lpcd, indeed quite a low figure for a class-I capital city. The current deficit in supply works out to be 41.87 percent of the supply.

To overcome the current shortage in supply and also to meet the increasing demand in future, the state PHED plans to take up work on another three WTPs, each of 6.81 MLD capacity and to be located at Irilbung, Canchipur and Potsangbam/Sekmai. The department also plans to tap water to the tune of 45.4 MLD from the ongoing Thoubal Multipurpose project (Dam) for supplementing the water supply (w/s) of Imphal in future. For the expansion and improvement of the distribution system, proposals for replacement of old pipelines and laying of additional new pipelines are made. Efforts are also made to improve the supply by controlling the leakages and wastages of water by repairing of leaking joints and construction of six more Zonal reservoirs/overhead tanks with total capacity of 4.54 million litres.

System operation

The whole Imphal is divided into 13 water supply (w/s) zones. Supply to the various zones are done from the various w/s schemes, various high and low level reservoirs (or pumping stations) located at various zones.

The supply to the various zones is restricted to one time supply of about three hours, either in the morning or evening. In some zones, even one time supply of three hours cannot be done daily and is done on alternate days.

Sources of Water of the City Water Treatment Plants

The present w/s of Imphal is obtained from six different sources out of which five are surface water sources and only one is groundwater source.

Surface water sources

Leimakhong River (13.5 km. from the plant) and Pollak stream (1.3 km. from the plant) feeds the Kangchup water treatment plant (WTP), located at 14 m. away from Imphal. The Imphal River which almost bisects the city by flowing in the heart of the city from north to south direction feeds Koirengei WTP (situated at the northern-most tip of the city), Minụthong WTP, Chinga WTP, Ningthempukhri WTP (these three are located in Municipal area), Canchipur WTP (situated at the southern tip of the city) and many other microplants which comes under RWSS. Iril River which also flows from North to South forms the eastern boundary of the city. This river feeds Porompat WTP (old + phase I & phase II). Singda dam, constructed across the river Singda is situated about 20 kms towards the western side of the city. It feeds the Singda WTP and partially to Kangchup WTP.

Ground water source

The Potsangbam and Sekmai area which is situated about 18 km have been found to have great potential for ground water. At present, it feeds the Potsangbam phase-I. The ground water potential of these areas is further enhanced by the availability of vast recharging area and also by the Sekmai River which flows nearby the area. There are further potential for tapping groundwater in these areas.

How to keep these sources alive?

We find that the whole of the Imphal w/s schemes (except the Potsangbam phase-I) is dependent on surface water of rivers and streams flowing in and around the city. Fortunately the catchment areas of the Valley Rivers still receive fairly good amount of rainfall[5] though rainfall seems to have got reduced for the valley.

It was not very long before when the hills which form the catchment area of these rivers and streams were covered with thick and dense vegetations (and forests) and these were regulating the flow of water into them (by first absorption of rainwater during rain and then slowly releasing it) assuring a reasonably good flow of water year round and also preventing soil erosions besides a host of other eco-protective functions of it. As population pressure on land kept on increasing, indiscriminate and ruthless deforestation took place unchecked and this, along with the practice of unscientific agricultural methods (like the 'Jhoom' cultivation) in the hills led to severe degradation of the catchment areas. Direct fallout of the above is that in recent times, even two -three days of heavy rainfall in the catchment areas makes them in spate, often overflowing and breaching their embankments and creating flood havocs and dry and drought conditions between the rains. The above situation has been attributed mainly to a sharp increase in the surface run-off rates. Thus, we have a situation here where even two-three days of heavy rainfall in catchment areas resulting in sleepless nights for the riparian population living in low-lying areas of Imphal and other parts of the central valley. Under the present circumstances, these people have been left with no option but pray for a regulated rain (if that is not asking too much!).

To make the existing Imphal w/s schemes sustainable from the water resource limit point of view, we could pick up a lesson or two from the amazing story of Lake Meiktila, an irrigation system in Myanmar which had a very unique history. The lake had lasted in a healthy state without silting up for nearly 900 years under the Burmese kings. The king had enforced very strict laws with the administration and control of the lake. One of the laws was enacted with the dual intention of ensuring a regular supply of water and preventing the entrance of silt in the lake... "*No person, on pain of death, was permitted to cut any jungle or to clear any land for any purpose whatsoever within 2 miles of the bank of a stream in the catchment area*" (Loucks, D.P. et al., eds 1999, p.20). However, when Burma came under British rule, many harshly enforced Burmese laws became obsolete and unfortunately the laws concerning the Meiktila Lake were amongst them. The beautiful and healthy existence of the lake came under grave danger during the time of British administration when the control over the lake became lax.

The above story brings out the crucial function of vegetations and forests in the catchment areas: firstly in assuring ample supplies of subsoil water and secondly prevention of erosion and thereby siltation in the river or stream flowing there.

Another thing which has made it all the more imperative to develop and properly manage the upstream watersheds is the coming up of barrages across Imphal and Iril Rivers. These barrages were constructed to enhance the availability of water especially during the lean season and mostly for the water supply. The barrages while enhancing the water availability, are also impeding and checking the flow of the water, making the river sluggish and thereby facilitating the siltation process.

The recent spurt in the agricultural activities (specially growing vegetables) taken up by some of the riparian population on the inner slopes of the earthen river embankments as well as on available space of the dry portion of the river bank during the lean seasons might also be aiding to erosion and siltation along the river courses. These bring about reduction in the storage capacity of the river, a higher probability of overflow and breaches along the embankments resulting in floods. Hence, the authority concerned should put a hold on these practices or those indulging in these practices should be persuaded to abstain from these activities.

The need for developing and conserving natural catchments or the water shed cannot be overemphasized. Involvement of community participation will be a vital key to the success of the above work with due recognition given to the role and responsibility of the people or stakeholders to protect and manage their catchment to preserve water and other natural resources that water gives life to. Local governance, sustainable use of natural resources and creation of additional/alternative sources of income/livelihood other than forestry based and jhum cultivation are critical to this act of balancing economic needs and protection of the resources in the water-shed. It will be through the above and also keeping them free from pollution[6] measures that we can successfully keep our water resources in our river and streams alive. Then only it will be possible for us and our future generation to avail of an uninterrupted service of these rivers and streams.

Coverage of the City Water Supply Schemes

As per record of the PHED, the number of official w/s connections for Imphal is 18398 which accounts for less than 20 per cent of its official count of total houses. It means that a massive proportion of the houses (more than 80 per cent) in Imphal do not have official w/s connection. Since there are no other agencies indulging in water supply through pipes, it means that a huge proportion of Imphalites are meeting their water need from public hydrants/illegal connections/ponds (community and/or private), rivers, streams, hand pumps or some other own arrangements. Table 1 gives a good idea of the sources of water for domestic usage for the state as a whole. The source of drinking water is a good proxy for source of water for domestic use as the two sources coincide in most of the cases.

Table 1
Distribution of household of Manipur by source of drinking water and each location

Sl. No.	*Source of drinking water*			*Within premises*		*Near premises**		*Away*	
		Total	*%*	*Total*	*%*	*Total*	*%*	*Total*	*%*
1.	Tap	116413	29.3	31174	7.8	63908	16.04	21331	5.36
2.	Hand pump	25270	6.4	1717	0.4	15283	3.84	8270	2.09
3.	Tube well	5251	1.3	700	0.2	3181	0.8	1370	0.34
4.	Well	25631	6.4	5309	1.3	13653	3.44	6669	1.66
5.	Tank, Pond, Lake	106565	26.8	7987	2.0	66418	16.73	32160	8.10
6.	River, Canal	70883	17.8	0	0.0	44358	11.17	26525	6.68
7.	Spring	40860	10.3	0	0.0	18641	4.70	22219	5.55
8.	Any other	6783	1.7	528	0.1	2396	0.63	3859	0.98
	Total	397656	100	47415	11.9	227838	57.30	122403	30.78

* For Urban area, within 100 m from the house & for Rural area it is within 500 m.
Source: Census of India, 2001.

Why such a poor official coverage?

Some parts of Imphal are covered under RWSS and there is no provision for individual connections in it. Going by the installed capacity of the RWSS operating in Imphal, it is estimated[7] that about 18680 houses fall under it. This partly explains the low number of connections.

The city also faces a very distressing and alarming phenomenon of the presence of a large number of illegal connections within it. In fact, according to reliable official source, the number of illegal connections will be about the same number as that of official connections. In fact, because of the rampant illegal connections, there are now quite a lot of connections which happen to be at the tail end of the supply line having gone completely dry or getting very little supply. The problem of illegal connections seems to be not so much with the water charge rate of Rs. 75 per month but the fact that the people wants to have it free.

As a matter of fact many people have started viewing the water supply system as an open access resource. People are able to have illegal connections with a small bribe passed on to the linesman of his area. The person thereafter starts enjoying the water, without even an iota of feeling guilty, on the contrary he seems to be quite proud of his act to achieve it.

The saddest part of the above story is that the society seems to be accepting it as a matter of fact. The absence of any strong social sanction against such happening may partly be because of the fact that water besides being an economic good, is also a social good and a critical input for human life. But the truth of the matter is that what is happening is just a reflection of the moral degeneration which has taken place in today's highly corrupt Imphal society.

In the long run, it is going to be the people who will be the ultimate losers. What is immediately needed is installation of some degree of governance in the system and a turn around in the people's attitude towards it. Otherwise, the system is surely heading towards the inevitable death as predicted by Hardin, "...Ruin is the destination toward which all men rush, each pursuing his own interest in a society that believes in the freedom of the Commons" (Stavins (ed.), 2000, p. 13).

People should stop playing with water before its turns into a proverbial fire. Under normal circumstances, people should give due recognition to the scarcity value of water and tailor their behavior accordingly.

Issues Concerning Financial Sustainability

To maintain and operate the w/s schemes requires continual financial support. The sustainable operation of a system depends on properly functioning infrastructures and the provision of funds for maintenance and personnel. Very often, the cause of under-performance or non-performance of a system is simply put on paucity of fund for its maintenance and operation, not to talk of up gradation of the system. If the under-performance or non-performance of the system, for one reason or the other continues for long it might finally lead to the closure of the system. To bring about financial sustainability to a system, one may have to explore ways and means existing within the system which can generate fund. Often the ways in which services are priced by publicly operated water resource systems have little to do with actual costs and benefits. Involvement of the private sector in planning and management of water development projects have been recommended from various quarters on the ground that it will lead to more efficient operation and services because there exist financial as well as social incentives to improve the performance of the system and its personnel. On the other hand the case of Singapore has shown that there is no a prior reason that public agencies will not deliver services efficiently and economically in a sustainable manner. Proper pricing of water is suggested for efficient and sustainable w/s system.

The following broad guidelines should be kept in mind while pricing water: (i) water should have the same price for all similarly situated users; (ii) there can be different classes of users but within class need the same price.

Along with the above, water as a social good and water as economic good needs to be distinguished and priced differently. To accommodate the above consideration, water may be categorized by quantity and types of use.

What one should bear in mind is that the market forces being brought in for efficiency and sustainable consideration of water use should not become an institution to deprive the basic minimum water requirement to the economically weaker section of the society. A suitable tariff policy needs to be framed which takes care of this aspect. One way is to provide certain minimum water at zero tariffs and the rate to be progressively made stiff with the quantity consumed.

Water is said to be the most subsidized good in the whole world. But in most cases the real benefit of the subsidy is being cornered by the rich section of the society and hardly reaching to the poor people. A hard look into the actual subsidy operation in the water sector is called for when one talks about desirability of cost recovery in w/s service for the system's sustainability.

Let us have a look at tariff collection of state PHED. In Manipur, consumers have been categorized in terms of types of connections and different rates are fixed according to type of consumers. In case of Imphal, what came out very glaring is the vast difference between potential tariff collection and actual tariff collection.

As per the official number and types of connections, the potential tariff collection for the year 2002 works out to an amount of 22.6 million rupees whereas the actual collection for the same year is a paltry sum of 4.215 million rupees. If we define efficiency in tariff collection as the ratio of actual collection to potential collection, we have a very poor figure of just 18.64 per cent efficiency. Such a low figure of efficiency in tariff collection should not be taken as solely reflecting citizen's dissatisfaction over the service. Thus, there exists a vast scope of improvement on this tariff front. A little tightening in the system or slightly modified mechanism than the prevailing one (with due consideration given to the ground reality) can bring to the system the much needed fund required for further improvement in its service. The need for developing an appropriate tariff collection system is there for all to see. A system which takes into account the income flow of the users may be developed.

NGOs or some local clubs may be involved who can collect fees weekly or monthly on a nominal commission basis. Here, we have talked within the existing tariff structure and have not really gone into the question of whether the current tariff rate reflects the actual costs and benefits.

Why Such a Big Revenue Gap?

In Imphal, as in most places in India, people are charged a flat rate irrespective of whether they are actually getting their full water supply or not. To begin with, the water supply in Imphal is erratic and inadequate (because of low pressure & very short duration of supply). Whether the water supply reaches a particular house does not depend on the water available in the pipe itself but on the pressure it is available at, the area where the house is located, the electricity available to pump the water and the number of illegal connections on the way. In most cases the water reaching the house is so inadequate that there is need to supplement from other sources. In such cases, the consumers by and large are reluctant or not willing to pay the monthly water charges. It has been observed that even those who are getting normal or near normal supplies because of their privileged location or some other reason also try to hide themselves behind the general non-performance of the public w/s and not clear their dues in time.

In various studies, it has been found that people in general are willing to pay for utility service if a satisfactory and reliable service is assured[8]. Hence, if the department wants to go for a revenue drive, the foremost thing is to bring a w/s system which can provide reasonably adequate water to the people. If this is too difficult a target at present situation, then in the context of Imphal, the revenue drive should begin from those w/s zones where the supply position has been reasonably normal, knowing fully that these normal w/s zones may change from time to time and the department has full knowledge regarding this.

The existence of large number of illegal connections and other undesirable practices of the consumers to avail of the water from the supply pipe lines are all within the common knowledge of the public and the authorities. Any means seem to be justifiable and rightful for the people in their attempt to get hold of such a basic and fundamental need of livelihood namely water. The department seems to be quite helpless in this regard. Not surprisingly, the people at large took the warning[9] of possible disconnection of their lines (if caught indulging in undesirable practices) very lightly.

The department could not execute the threat, showing its helplessness and failure to infuse any semblance of governance in the system. Clearly, something needs to be done here: either empowering the PHED to take up action against the defaulters or if they are already legally empowered for such action, the ground reality which is stopping them from exercising these powers and the need to devise a mechanism to streamline the system after taking account of the ground reality.

We reemphasize the need of raising public awareness regarding the scarcity value of water, the cost involved in treatment of water etc so that they stop seeing and demanding water as a free good. Even those who are getting highly subsidized water supply to the extent of almost free should (or made to) realize that the subsidy, involves an opportunity cost. The cost could be in terms of roads, educational or health facilities etc. Thus, everyone in the society in today's context should accept that water cannot ever be a free good in the sense of not needing to give up something of value to obtain more of it. At the same time, everyone involved in water resources management system has an obligation to see that water is provided in sufficient quantities and qualities, at acceptable prices and reliability to meet the demand of the day and in the future.

Now, let us look at the distributional aspect of the water supply in the prevailing scenario.

The Cost of Water Across the Population

We implicitly assume here that the upper section of the society in general have better access to the w/s because of their general privileged house location and more resources to appropriate the system. In all likelihood they would be having more powerful pumps compared to their poor cousins to draw water from the supply line, more storage spaces, more resources to bribe the system in case of need, etc. Again in case of water supply failure, they can opt for bulk purchase through tanker service. The lower half of the society has to suffer the inadequate and erratic supply and have to supplement through small retail purchases. We are aware of the cases of some rich people whose houses happen to be at the tail end of the supply line and also due shortage of storage space have to depend on small retail purchases. There are also few cases of economically poor people who on account of prime location of their houses and/or illegal connections enjoy all the water they require.

Let us try to estimate the cost of water across the various sections of the population. Consider a family of say four members with w/s connection. At the present supply position of the city (i.e. approximately 79.9 lpcd), the family gets about 9588 litres per month from the public w/s. Since the monthly charge for an individual connection is Rs.75 the cost to this family works out to be a mere 7.82 paise per 10 litre. For those who are able to acquire the tanker supply of 9000 and above, the cost of water works out to be 35-39 paise per 10 litre whereas for 4500 litre tanker supply, the cost is 44 paise per 10 litre.

On the other hand, the poor people without much storage space at home as well as not having much money to spare for water at any point of time have to fall back on retail purchase where price ranges from Rs. 1 to Rs. 3 per 10 litres. Thus, we see that the water from supply line is the cheapest followed by the water from tanker service and the costliest is from retail purchase. Though the population at large gets affected because of the failure or ineffectiveness of the public w/s system, undoubtedly it is the poor who gets the hardest punch from it.

And coming to the plight of the poor people who are supposedly being supplied free water on public hydrants; they generally have to spend long hours to get their share of few bucketfuls of water. If the waiting time is allowed to be valued here, the cost of water to the poor will turn out be higher than the rich people as a study conducted in Dehradun[10] shows. Water, thus seems to be always available to the rich at a much cheaper rate than to the poor.

The prevailing water distribution system without any exception seems to be heavily tilted in favor of the rich. This reality is against the backdrop of the generally accepted principle that pricing of water (or the cost of water to the consumer) should reflect social concerns and sustainability issues and in any case water for basic need for health and hygiene and livelihood should be available at low cost. It is an irony that even the situation where the government apparently subsidizes the poor by providing a basic minimum amount of water free of charge through public stand post, does not prove to be an exception to the above observation.

Another convenient source of water which could be tapped by Imphalites is the roof water (RW), the rainwater falling over the roof tops.

Roof Water (RW) Harvesting

Imphal is a low rise and thinly spread out city. High rise, multi-storied residential buildings are almost non-existent. Many of the houses have sloping roofs made of GI corrugated sheets, which is quite ideal for a place with such heavy rainfall. For these houses with sloping roofs, a trough like channel made of GI sheets may be fixed at the lower end of the sloping roof-tops for RW harvesting. These simple but very effective structures have been quite popular and been used since quite a long time in Imphal. As a matter of fact, there will be few people in Imphal who is not aware of this method of RW harvesting.

RW harvesting is very suitable option for Imphal on many counts namely (1) its average annual rainfall is around 1200 mm spread over 6-7 months as per meteorological data of Imphal obtained from Tulihal and ICAR Station. (2) there are already many houses with sloping GI corrugated sheet roofs[11] and addition of the above simple structure of RW harvesting will not involve much additional capital cost nor any specialized know-how for it (3) most of the residential houses are all small and owner-occupied houses and hence ideal to make RW harvesting arrangements according to the need of individual units and finally; (4) the relatively pollution free atmosphere.

The rivers and streams which are the present main sources of fresh water for w/s of Imphal are all very small and of limited volume. Because of their size and limited capacity these sources cannot be exploited beyond a certain point and hence we need to look for new sources to meet the increasing demand in future. Utilization of RW as a source in an effective way can go a long way to ease the pressure of future demand. From sustainability angle also, this option sounds very fine.

In most of the houses, the present storage arrangement for the RW harvested is quite small in capacity and hence only very limited quantity can be harvested and stored. The limited water so collected is used directly for all kinds of domestic purposes but unfortunately because of the small storage capacity, this harvested RW gets consumed within the rainy days and nothing is left for later non-rainy days. If the capacity of the storage is increased, then the water need for all domestic use for quite many days may be met from it. If some engineering mind is to put for upgrading[12] the existing RW harvesting structures and larger tanks or reservoirs are arranged to store the RW harvested, then this source of freshwater can serve Imphal very well. RW harvesting in Imphal is currently being done only at residential buildings and this needs to be taken up in offices/institutional or other public buildings as well. The advantages of RW harvesting for domestic and urban use includes savings in water costs, low installation cost, non-dependence on large infrastructural system, availability of extra water for emergency use and capability of preventing excess water from flowing into particular local ecosystems.

In many studies on water problems currently faced by cities such as Chennai, Kochi, Rajkot and other places, roof water and surface run-off harvesting have been suggested as the suitable remedies. In fact, some very successful and striking rainwater harvesting programmes[13] have already caught the imagination of a large section of people all over the world.

Another source of fresh water which has been and continues to be indispensable to the life of the people of Imphal is the ponds or the Pukhris as locally known. These traditional water harvesting structures have proved to be very efficient in capturing and storing rainwater. In the face of inadequate and irregular water supply in most part of Imphal, the service being catered by the Pukhris in meeting the water needs of its citizens is tremendous.

Though the private ponds have almost completely disappeared from the Imphal Municipal area and some of its fringes, community ponds still have a very strong presence there. In fact, the need of the community ponds (on the face of the ever-worsening w/s situation) seems to have grown and a large section of Imphalites depends on it for their day to day existence. Though presently things are working fine for the community ponds but organization with formal structure and inbuilt incentive may be needed to be developed in the future to take care of the community ponds for its sustainability.

Going beyond the fresh water sources, another source of water which is becoming very common and great attention is being paid in many cities and some other water scarce regions is the possibility of additional water being made available from treatment and reuse of sewage water and effluents from industry. This option is of very little significance in the present situation of Imphal.

Demand Management Strategies

Demand management addresses the ways and various methods available to promote more desirable levels and patterns of use. Water conservation (use reduction) measures and water pricing policies are two instruments of water demand management. In the context of water demand for domestic use, popularizing and installation of toilet of smaller model can save lots of water as the water consumption in standard model toilets is unnecessarily very high[14]. Water education is very essential for making demand reduction. Only when the scarce value of water is drilled into the mind, people would become conscious of saving water and hence readily take up works of the nature of detecting and repairing leaks, economizing when watering plants and flowers, washing clothes and cars etc and sanitation purposes like bathing and washing floors etc.

One can use the pricing policy as well. Though it may not have a great impact on revenue, the act of linking the water price to the amount of water used[15] has the desirable effect of reduction in cases of profligate consumption. Pricing when being used for demand management, one should take care of the social concerns by making a lower slab of water use for which the rate is affordable by the people of lower income or those with low capacity of payment and the progressive rate can be made very steep in accordance with the quantity of water use, at the upper end[16].

Finally, in what ever way we try to solve the water problem (i.e. excess of demand over supply or the quality of available water), whether it is from the supply side or the demand side or a combination of the two, we have to arrive at the solution without any compromise on quality of life and health aspect of the people of today and tomorrow.

Conclusion

We have discussed at length the various sources of fresh water available to the people of Imphal, which could be tapped or being tapped for enhancement in water availability. The two broad ways for enhancement in water availability which comes implicitly in the paper are (i) strengthening the public water supply system in terms of its coverage, improvement in its performance (adequacy and reliability factors); (ii) making better and more effective utilization of the other options like roof water harvesting, the ponds, river and canals.

We had seen the dismal scenario in the coverage and the revenue collection front of the public water supply system. Huge fund will be required if the first option is to be taken up even in a partial and phase manner. As the coffer of the state government is almost always empty these days without much hope of improvement in near future, one need to seriously study and explore the various possible forms of public/private partnerships (PPP) for Imphal water sector. As it was emphasized in second world water forum, the notion of PPP is quite different than privatization of water rights. We should also try to generate fund from within the department. This should include improvement in revenue collection as well as cut down on its expenditure.

There is need to tighten up the tariff collection activities and also to evolve a more effective and successful mechanism for the above. In our drive to collect more revenue, one should not forget the responsibility of a minimum provision for drinking and sanitation purposes. In fact, the state has a constitutional obligation towards its citizens for provision of safe drinking water. Beyond the basic requirement of water for life and health water could be looked up as an economic good and pricing and allocation done accordingly. Help of local clubs and organizations can be taken to tackle the problem of illegal connections, non payment of water charges and pilferage of water.

As things stand today, the residents of Imphal will have to wait for quite a long time before an effective and reliable water supply comes up (if ever it happens). Hence the need and importance of the other options to meet the deficit water supply is quite evident. As mentioned earlier roof water harvesting is very good and viable option to meet a substantial part of the domestic water requirement. Regarding the rivers and streams which are flowing in and around Imphal which have been intensively used for various w/s schemes as well as directly by the riparian population, care should be taken not to pollute them. The institution of community ponds has to be kept alive and strengthened. Finally, we must remember that these fresh water bodies besides being sources of water for direct consumption, also perform many ecological and environmental functions which according to some is essential for the continual existence of the varied life forms including human beings (Tilman and Downing, 1994; Naeem et al., 1994; Gowdy, 1997; Randall, 1994).

The author would like to end by emphasizing the need for a clear distinction between water as a social good to that of it being an economic good. The requirement of water as a basic and critical input to human life clearly falls within the social arena of water. The government should not shy away from its responsibility in this arena of water, whatever are the arguments in favor of greater role of private sector in the overall water sector.

NOTES

1. There are countries like Argentina and Brazil from the developing world and Germany, France, Japan and UK of the developed world where water usage in domestic sector is of quite high order, ranging from 14-20% of the total water usage.

2. In fact, rainfall recorded at IFCD, Imphal shows the number of years with annual rainfall less than 1000mm for the period 1972-91 as 4 whereas the corresponding figure in the last 11 years have alarmingly shot up to 8. Though the average annual figure for the last decade remains around 1000mm, the above observation is worth noting in any discussion of water availability in Imphal.

3. Unregistered population here roughly refers to those temporarily residing in Imphal but not included in the census and also those residing outside Imphal but engaged in economic activities based in Imphal. Basically, it is the average number of persons, not included in Imphal population as per census but who spend a good part of their day time (and for some even night time) in Imphal.

4. The leakage loss for Delhi water supply system is reported to be 40% though the Delhi Jal Board puts it at 20% (Everything about Water, March-April 2001, N. Delhi, pp. 27).

5. Average annual rainfall recorded in Kangpokpi (in Senapati district) for the decades 1982-1991 and 1992-2001 were 1417.5 mm and 2090.5 mm respectively whereas the corresponding figure for Litan (in Ukhrul district) were 1541.5 mm and 1190.7 mm. The catchment areas of rivers and streams flowing in Imphal valley fall in these districts.

6. The water quality of the rivers and streams of the valley being used for water supply and also those of community ponds are found to be of high order. When we compared the water quality of Imphal River at

two points along its course in the city, the water quality seems to help slightly deteriorated though not in the alarming scale. The two points of reference are Koirengei (a northern point of the city) and Mahabali (a central point in the city) of Imphal River. Care should be taken to minimize the polluting activities along the city stretch of the river.

7. The total capacity installed under RWSS is 9.32 MLD @ 40 lpcd. That means roughly about 1, 8000 people will be covered. Going by the houses per capita in non-municipal area of Imphal, the above figure translates to about 18680 houses.

8. We have the cases of Andhra Pradesh where people in a democratic setup have accepted the 300% hike in irrigation charges for a improved system. Also, a capacity 21 study by Nagpur based National Environmental Engineering Research Institute found that people of Delhi are willing to pay for clean water.

9. It was conveyed through advertisements brought out by PHED in many of the prominent local dailies for 20 to 25 days during January-March, 2003.

10. Average cost of the people connected to supply system were found to be Rs. 4-5 per cu.m while the poor using public taps, it was Rs. 40 per cu.m (time was valued at Rs. 3.50 per hr or 80 percent of the minimum wage rate.

11. For the Manipur state, 58.9% of the total households are found to be having G.I., metal or asbestos sheets in their roof. The figure for urban areas is 72% (census of India 2001). The corresponding figures for Imphal are expected to slightly higher than the state figures.

12. Upgradation should also take care of the aesthetic aspect of the structure. For many in urban areas, it might be this aspect which is acting as a hurdle in the installation of these structures in their houses. Also, the fact that existing system is so simple and straight forward might not please or appeal to the urban mindset. Clearly, the people need to be convinced about the philosophy behind RW harvesting.

13. The story of how Tarun Bharat Sangh and the people of Alwar in Rajasthan under the guidance of Rajendra Singh took to rainwater harvesting and made a river flow again; similar stories repeated in rainwater harvesting programs taken up in areas of MP as well. The objective behind these programs is harvesting monsoon however meager.

14. We have the Mexico City case wherein replacement of 350,000 toilets with smaller 6l models resulted in saving enough water to meet the household needs of 250,000 additional residents.

15. In Beijing water price is linked to the amount of water used. Water consumption quotas and fines for excess use are set. In Bogor, Indonesia a 30% hike in water fees resulted in a 29% decrease in water consumption. In Waterloo, Canada also water use per capita declined by nearly 10% due to high water prices, distribution of water savings devices and public education.

16. The private sector should not blindly be looked upon as the only solution to reduce water-use wastage. One could explore the option of empowering the community to impose a price on water. Outright privatization of water, in all probability will lead to violation of the basic right of access to water for the majority poor and weaker sections. And this fear is not unfounded.

REFERENCES

Annual Administration Reports, 1999-2000 and 2000-01, Government of Manipur, PHED.

Clean Water, Environmental governance-1, Indira Gandhi Institute of Development Research, Mumbai.

Coase, Ronald (1969), The Problem of Social Cost, in Stavins, Robert N. (ed.), *Economics of the Environment: selected readings*, fourth edition, W.W. Norton & Company, New York, pp. 23-49.

Everything about water, March-April 2001, N. Delhi, pp. 27.

Gowdy, John. M (1997), The value of Biodiversity: Markets, Society and Ecosystems, *Land Economics* 73(1), pp. 25-41.

Hardin. Garett, (1968), The Tragedy of the Commons, in Stavins, Robert N. (ed.), *Economics of the Environment: selected readings*, fourth edition, W.W. Norton and Co., New York, pp. 9-22.

Loucks, Daniel P. and Gladwell, John S. (eds.) (1999), *Sustainability Criteria for Water Resource System,* Cambridge University Press, U.K.

Manipur Gazette No. 198 (A), (1994), Government of Manipur, Secretariat, MAHUD Department.

Masters, Gilbert M. (1998), *Introduction to Environmental Engineering & Science.* Prentice Hall of India Pvt. Ltd., New Delhi.

Murty, M.N., James, A.J. and Misra, Smita (1999), *Economics of Water Population*, Oxford University Press, New Delhi.

Randall, Alan (1994), The value of Biodiversity, *Ambio* 20(2), pp. 64-68.

Singh, Ksh. Jhaljit (2003), The water Supply in Imphal city and its Suburbs: Its economics and environmental Implications, in Chopra, K., C.H.Hanumantha Rao and Ramprasad Sengupta (ed), *Water: Resources, Sustainable Livelihoods and Eco-System Services*, Concept Publishing Company, New Delhi.

Wade, Robert (1987), The Management of CPR: Collective Action as an Alternative to privatization or State Regulation, *Cambridge Journal of Economics,* vol II, pp. 95-106.

14

Border Trade at Moreh-Tamu Sector: Boon or Bane for Manipur?

N. Bhupendro Singh

Introduction

Looking into the prevalent scenario in the North East India, its physical realities fueled by the changing contour of world economies and emergence of new regional order, a strong argument has been put forth for opening the North Eastern frontier of India. It has been argued that a closer national integration with the Indian Union can be fostered only when the region has been freed from the shackles of economic backwardness and geographical isolation. The opening of North Eastern frontier would also provide an opportunity to integrate the region's economy with that of neighbouring countries thereby facilitating in the revival of the regional economy. It would be an opportunity for the mainland industrial units to explore the booming South Asian market, and also to counter the Chinese dominance in the region. Such exercises would gain centrality and visibility of the region. With these objectives the 'Look East Policy' was initiated by the Government of India (GOI) in 1991. As a part of the policy, trade agreement was signed between the Governments of India and Myanmar on 21 January 1994 which became operational on 12 April 1995 in the Moreh-Tamu sector based on the barter trade mechanism of 22 items[1], mostly agricultural or primary commodities produced in the two trading countries.

The opening of border trade at Moreh-Tamu sector is expected to play a significant role in building up the economy of Manipur in particular and North East in general. It, however, cannot be hailed as an unmixed boon for the state. While a wide range of goods transported through this route are being displayed in every market place for the consumers to choose, there is hardly any sign of improvement in the local manufacturing sector for export. Instead the state has become a transit corridor for all sorts of contraband items such as drugs and narcotics, human trafficking, money launderings, gun running, smuggling, etc which have a lot of negative social impacts. This has generated two of the most pertinent questions; firstly, will the state remain as a mere transit corridor of the goods of mainland India, market for the products of Myanmar and other third countries and route for negative items? If so, there may not be any significant improvement in the economy of the state and region as a whole in the near future rather being a bane to the society. Secondly, is the state actually striving to strengthen its resources-industry linkage in which it has comparative advantage so as to boost trade and economy?

The present study is an attempt to assess the twelve years experience of border trade opening and its implications on the economy of Manipur. The study would also examine the prospects of optimizing the gain from trade opening. The study has been organized into four sections including introduction. Section two discusses the volume and composition of border trade. In Section three an assessment of the economy of Manipur in the post trade opening has been made. Suggestions to optimize the positive trade benefits have been presented in section four.

Volume and Composition of Trade

Historically, there has been exchange of goods informally between the local populations in the border areas of the two countries. The formalization of trade between the two countries has not been able to contain the informal exchange of goods being followed traditionally rather it resulted into an increase in informal trade. Thus, an analysis on the volume and composition of trade flow needs to be examined for both formal and informal trade.

Formal Trade

The trend of the volume of border trade at Moreh-Tamu sector vis-à-vis Indo-Myanmar international trade is given in appendix. Following the trade agreement between the two countries there has been a sudden increase in the formal trade across the Moreh-Tamu sector in the initial three years. The volume of trade increased from Rs. 15.84 crore in 1995-96 to Rs. 57.53 crores in 1997-98. It, then, declined sharply in the subsequent four years only to recover again in the following years. In most of the years the proportion of export in the total volume of trade is more than the proportion of import from Myanmar. Contrarily, the volume of Indo-Myanmar international trade has increased from Rs. 785.9 crore in 1996-97 to Rs. 4174.69 crore in 2006-07 at an annual compound growth rate of 17.69% (with the growth rate of 17.17% in export and 17.80% in import). Over the years the share of India's export in total volume of trade varies from 14 to 22% only.

The composition of trade basket is much more diversified in the initial years of trade opening than in the later years. In the initial years, wheat flour, seeds, soyabari nuggets, rose powder and cumin seeds were the major export items while betel nuts, chick peas, turmeric, mustard seeds and red kidney beans were the major import items. In the later part, the number of items traded both in exports and imports have reduced drastically. The major exports items have also shifted to buffalo appall, soyabari nuggets, wheat flour and cumin seeds while betel nuts have remained as the major import item. Almost all the items exported are the products which are transported from mainland. There is no locally manufactured item in the export basket.

The imposition of restriction by Myanmar authorities that exports from India should precede imports from Myanmar (w. e. f. 26th November 1997) has not hampered the flow of goods at the Moreh-

Tamu sector. The decline in the formal trade at Moreh-Tamu sector may be attributed to the rigidities in the existing trade agreements such as limited size of the trade basket, barter trade mechanism, recording of trade transaction in hard currencies and over valuation of Myanmarese currency (Kyat) in the official exchange rates and more importantly the attitude and approach of the GOI towards this region and beyond.

It can be attributed partially to the ever deteriorating law and order situation in the state in particularly and Northeast in general, lack of proper infrastructure, poor border management, imposition of various unauthorized taxes (both by government's machineries and numerous insurgent groups operating in Manipur and adjoining states) leading to high transportation cost and risk involved with the life of the trader. All these factors have led to the growth of informal trade, a classic case of bad trade driving out good trade.

Informal Trade

The volume of informal trade, as the name suggests itself and composition of these trade flows are difficult to accurately gauge. An impressionistic assessment on the varieties of goods available in Imphal market and the volume and items seized by the custom authorities reveal that the volume of informal trade is manifolds more than the volume of formal trade. Singh, (2009a) attempted to estimate the volume of informal trade during 2000-01 to 2004-05.[2] According to his estimate the volume of informal trade flow increased by Rs. 2,385 lakh i.e. from Rs. 16,587 lakh in 2000-01 to Rs. 18,972 lakh in 2004-05. If the value of smuggled items and drugs and narcotics flowing across the border is added then the volume of informal trade is likely to be much larger than the one estimated.

The main export items include food drinks, medicine, chemical and fertilizer, motor bike, bicycle and its parts, CI sheet, etc. These items are manufactured in mainland India. The major negative items crossing the border are animal parts and ephedrine - precursor chemical used in manufacturing Amphetamine Type Stimulants (ATS) drugs.

Other than vegetables the local manufactured products cannot find a place in the export basket which implies a weak resource base industry in the state.

The composition of import basket is increasingly diversified after the formal opening of border trade. Many products manufactured in third countries such as China, Taiwan, Thailand, South Korea, etc. available in the state are also imported through Myanmar. The main import items are textiles and readymade garments, foot wear, generator, inverter, battery, emergency lamp, fan, TV, radio, tape recorder, DVD player, camera, crockeries, plastic products, food and beverages, cosmetic and toiletry, precious stones, candle, detergent, wooden furniture, etc. Further, many negative items such as drugs and narcotics, pornographic CDs, counterfeit currency, small arms, etc. are also smuggled into the state. While the quantum of the flow of negative items is difficult to measure, its impact is increasingly being felt in the state. It distorts the social fabrics as discussed in the subsequent section.

Gains from Border Trade

Conceptually and practically trade opening is associated with specialization in production activities, better economic performance, higher employment, higher income and diversification of consumption basket. The trade opening should have direct bearing on transport storage and communication, trade, hotels and restaurants, banking and insurance, construction and manufacturing sectors of the state NSDP. The higher growth rate of income originating in different sectors of the state economy would ultimately have positive impact on NSDP and hence on PCI of the state. The annual compound growth rate of income originating in different sector of the state, NSDP and PCI during 1995-2004 is shown in Table 1.

Table 1

Sectoral compound growth rate of NSDP during 1995-2004

Sector	*b*	$\overline{R}^2$	*c*	*Growth Rate*	*Remark*
Agriculture	0.030811	0.9002	-0.00273	3.13	Decelerating
	(9.0666)*		(-2.7326)**		
Fishing	0.050317	0.7790	-0.008693		
	(5.3103)*		(-3.7985)*	5.16	Decelerating
Manufacturing	0.080615	0.9552	-0.000108	8.40	Construction
	(13.8896)*		(-0.0441)		
	0.096517	0.8435	0.00787	10.13	
	(7.0369)*		(1.5828)		
Transport,	0.101579	0.9899	0.001756	10.69	
Storage &	(29.6783)*		(1.3667)		
Communication					
Trade, Hotels	0.030942	0.5762	-0.006954	3.14	Decelerating
and Restaurants	(3.6382)*		(-2.837)**		
Banking &	0.117839	0.9143	0.002796	12.51	
Insurance	(9.8504)*		(0.5656)		
Real Estate	0.051677	0.9967	0.000691	5.30	
	(52.4169)*		(2.1274)**		Accelerating
Public	0.055641	0.8146	-0.004351	5.72	
Administration	(6.3679)*		(1.3167)		
Other Services	0.05826	0.8170	-0.003843	6.00	
	(6.4177)*		(-1.0823)		
NSDP	0.056897	0.9687	-0.002116	5.85	
	(16.717)*		(-1.7699)		
PCI	0.03584	0.9271	-0.001995	3.65	
	(10.744)*		(1.6745)		

Note: 1. * & ** implics significance at 1% & 5% respectively.

2.The annual compound growth rate is given by (e^{b-1}) 100 where b is estimated by using log linear model, log Y = a + bT and to examine the pattern of growth, i.e. accelerating or decelerating growth rate log linear model, log Y = a + bT + cT^2 is used.

In the post trade opening period banking and insurance, transport, storage and communication, construction and manufacturing sector have grown at an annual compound growth rate of 12.51%, 10.69%, 10.13% and 8.40% respectively. The sectoral contribution of these sectors has also increased, more particularly construction sector whose share has increased from about 10% of the NSDP in 1995 to about 16% in 2004. Unfortunately, even at this pace of growth there is hardly any sign of improvement in physical infrastructure particularly roads whose conditions are worsening day by day. The conditions of all the national and state highways are in pathetic condition and not surprisingly the state is placed at the lowest rung in the state-wise infrastructure index. Then, the question is, where have all the growth gone?

The growth rate achieved by manufacturing sector is quite impressive but it is mainly due to the higher growth rate of unregistered component which grows at the rate of 8.62% per annum while registered component grows at an accelerating rate of 1.94% per annum. There is a marginal improvement in the NSDP share of manufacturing sector from 7.5% in 1995 to 8.9% in 2004. Neither the border trade nor the Industrial Policy of 1996[3] could attract adequate private investments to foster the local manufacturing units so as to provide necessary growth impetus to the economy of Manipur. Further, the growth rate of agriculture sector which is supposed to be the main source of locally manufactured exportable item is not quite impressive. It grows at the decelerating rate of 3.13% per annum while its NSDP share declined from 30% in 1995 to 23% in 2004. Similarly, trade, hotels and restaurants sector grows at 3.14% per annum but at the decelerating rate. The NSDP share of this sector has also declined from 11% in 1995 to 9% in 2004. The low growth rate of this sector may be attributed to weak resource base industry and predominance of informal trade over formal trade. Without locally manufactured products in the export basket, positive benefits from trade are unlikely to be optimized and the state would remain a mere transit corridor of the mainland products and market for the imported products from Myanmar and other third countries.

The high growth rate of banking and insurance may be partly due to the state government's policy to disburse the employees' salaries through bank accounts, development of internet banking facility which has become a much cheaper and faster mode of money transaction and remission, implementation of self employment generation programme such as special employment generation programme (SEGP) which has a positive impact on real estate sector and increase in insecurity of life due to lawlessness in the state. Perhaps part of the explanation goes to the formal opening of border trade. In other words, border trade may have facilitated the growth of personal income, most likely from the income generated out of negative activities, and hence growth of wealth and capital assets in the state.

The agriculture sector continues to be the major source of livelihood of the people of Manipur. Though the share of agriculture in NSDP has declined sharply, the number of population attached to this sector continued to be high. Over 67% of population is still dependent on this sector. Table 2 shows the number of persons employed in trade, hotels and restaurants and manufacturing sector.

In the urban areas, among the usually employed persons (PS+SS), the percentage of persons (male and female) employed in trade, hotels and restaurants have increased consistently. While in the rural areas the same have gone down in the initial years of trade opening only to recover in the subsequent years/round. Similarly, the percentage of persons employed in manufacturing sector also declined initially both in urban and rural areas. Traditionally small business and unregistered manufacturing units, both in rural and urban areas, are mainly dominated by female employees. Further, the number of persons employed in urban area is much higher than the rural area. It implies that the formal opening of border trade has failed to attract more employment in manufacturing and trade, hotels and restaurants from rural population. In the rural areas agriculture continued to be the main sources livelihood. Though the percentage of usually working persons employed in agriculture sector have reduced from 75 percent in 1999-00 to 69 percent in 2004-05 but is still higher than 1993-94 figures of 64 percent. One plausible reason for low rate of employment

Table 2

Percentage of working population employed in the principal and subsidiary status (PS+SS) taken together

Round/Year	*Trade, Hotels & Restaurants*						*Manufacturing*					
	Rural			*Urban*			*Rural*			*Urban*		
	M	*F*	*P*	*M*	*F*	*P*	*M*	*F*	*P*	*M*	*F*	*P*
50th Round												
(1993-94)	3.8	5.6	4.5	10.8	19.5	13.7	3.7	26.2	12.3	4.4	34.2	14.4
55th Round												
(1999-00)	2.7	5.8	3.7	16.4	27.4	19.9	2.2	18.6	7.4	5.5	21.5	10.5
61st Round												
(2004-05)	5.3	8.7	6.6	17.0	26.1	20.0	3.1	17.2	8.6	7.8	29.0	14.8

Note: M = Males, F = Females, P = Persons
Source : NSSO, 50th, 55th and 61st Round.

generation may be due to predominance of informal trade in which many people might have opted these occupations as a part-time job. Further, reduction in profit margin due to heavy unauthorized tax collection from the traders and risk involved with the present law and order situation and ever dilapidating road conditions have made these two sectors less attractive venture.

Table 3
Per capita monthly consumption expenditure (Rs.) in the rural and urban areas of Manipur

Item	*1993-94*		*1999-00*		*2004*	
	Rural	*Urban*	*Rural*	*Urban*	*Rural*	*Urban*
Food	202.14 (67.48)	203.94 (63.82)	339.43 (63.12)	399.18 (56.40)	328.82 (50.14)	375.50 (47.13)
Non-Food	97.43 (32.52)	115.61 (36.18)	198.36 (36.88)	308.59 (43.60)	327.04 (49.86)	421.30 (52.87)
Total	299.57 (100)	319.55 (100)	537.80 (100)	707.77 (100)	655.86 (100)	796.80 (100)

Source: NSSO, 50th, 55th and 60th Rounds.

The average per capita monthly consumption expenditure on food and non-food items increased at a faster rate in the initial years of trade opening. However, during 1999 to 2004 the average consumption expenditure on food items declined in absolute term both in rural and urban areas. The contraction in the per capita monthly consumption expenditure on food items calls for a thorough investigation as the same is not only higher but also growing at the national level. Contrarily, the consumption expenditure on non-food items increased consistently much faster than the food items. In 2004 non-food items consists of 50% and 53% of the total per capita monthly consumption expenditure in rural and urban areas respectively. The faster increase in per capita consumption expenditure on non food items may be attributed to increase in consumer satisfaction in the form of cheaper price, easy handling, style and packaging of the wide range of imported products from Myanmar and other third countries. Thus, in the post trade opening period a significant change can be observed only in the per capita consumption expenditure on non food items. But the most disturbing fact is the increase in consumption expenditure on pan, tobacco and intoxicant items which will have negative impact on the society.

With varieties of goods imported from Myanmar and other third countries available in every market place, the consumption baskets of many families of the state are becoming more diverse. Thus, opening of border trade has led to an increase in consumer's satisfaction, generated more employment and income. It, however, would be wrong to hail the opening of border trade as a boon for the state.

Despite the positive benefits of opening of the Moreh-Tamu sector the negative effects generated by the many negative items crossing the border have increasingly destabilized the society. The predominance of informal trade across the long porous border has opened the floodgates of drugs and narcotics - opium, heroin and Amphetamine Type Stimulants (ATS) - to the state. The Moreh-Tamu sector has become safe corridor for transportation and exportation of these drugs. The frequent seizures of these items in the state substantiate this. It has also been reported that mini heroin factories have started coming up near Tamu and Namphalong close to Manipur border and area under poppy cultivation is rising in the countryside of Arunachal Pradesh, Nagaland and Manipur. Booming drug trade and rise in domestic cultivation of opium have led to sharp increase in the number of intravenous drug users (IDU) in the state. According to Altsean-Burma (2004), 30% of intravenous drug users in India are located in the Northeast which accounts only 3% of the country's total population. The number of IDUs in Manipur alone has increased from 9,314 in 1999-00 to 37,996 in 2006-07. With a significant portion stemming from drug users (over 40%), the number of HIV infected persons has sharply increased from 1,505 in 1999 to 29,147 by March 2008.[4] The HIV/AIDS epidemic has become a major political and social challenge in the state.

Along with drug trade other negative activities such as smuggling, human trafficking, gun running, and money laundering, etc. have also increased. There is an escalation in the activities of criminals masquerading as insurgents. Abduction, kidnapping, extortion, killing, bandh, strike and curfew have become the order of the day. Such activities perpetuate a climate of disorder, absence of the rule of law and corruption which has destabilized the society and dislocated the fabric of social harmony. These, along with poor governance have made the state an unfavourable destination for investment and have stifled entrepreneurship. The size of the positive benefits from trade depends upon the social, political and economic condition of the trading state/country. At present, the social cost of opening border trade seems to be more visible than the economic gain. In short, border trade at Moreh-Tamu sector is economically benign but socially malign.

Suggestions

The formal trade at Moreh-Tamu sector has almost been driven out by informal trade due to over-regulation, limited size of trade basket, overvaluation of Myanmarese currency in the official exchange rate coupled with the absence of rule of law and lack of proper infrastructure in the state. While import basket is increasingly diversified, the local manufactured products are hard to find in the export basket.

The optimization of positive benefits and minimization of negative gains require restriction on the flow of negative items vis-à-vis removing the maladies of formal trade. An enabling environment for formal trade to develop requires the rule of law, adequate infrastructure, efficient management of borderland, liberal trade law and more items in the trading basket. The quality of governance in the state needs a drastic improvement.

It is evident that growth in most of the fast growing countries in the recent time is export led. Without the local manufactured products in the export basket, more trade would not serve much of the objective. The state needs to strengthen its resource base industries and to encourage private investment. Though the resources available in the state are more or less comparable with that of the neighbouring countries, it would be worthwhile to strengthen the resource base industries in the state. Concurrently, the mainland export industries should be encouraged to open its units in the state.

Considering the gravity of the problems affecting the state and the region as a whole, the central government should be more responsive to the policy initiative. Justice delayed is justice denied. Rather than shrinking behind the defensive siege mentality, the outlook and approach of the central government towards this region and beyond need to change. The problem of insurgency must be resolved sooner than later. At the same time the region should be freed from all the archaic laws such as Protected Area Permit Act (PAP) and Armed Force Special Powers' Act (AFSPA) which are specially designed for the region in the name of protecting the identities of the inhabitance. With the speed of changes taking place in this era of globalization, slow pace of change restricts the positive trade benefits and compound the problems affecting the region.

NOTES

1. Recently 18 fresh items have been added to the existing tradable 22 items. The items include bicycle parts, life saving drugs, fertilizers, insecticides, cotton fabrics, stainless steel, utensils, menthol, agarbatti, cosmetics, leather footwear, paints and varnishes, sugar and salt, mosquito coil, bulb, X-ray and photo paper and imitated jewelleries.

2. For more detail on the methodology followed in the estimation of the volume of informal trade and composition of informal trade basket see Singh, Th. Priyokumar (2009) "Informal Trade along Myanmar-Manipur (India) Border: Magnitude and Composition of Trade Flows" in Singh, E. Bijoykumar and Ksh. Jhaljit Singh (eds). *Challenges of Economic Policy in Manipur: Essays in Honour of Prof. M. Iboton Singh*, Akansha Publishing House, New Delhi.

3. The benefits accrued from The New Industrial Policy of Manipur 2002 are yet to be reflected in the literature.

4. The growth of HIV/AIDS epidemic in the state is also fuelled by increasing number of female sex workers who plays a significant role in the flow of informal trade. It is learnt that these sex workers are often used as bargaining chips by the traders to custom and excise

official, policemen and transporters in the process of transportation of illegal items. Policemen, traders, transporters and migrant workers who have unprotected sex often carry the virus to their home.

REFERENCES

Altsean-Burma (2004): *A Failing Grade: Burma's Drug Eradication Efforts*, http://www.altsean.org/Docs/PDF%20Format/Special%20Reports/Failing%20Grade.pdf

Bezbaruah, M. P. (2007): "Indo-Myanmar Border Trade: The Stakes for North East India", *Dialogue*, vol. 9, no. 1, July-September, http://www.asthabharati.org/Dia_July07/m.p.%20bez%20.htm.

Devi, M. Binota (2009): "India's Look East Policy and Indo-Myanmar Border Trade", in Singh, E. Bijoykumar and Ksh. Jhaljit Singh (eds.), *Challenges of Economic Policy in Manipur: Essays in Honour of Prof. M. Iboton Singh*, Akansha Publishing House, New Delhi.

GOI (1997): *Transforming the North East: Tackling Backlogs in Basic Minimum Services and Infrastructure Needs*, High Level Commission Report to the Prime Minister, Planning Commission, http://planningcommission.nic.in/reports/genrep/ne_exe.pdf.

Grare, Frederic and Amitabh Mattoo (2003): *Beyond the Rhetoric: The Economics of India's Look East Policy*, Manohar Publishers & Distributors, New Delhi.

Khanna, Sushil (2005): *Economic Opportunities or Continuing Stagnation*, http://www.manipuronline.com/Economy/November2005/stagnationoropportuny18_1.htm

NSSO: *Employment and Unemployment Situation in India*, Various Rounds.

NSSO: *Household Consumption Expenditure in India,* Various Rounds.

Singh, Th. Priyokumar (2009a): "Informal Trade along Myanmar-Manipur (India) Border: Magnitude and Composition of Trade Flows", in Singh, E. Bijoykumar and Ksh. Jhaljit Singh (eds.), *Challenges of Economic Policy in Manipur: Essays in Honour of Prof. M. Iboton Singh*, Akansha Publishing House, New Delhi.

Singh, Th. Bharat (2009b): "Indo-Myanmar Border Trade: Issues and Opportunities", in Singh, E. Bijoykumar and Ksh. Jhaljit Singh (eds.),

Challenges of Economic Policy in Manipur: Essays in Honour of Prof. M. Iboton Singh, Akansha Publishing House, New Delhi.

UNDP (2005): *Trade and Development*, UN Millennium Project, Task Force on Trade, London.

Upadhyay, Archana (2006): "Terrorism in the North-East: Linkages and Implications", *Economic and Political Weekly*, Vol. 41, No. 48, pp. 4993-4999.

Verghese, B. G. (Undated): *Unfinished Business in the North East: Pointers Towards Restructuring, Reform, Reconciliation and Resurgence*, Seventh Kamal Kumari Memorial Lecture, http://www.freeindiamidia.com/economy/19_june_economy.htm

Yumnam, Amar (2007): "Indo-Myanmar Trade through Moreh: Status and Assessment" in Gurudas Das, et al (eds) *Indo-Myanmar Border Trade: Status, Problems and Potential*, Akansha Publishing House, New Delhi.

Appendix

Volume of Moreh-Tamu and Indo-Myanmar bilateral trade

(Rs. in lakh)

Year	*Moreh-Tamu Trade*			*Indo-Myanmar Trade*		
	Export	*Import*	*Total*	*Export*	*Import*	*Total*
1995-96	1,045	539	1,584	-	-	-
1996-97	3,171	1,518	4,688	16,046	62,904	78,590
1997-98	2,245	3,508	5,753	18,326	83,253	1,01,579
1998-99	506	374	880	12,672	73,101	85,773
1999-00	326	368	694	14,776	74,356	89,132
2000-01	529	19	549	24,081	83,004	1,07,085
2001-02	125	830	955	29,041	1,78,572	2,07,613
2002-03	367	1,215	1,582	36,332	1,62,629	1,98,961
2003-04	875	806	1,681	41,193	1,87,947	2,29,139
2004-05	564	501	1,065	50,860	1,82,383	2,33,243
2005-06	410	330	740	49,010	2,32,863	2,81,873
2006-07	6,213	178	6,391	63,375	3,54,095	4,17,469

Note: * Estimate for April-December

Source: Department of Industry, GOM and Department of Commerce, GOI.

15

Trade and Industrialization in Manipur: The Post-Liberalization Scenario

Th. Priyokumar Singh

Introduction

Trade and investment play a significant role in the process of transition from a predominantly agriculture-based backward region to an advanced industrialized region. However, global trade and investment pattern tend to benefit capital intensive industries that can capture markets across the border and disadvantage labour-intensive small enterprises. This kind of disadvantage is being faced by small enterprises in Manipur as employment intensive domestic products have been replaced by the import of similar products from outside the state made by using more capital intensive production methods. Trade liberalization formally or informally has preceded industrialization in the state even though the reverse would have been preferred. The emerging pattern of trade does not favour the state as far as transfer of knowledge, technology and financial resources from external sources are concerned and put the industrialization process in Manipur on a slow track. Moreover, free trade must be accompanied by complementary domestic policy reforms, without these its benefits may be greatly reduced (Dean, 2003).

This study is an attempt to examine any kind of linkage between the emerging pattern of trade and the industrial development in the state particularly in the post liberalization period. It is divided into five sections. Section II is an examination of the pattern of trade in Manipur. Section III gives a brief scenario of industrial sector in the state. The following section gives the pattern of linkage between trade and industrialization in the state while Section V concludes.

The Emerging Pattern of Trade in Manipur

Emerging pattern of trade in Manipur has been lopsided; the volume of imports has far exceeded the volume of exports. From essential item to luxury item the state is dependent on import and its exports have been negligible. Trade under consideration in this study includes inter-state trade, i.e. trade between Manipur and the rest of the country, and the Indo-Myanmar border trade via Manipur. Both formal and informal trades are considered.

Inter-state Trade

India is a big country in terms of size and population. There is diversity in the factor endowment of different regions or states as a result of which the magnitude of its inter-state and intra-state trade is high. Analyzing the role of such kind of trade activities in the economic development of Manipur will be worthwhile in better understanding of its growth pattern. In Manipur the increasing demand for goods cannot be met by its own production and, thus, all kinds of goods are imported from other parts of the country to meet day to day needs of the people. The emerging pattern of trade has intensified since 80's and more significantly in the post liberalization period as the period witnessed deteriorating productive base in the state. There has been large import of all kinds of goods from mainland India and Myanmar accompanied with negligible volume of export to other states. During 80's the main items of export were maize, dalchini, ginger, chilly, cabbage, fruits, bull and buffalo, etc. for which data are available at Market Intelligence Department, Govt. of Manipur. Data of export in 90's are not properly available and one of the reasons given by the said department for not maintaining data from the middle of 90's is due to irregularities of export flow and drastic decline in its volume. On the other hand, import data are available which revealed a manifold increase in the import volume as well as the number of items. Volume of inflow and outflow of goods of Manipur in some particular years can be observed from Tables 1 and Table 2.

Table 1

Volume of some goods exported by Manipur to other states (1990-94)

Items	*1990*	*1991*	*1992*	*1993 (Up to March)*	*1994 (Up to May)*
Maize	277.20	2654.40	4250.40	1040.00	2220.00
Dalchini	3477.00	5778.00	7577.40	1756.00	14218.00
Cauliflower	790.40	3134.40	5010.40	875.00	1739.00
Cabbage	2248.80	1591.20	4031.20	2808.00	3732.00
Ginger	3030.50	13267.00	3916.00	4519.00	20847.00
Other Veg. items	2071.00	5083.00	10912.00	6341.00	N
Chilly	662.80	696.00	2400.00	480.00	1240.00
Bull	293	2121	2016	324	N
Buffalo	102	574	478	88	N

Source: Export-Import File, Market Intelligence Department, Imphal.
Note: 1) Bull & Buffalo are in numbers, and the rest are in quintals.
2) N- Data not available.

Table 2

Volume of inflow and outflow of taxable goods of Manipur from and to other States (1999-2002)

Year	*Inflow (Rs.)*	**Outflow (Rs.)*	*Total (Rs.)*
1999-00	196,54,98,204	50,60,904	196,95,59,108
2000-01	291,84,14,339	15,91,16,415	307,75,30,754
2001-02	257,76,28,283	10,44,74,057	268,21,02,340

Source: Singh, (2002)
* Most of the goods are those coming from Myanmar via Moreh under the border trade transactions.

Indo-Myanmar Border Trade via Manipur: Formal Border Trade

The much hype Indo-Myanmar border trade was signed on 21st January 1994 and the trade has been formally opened on 12 April 1995. Moreh in Manipur and Tamu in Myanmar are two adjoining towns engaged in trading activities. The trend in its trade flow has fluctuated since then as observed in Table 3 and Figures 1 and 2 respectively. The main items of export have been wheat flour, cumin seed, soyabari, suman rose powder, aniseed, etc. and that of the imports have been betel nut, dry ginger, turmeric, pulses, beans, khangra (timber), etc.

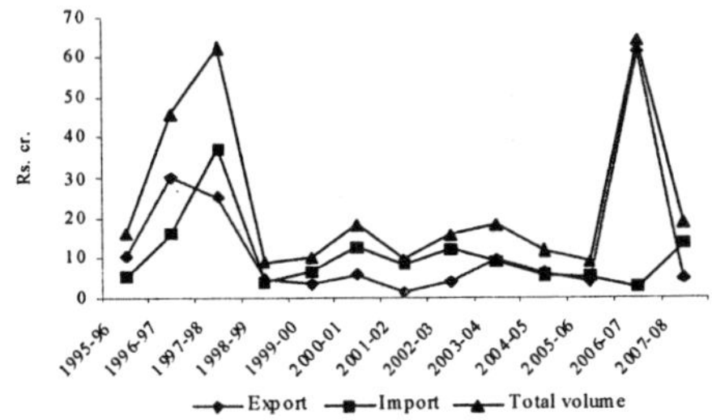

Fig. 1: Export, import and total value of formal border trade via Manipur (1995-96 to 2007-08)

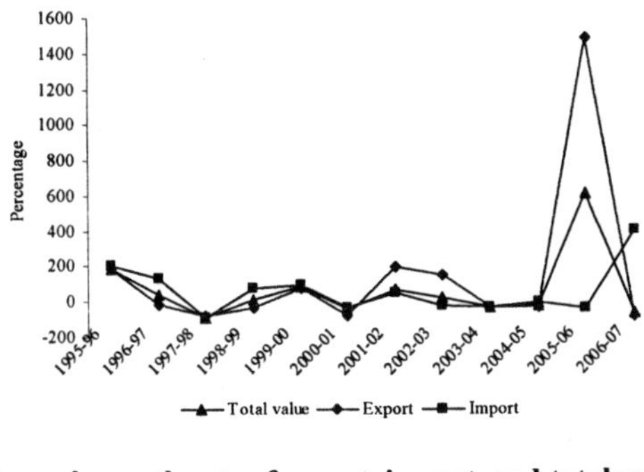

Fig. 2: Annual growth rate of export, import, and total value of Indo-Myanmar formal border trade via Manipur (1995-96 to 2007-08)

Table 3

Volume of Indo-Myanmar (formal) border trade via Manipur

Year	*Export* (*Rs.*)	*Import* (*Rs.*)	*Trade balance* (*Rs.*)	*Total volume* (*Rs.*)	*Annual Growth Rate (%)of*		
					Export	*Import*	*Total*
1995-96	104532984	53905477	50627507	158438461	-	-	-
1996-97	297896037	161712506	136183531	459608543	184.98	199.99	190.09
1997-98	251667199	371955314	-120288115	623622513	-15.52	130.01	35.69
1998-99	48842680	37456152	11386528	86298832	-80.59	-89.93	-86.16
1999-00	33106687	65277518	-32170831	99384205	-32.22	74.28	15.16
2000-01	56884434	124175222	-67290788	181059656	71.82	90.23	82.18
2001-02	12905545	81393813	-68488368	94299458	-77.31	-34.45	-48.36
2002-03	38487310	119092960	-80605650	157580270	198.22	46.32	67.11
2003-04	94582647	88591062	5991585	183173709	145.75	-25.61	16.24
2004-05	61270400	54818676	6451724	116089076	-35.22	-38.12	-36.62
2005-06	38666699	52115866	-13449167	90782565	-36.89	-4.93	-21.80
2006-07	612652642	26964981	585687661	639617623	1484.45	-48.26	604.56
2007-08	49374078	134673330	-85299252	184047408	-91.94	399.44	-71.23

Source: Department of Revenue, Office of the Assistant Commissioner, Customs Division: Imphal, Ministry of Finance, GOI.

Under this trade arrangement, the state mainly serves as a transit point as export items originate from other states. The people of the state have not been able to participate meaningfully in it either as a trader or as an exporter of locally produced goods in significant volumes. One of the important factors for lack of local participation is due to the unfavorable trading environment of formal trade prevailing in the state, viz. difficulties in securing import/export licenses, procedural delays at the customs, processing cost and inconveniences in the bank, difficulties in the movement of merchandise in bulk, etc. Besides, there is no any special provision favoring local people and products to enter into the trade arrangement.

The growth rate of this trade is analyzed for the whole period (1996-2008) and the two sub-periods i.e. 1996-2000 and 2000-2008 respectively. The estimated values show that there is insignificant growth in the whole and the two sub-periods. Further, the rate of change in the growth rate is also analyzed and the estimated values as shown in Table 4 which indicates that the growth rate neither accelerates nor decelerates in the whole and two sub-periods.

Table 4

Rate of change in the growth rate of Indo-Myanmar (Formal) border trade via Manipur

Periods	*Estimates of*			*Remark*
	a	*b*	*c*	
1995-2008	19.9348 (28.9453)	-0.3349 (-1.4803)	0.0227 (1.4419)+	C
1995-2000	17.8694 (10.2161)	1.5097 (1.1326)	-0.2950 (-1.3536)+	C
2000-2008	19.9148 (21.9261)	-0.3332 (-0.7989)	0.0239 (0.5869)+	C

Note: 1) The model is $\text{Log } Y = a + bt + ct^2$
2) + insignificant t-values, C - Constant Growth rate

Informal Border Trade

Informal trade has been taking place for a long time along the border at a large scale involving large number of local people. Here also local products are not exported to Myanmar on a regular basis, but a large volume of goods are imported from Myanmar. These goods are either produced in Myanmar or countries like China, Korea, Taiwan, Singapore, Thailand, etc. The wide range of commodities imported are electronic goods, clothing items, household materials, beverages & edible items, tools and machines, fuel, teak, precious stone, etc. The transacting environment of such trade is quite favorable in the state as there is easy entry into the activity, less risk of seizure of imported goods, quick realization of return, large market size of imported goods, etc. The volume of import under this form of trade has increased from Rs. 162 crores in 2000-01 to Rs. 186 crores in 2004-05 but that of export volume during the period is almost stagnant at around Rs 3.9 crores annually (Singh, 2002).

The Scenario in the Industrial Sector of the State

In the modern liberalized economy, economic development of a region largely depends on the growth of industrial sector and it is often remarked that without rapid industrialization economic development is almost impossible. However, the industrial scenario in the state is quite worrisome in regard to its growth and contribution towards the state domestic product. The manufacturing sector contributes hardly 9% of the NSDP in the year 2005-06. Most of the public sector undertakings that existed earlier in the state had already been closed down for a variety of reasons.

The situation brought the state to depend on small scale industries (SSIs) for expansion of its production and employment in the industrial sector. The growth of SSIs over the years has been increasing from 7392 units in 1991-92 to 9993 units in 2003-04, and employment generated increased from 36910 to 51842 in the period.

Table 5
No. of units, investment, employment and production of manufacturing industries in Manipur (1991-2006)

(Rs. in lakhs)

Year	*No. of Units*	*Total Invest*	*Total Emp. (persons)*	*Total Production*
1991-92	253	193.00	3523	870.00
1992-93	304	-	1490	-
1993-94	400	113.00	1280	980.00
1994-95	245	167.00	3040	646.00
1995-96	272	130.00	1680	743.00
1996-97	298	128.00	1618	685.00
1997-98	178	121.00	1004	549.00
1998-99	152	81.00	924	394.00
1999-00	175	166.00	1128	736.00
2000-01	191	160.00	975	504.00
2001-02	89	87.00	468	390.00
2002-03	105	142.00	638	545.00
2003-04	105	162.97	582	384.07
2004-05	158	201.22	1015	470.60
2005-06	113	188.80	862	593.26

Source: Statistical Abstract Manipur 2007, p-242.
Directorate of Economics & Statistics, Government of Manipur.

Industrial Sickness in Manipur

In the promotion of economic growth of a region, due consideration is always given in its industrial growth. But industrial growth will be realized in positive sense only when industrial sickness is timely checked. The reasons for industrial sickness are of a varied nature and may vary from region to region, size to size of units and product to product. Any decline in internal cash generation is possible due to drop in production, poor cash management, increase in cost of production, etc. The causes of industrial sickness can be broadly classified as endogenous or internal and exogenous or external factors.

Industrial sickness is a major concern in the industrialization process of the state. Many public sector undertakings have already closed down after becoming sick due to paucity of fund for maintenance. Some important endogenous factors causing sickness in SSIs in the state are poor quality of management, inadequacy of finance, lack of quality control, etc. The important exogenous factors are unfavorable investment climate, lack of skilled manpower, raw material shortage, inability to access and capture external market etc. However, degree of seriousness of the cause of sickness in the state is more with exogenous factors than the endogenous factors. In spite of its complex phenomenon, removing unfavorable investment climate is a priori in speeding our industrial growth. By attracting foreign investment like that of Thailand's initiative towards north eastern states of India under its Look West Policy launched in 1997, industrialization process in the state can be stimulated.

In fact, one of the factors leading to closing down of industrial unit in the state is its lack of competitive strength with the imported product not only in external market but also in home market. The industries that were closed down in the state in the pre liberalization period included iron, glass, paper, salt making, etc. In the post liberalization period particularly in the recent past, new type of industries that are being closed down include candle, soap, battery, polythene bag, shoe making etc. All these are the result of extra legal trade liberalization prevailing in the state.

Share of Trade and Manufacturing in NSDP

In the empirical analysis regarding contribution of trade and industry in NSDP, the real income originating in trade, hotel & restaurant together (due to non availability of separate data of trade) and manufacturing have been taken as proxies of trade and industry respectively. Since NSDP data at constant (1993-94) prices is being used for empirical analysis, the reference period for discussion begins from 1993 onwards. When the value of NSDP at (1993-94) prices increased from Rs. 114144 lacs in 1994 to Rs. 197936 lacs in 2005, that of trade and manufacturing increases from Rs. 13899 lacs to Rs. 18265 lacs and from Rs. 8437 lacs to Rs. 17571 lacs respectively. However, the percentage share of trade in NSDP decreased in the same period from 12.18% to 9.23%. But that of manufacturing increased from 7.39% to 8.88 % (Table 6).

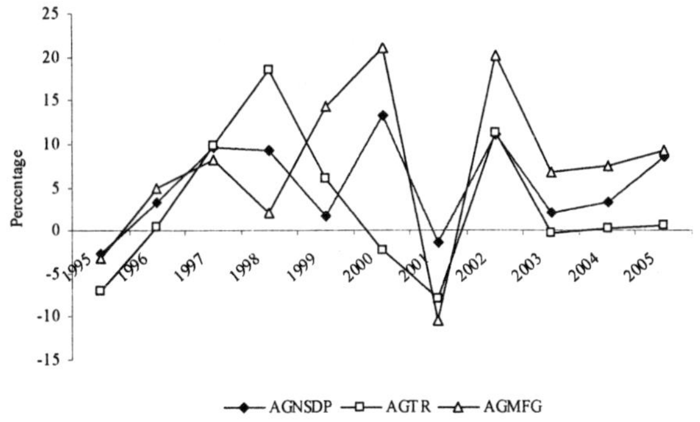

Figure 3:Annual Growth Rate of NSDP, Trade and Manufacturing (1994-2005) in Manipur at constant (1993-94) prices

The compound growth rate and pattern of growth rate of trade and manufacturing for the whole period i.e. 1994-2005 and the two sub periods i.e. (1994-2000) and (2000-2005) are estimated with regression analysis. The estimated values of respective sectors and periods are shown in Table 7. The growth rate of trade for the whole period is estimated as 3.39% and that of manufacturing is calculated as 7.61%. The rates of change of growth in both sectors are found neither accelerating nor decelerating in the whole and first sub-period. However, both sectors are found accelerating in the second sub-period i.e. (2000-2005). Regarding the two components of manufacturing only the growth of unregistered sector is found significant with 7.78% but the rate of change of growth of these two components are also found stagnant.

Table 6

Share of trade and manufacturing in NSDP of Manipur (1993-2005) at Constant (1993-94) prices

(Rs. lakhs)

Year	*NSDP*	*NSDP originating from*				*% Share of trade in NSDP*	*% Share of Mfg. in NSDP*	*Annual growth rate of NSDP*	*Annual growth rate of trade*	*Annual growth rate of Mfg.*
		TRADE	*MFG*	*R_MFG*	*UR_MFG*					
!994	114144	13899	8437	218	8219	12.18	7.39	-	-	-
1995	111030	12921	8164	240	7924	11.64	7.35	-2.73	-7.04	-3.24
1996	114737	12972	8570	331	8239	11.31	7.97	3.34	0.39	4.97
1997	125788	14245	9269	455	8814	11.32	7.97	9.63	9.81	8.16
1998	137364	16871	9448	209	9239	12.28	6.88	9.20	18.43	1.93
1999	139636	17878	10800	168	10632	12.81	7.73	1.65	5.97	14.31
2000	158117	17748	13061	92	12969	11.22	8.26	13.24	-2.32	20.94
2001	155850	16344	11683	128	11555	10.99	7.50	-1.43	-7.91	-10.55
2002	173015	18173	14030	193	13837	10.50	8.11	11.01	11.19	20.09
2003	176555	18125	14979	276	14703	10.27	8.48	2.05	-0.26	6.76
2004	182284	18162	16093	393	15700	9.97	8.83	3.24	0.20	7.44
2005	197936	18265	17571	416	17155	9.23	8.88	8.59	0.57	9.18

Source: CSO, GOI, Available online at http:// www.mospi.nic.inThe annual growth rate of real income of both trade and manufacturing are fluctuating throughout the whole period. The annual growth rate of trade is found highest i.e. 18.43% in 1998 and lowest i.e. -7.91% in 2001, and that of manufacturing is highest i.e. 20.99% in 2000 and lowest i.e.-10.55% in the next year 2001.This pattern of growth can be observed with the Figure 3.

Table 7

Growth rate and rate of change in the growth rate of trade and manufacturing in Manipur (1994-2005)

Periods	*Growth Rate*		*Pattern*	
	Trade	*Manufacturing*	*Trade*	*Manufacturing*
1994-2005	3.39	3.39	Constant	Constant
1994-2000	4.69	4.69	Constant	Constant
2000-2005	6.34	6.34	Acceleration	Acceleration

Note: 1) The model is Log Y = a+ bt for estimating growth rate and Log Y = a + bt + ct^2 for estimating rate of change in the growth rate.
2) The year 1994 represent the financial year 1993-94.

Pattern of Linkages between Trade and Industrialization in Manipur

Linkages between trade and industrialization can be examined in two ways. One is to examine the impact of manufacturing on trade while the other is the other way i.e. the impact of trade on manufacturing. These analyses are done empirically as follows.

Impact of manufacturing on Trade

The impact of manufacturing on trade is measured by elasticity. The elasticity measured after correction of autocorrelation using Newey West procedure turns out to be positive and statistically significant for manufacturing and its component unregistered manufacturing. This shows that manufacturing and its component unregistered manufacturing have significant impact on trade suggesting that trade in the post liberalization period is influenced by the growth of manufacturing particularly by the unregistered manufacturing. But, registered manufacturing does not have any significant impact on trade in this period.

Table 8
Impact of manufacturing on trade

Sectors	*Estimates of*		$\overline{R}$	*D-W*	*Remark*
	a	*b*			
MFG	6.4026 (11.1552)	0.3547 (5.8230)*	0.8709	1.5108	MA(2)
R-MFG	10.2088 (22.5309)	-0.0603 (-0.9895)	0.6929	1.5072	AR(1)
UR-MFG	6.4432 (11.9883)	0.3511 (6.1427)*	0.8819	1.5235	MA(2)

Note: 1) The Model is Log (Trade) = a + b Log(X),
where X represent MFG or R-MFG or UR-MFG as the case may imply.
2)The problem of Autocorrelation is corrected by Newey West Method.
3)* Significant at 1% level.

Impact of Trade on Manufacturing

In general, trade influences manufacturing sector in many ways, viz. adoption of new cost-saving technology, growth of certain manufacturing units, processing of raw materials which are not available in a region, economies of large-scale production etc. All these ultimately induce higher production level, income return and rapid industrialization. The impact measured by elasticity shows that trade does not have any significant impact on manufacturing and its components. It indicates that the growth in manufacturing in the post liberalization period is not influenced by the growth of trade in the state.

The above findings may substantiate the view that the emerging pattern of trade provides only a wide variety of goods for consumption at cheap prices which in fact discourage research and innovation activities in the state. The favorable transacting environment of informal border trade attracts the people in trading activities rather than influencing them toward its own production. Basic gains from trade that are being enjoyed from inter-state trade and border trade are not significantly associated with its industrialization.

Table 9
Impact of trade on manufacturing and its two components i.e. registered and unregistered manufacturing

Regressands	*Estimates of*		$\overline{R}$	*D-W*	*Remark*
	a	*b*			
MFG	3871.442 (9.2800)	0.5291 (1.4037)+	0.8901	2.5866	AR(1)
R-MFG	17.4370 (1.2212)	-1.2334 (-0.8382)+	0.2945	1.5298	MA(1)
UR-MFG	2.0820 (0.3579)	0.6001 (1.6256)+	0.8989	2.5956	AR(1)

Note: 1) The Model is Log (X) = a + b Log (Trade) where X represent MFG or R-MFG or UR-MFG.
2) + statistically insignificant.
3) The problem of autocorrelation is corrected by Newey West Method.

Conclusion

Discussions made so far indicate that there exists extra legal trade liberalization in the state and the pace of trade liberalization has preceded industrialization. The emerging pattern of trade does not favor the state as far as transfer of knowledge, technology and financial resources are concerned. In fact, it discourages industrialization and the state has become a captive market of outside products.

The problem of closure of many industries in the state under pressure from the emerging pattern of inter-state trade is compounded by the extra legal liberalization of border trade in the post liberalization period. A new strategy like the public - private approach is needed for rapid industrialization of the state so as to reduce its dependency on outside products. Besides, there is a genuine need for people to nurture such industries by buying the goods produced by them.

REFERENCES

Carr, M and M.A. Chen (2001): "Globalization and the informal economy: How global trade and investment impact on the working poor", *Women in Informal Employment, Globalizing & Organizing*. WIEGO, May.

Dean, Judith M. (2003): "Why trade matters for the poor", International Economist Research Division Office of Economics, US International trade Commission. Prepared for the 20th Anniversary Conference Association of Christian Economists, Jan. 5 -6, Washington D C.

Govt. of Manipur (2007): *Economic Survey of Manipur 2006-07*, Directorate of Economics and Statistics.

______________(2008): Statistical Abstract: Manipur 2007, Directorate of Economics and Statistics.

Meetei, L. Sanatomba (2007): "Impact of Industrial policies on industrialization in Manipur since 1982", Unpublished Ph.D. thesis, Manipur University.

Nayak, S.S. and R.N.Misra, R.N. (2006): "Sickness in Small-scale Industrial Units and Its Revivals", *Orissa Review*, Sept. - Oct. pp. 59-61.

Shekhar, V (2008): "Thailand's Investment in India's Northeast: Strategies, Potentials, and Risks, Research Papers Institute of Peace and Conflict Studies, New Delhi, April.

Singh, Kh. Tomba (2002): "Industrial Sickness in Manipur - A Case Study of Small Scale Industries", Unpublished Ph.D. thesis, Manipur University.

Singh, Th. Priyokumar (2002): "Inter-State and Regional Trade of Manipur (1950-2000)", Unpublished Ph.D. thesis, Manipur University.

______________(2008): "Informal trade along Myanmar-Manipur (India) border: Magnitude and Composition of Trade Flows" in Singh, E. Bijoykumar and Ksh. Jhaljit Singh (eds), *Challenges of Economic Policy in Manipur*, Akansha Publishing House, New Delhi.

Venables, A.J. (2000): "Cities and Trade: External trade and internal geography in developing economies", Background paper written for the World Development Report 1999.

16

Inter Sectoral Linkages and Implications on Growth: The Manipur Experience

L. Sanatomba Meetei

Introduction

The growth process of the Indian economy has witnessed a declining share of agriculture along with a gradual increase of industry and a sharp rise of services in its national income. The sixty year old growth process of the country since her independence reveals that agriculture and services have interchanged their positions in regard to their respective shares in the national income. However, agriculture still continues to be the mainstay of the Indian economy in terms of its high share in employment and livelihood creation. The (2001) Census report shows that 59.9% of the total workforce is being engaged in agriculture and allied services in the country.[1] Thus, it has been a matter of concern for various policy makers and economists on whether agriculture is still the engine of growth of the Indian economy or industry should be given more weightage than agriculture and how tertiary sector is being linked up with the two sectors. Given this perspective, the present paper is an attempt to analyse the inter sectoral linkages in the context of Manipur on one hand and how far the sectors have contributed to her growth process on the other. Given the hypothesis that Manipur is not an industrialised state on account of low share of industry in its state income as well as employment, it becomes imperative to study how the growth process of the state has undergone changes through the years. The period of study of the present paper is from 1994 to 2005.[2]

The paper is divided into five sections. Section two analyses the sectoral performance of the state. Section three is devoted to analyzing the impacts of different sectors and sub-sectors on real NSDP of the state. Section four deals with sectoral correlation analysis with a view to reflect the inter sectoral linkages in the state. Implications of the findings of the study for policy reforms and some conclusions drawn from the present study are given in the last section.

Sectoral Performance

We begin with an analysis of the shares of the various sectors of the economy of the state grouped into primary, secondary and tertiary sectors. The relative contributions of agriculture, industry[3] and services are also found out. The service sector has been further subdivided into four categories viz. transport, storage and communication; trade, hotels and restaurants; finance related services; and social and personal related services. The sectoral contributions to the state economy are presented in Table1. Figure 1 depicts the shares of three major sectors i.e. primary sector, secondary sector and tertiary sector in the real NSDP of the state while figure 2 shows the relative shares of the components of the tertiary sector.

It is evident from the Table 1 that during the last 11 years the structure of the economy of Manipur has undergone changes in favour of the secondary and tertiary sectors at the expense of the primary sector. Whereas the contribution of the primary sector to the real NSDP of the state has declined from around 38% in 1993-94 to 28% in 2004-05, the secondary sector and the tertiary sector have risen from 15.7% and 46.4% in 1994 to 23.1% and 47.4% in 2005 respectively. While the increase in the share of the secondary sector's share has been substantive, it has been almost marginal in the case of the tertiary sector. So, there is an impression that the decrease in the primary sector's share has been compensated through the rise in the secondary sector's share. However, as we can see from the column 6 of the table, industry in Manipur has nothing to do with it because its share has remained more or less stagnant from 7.4% in 1993-94 to around 9% in 2004-05.The major share of the secondary sector comes from the construction sub-sector as can be seen from the table given in the appendix. Regarding the tertiary sector, public administration and other private services are contributing larger shares. In 1993-94, the sub-sector's share was 25.6% and it further rose marginally to 27% in 2004-05 and both the figures are more than half of the total share of the tertiary sector in the state income. The shares of vital sectors of an economy such as transport, trade, banking, etc have been very marginal. One striking feature is that the share of trade, hotel and restaurants has actually decreased from 12.2% of the total state income in 1993-94 to 9.25% in 2004-05 which is an indication of nothing but a telling commentary on India's Look East Policy and subsequent opening of trade corridor with the South East Asian countries.

Table 1

Relative shares of different sectors in real NSDP of Manipur

(p.c.)

YEAR	*PRI*	*SEC*	*TERT*	*AGRI*	*IND*	*TSC*	*THR*	*FINS*	*SPRS*
1	*2*	*3*	*4*	*5*	*6*	*7*	*8*	*9*	*10*
1993-94	37.9	15.7	46.4	31.2	7.4	3.4	12.2	5.2	25.6
1994-95	37.1	15.5	47.4	30.5	7.3	3.6	11.6	5.3	26.9
1995-96	35.8	16.6	47.6	29.7	7.5	3.5	11.3	5.2	27.6
1996-97	34.6	17.5	47.8	29.2	7.4	3.5	11.3	5.4	27.6
1997-98	35.4	16.4	48.2	28.0	6.9	3.6	12.3	5.3	27.0
1998-99	35.6	17.8	46.6	27.3	7.7	3.8	12.8	5.4	24.6
1999-00	31.1	20.1	48.7	25.9	8.3	3.4	11.2	5.1	29.0
2000-01	33.4	16.8	49.8	27.7	7.5	4.2	10.5	5.3	29.8
2001-02	31.0	19.5	49.4	25.7	8.1	4.2	10.5	5.4	29.3
2002-03	29.6	22.8	47.6	24.4	8.5	4.6	10.3	5.9	26.8
2003-04	29.4	23.4	47.2	24.4	8.8	4.9	10.0	6.1	26.2
2004-05	28.0	24.6	47.4	23.1	8.9	5.0	9.2	6.2	27.0

Note: PRI: Primary; SEC: Secondary; TERT: Tertiary AGRI: Agriculture; IND: Industry; TSC: Transport, Storage & Communication; THR: Trade, Hotels & Restaurants; FINS: Banking, Finance & Real Estate; SPRS: Public Administration & Other Services
Source: Calculated from appendix.

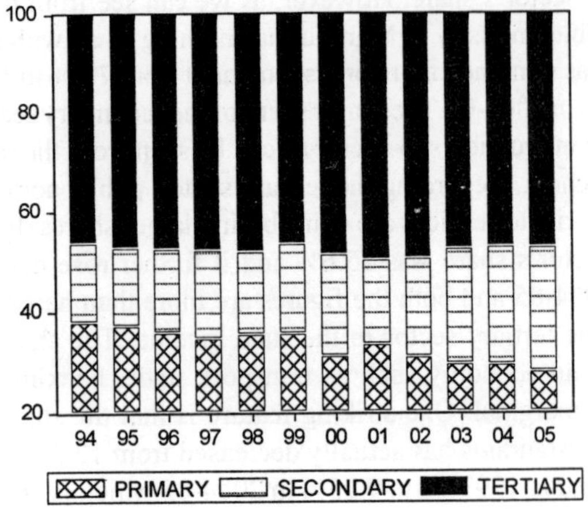

Fig.1: Relative shares of major sectors in the State NSDP (p.c.)

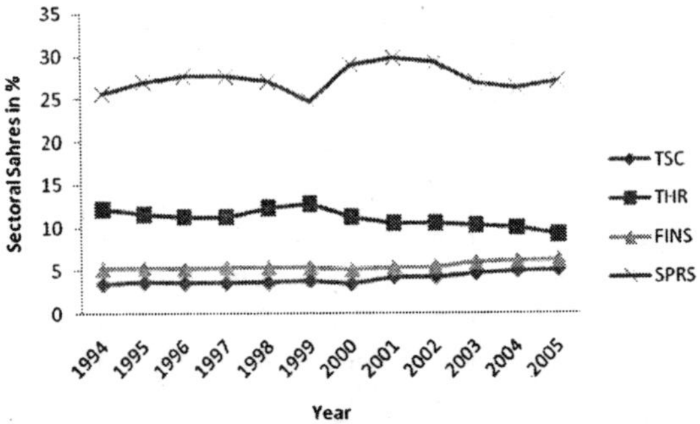

Fig. 2: Relative Shares of Services in Real NSDP (p.c.)

Having studied the performance of the various sectors in terms of their respective shares in the state income, we now turn our analysis on the sectoral growth[4] of the state. The growth rates of the various sectors and sub-sectors of the state economy along with their pattern of growth[5] are given in Table 2.

Table 2
Sectoral Growth Rate of Manipur: 1994-2005

Sector/Sub-Sector	*Growth rate (p.c.)*	*Pattern*
Agriculture	2.9	**
Forestry & Logging	*	**
Fishing	5.4	Deceleration
Primary	2.8	**
Manufacturing	7.6	**
Regd. Manufacturing	*	**
Un-regd. Manufacturing	7.8	**
Construction	11.4	**
Secondary	10.0	**
Transport, Storage & Communication	9.4	Acceleration
Trade, Hotels & Restaurants	3.4	**
Banking & Insurance	10.8	**
Real Estate	5.2	**
Public Administration	5.9	**
Other Services	6.0	**
FINS	7.1	Acceleration
SPRS	5.9	**
Tertiary	5.8	**
NSDP	5.6	**
Per Capita Income	3.4	**

Note: 1.* indicates insignificant growth rate at 1% & 5% levels of significance
2.** indicates constant growth at 1% and 5% level of significance

Source: Estimated from appendix.

As shown in table 2, the real income of the state has been growing at an annual growth rate of 5.6% during 1994 to 2005. Among the broad sectors, secondary sector has attained the highest annual growth rate of 10.00% which is due to an annual growth rate of 11.4% of the construction sub- sector. Tertiary sector has grown at par with the state income at 5.8% per annum. The growth rate of industry in the state during the period is also healthy at the rate of 7.6% per annum with its un-registered segment growing at a little higher at 7.8%. There is no growth at all of the registered industry in Manipur. The absence of growth of the registered segment of industry in the state is an indication of the domination of the industrial scenario in Manipur by the small and cottage industries. It can also be confirmed from the share of this portion of industry in the table given in the appendix. The medium and large industries have not developed. Therefore the role of cottage and small industries in the industrialization process of the state cannot be underestimated. The sector which has suffered the most in the state is the primary sector with an annual compound growth rate of just 2.8%. The agricultural sub-sector also grew at an annual compound growth rate of 2.9%. It has serious policy implications as far as the economy of the stats is concerned from two points- one, the virtual absence of any medium and large industries in the state which cannot be taken for granted to play a major role in her development process, and, two, a high share of public administration and private services which are not directly related with the real productive capacity of the economy.

Regarding the pattern of growth of the sectors in the state by using the hypothesis of acceleration and deceleration, the econometric results show that only two sub-sectors i.e. transport, storage & communication and finance related services grow with acceleration during the period under study. This means that transport storage & communication with a healthy growth rate of 9.4% per annum is expected to grow even faster in the years to come. The same is the case with finance related services also. As for the fishing sub-sector, its growth rate is likely to slow down with time. All the remaining sectors along with the broad sectors grow at constant rate whereas fishing sub-sector has grown with deceleration. The whole argument is being shown in Table 2.

Impact of Sub-sectors on Real Income

We have seen in the preceding section that it has been the primary sector and more importantly the agricultural sector which has declined the most in Manipur in terms of the share in real NSDP and growth rate. The deterioration in the sector's share in real NSDP has been accompanied by a low level of growth during the last years. The economy has been dominated by the tertiary sector with nearly half of the state's income coming from this sector. In view of this perspective, an attempt has been made in Table 3 to estimate elasticity of the different sub-sectors of the tertiary sector with the remaining sectors of the economy. The economy has been classified into as (i) The broad tertiary sector, (ii) Commodity sector comprising of primary and manufacturing sectors, and (iii) Rest of the economy which is real state income less commodity sector.[6]

Table 3

Sectoral elasticities of tertiary sector with others

Independent Variable	*Elasticity*					
	Commodity Sector	*Adj.R^2*	*D-W*	*Rest of the Economy*	*Adj.R^2*	*D-W*
TSC	0.390 (5.301)*	0.93	1.36	0.721 (13.090)*	0.94	2.11
THR	0.506 (10.420)*	0.98	2.03	0.436 (7.909)*	0.91	2.97
BI	0.264 (6.345)*	0.97	1.58	0.603 (10.945)*	0.91	1.00
RA	0.716 (11.707)*	0.92	1.19	1.305 (17.226)*	0.96	2.72
FINS	0.052 (8.086)*	0.95	1.61	0.885 (15.800)*	0.98	2.17
SPRS	0.589 (9.153)*	0.88	1.71	1.130 (16.496)*	0.96	1.75
Tertiary Sector	0.648 (16.783)*	0.96	1.90	1.172 (30.965)*	0.99	1.10

Note: 1.BI- Banking & Insurance; RA- Real Estate
2.Figures in parenthesis indicate value of t statistics.
3.* indicates significant at 1%.

We can see from the above table that all the sub- sectors and the tertiary sector as well have significant elasticities. We can also see from the above table that all the sub-sectors of the tertiary sector as well as the broad tertiary sector have significant impacts on the commodity and rest of the sectors of the economy. Real Estate has the highest elasticity with the commodity sector and rest of the economy sector as well with 0.716 and 1.305 respectively. The sub-sector of the tertiary sector which has the least impact on the commodity sector emerges out to be FINS while it turns out to be THR on the rest sector. Another important observation is that the coefficient of elasticity of all the sub-sectors and the broad tertiary sector in regard to the rest of the economy are larger than that in respect to the commodity sector except in the case of THR. This means that tertiary sector has larger impact on the rest sector than on the commodity sector. The exception in the case of THR is that it has larger impact on the commodity sector than on the rest sector. It explains the validity of the hypothesis that the trade items of the state are more to do with agricultural related activities because of the fact that she has a weak industrial base. Having estimated linkages of the tertiary sector with the other sectors, our next attempt is to estimate the elasticity of real state income of the state. It is examined by adopting the following specifications:

(1) $\text{Log(Real NSDP)}_t = a + b \text{ Log (Sector)}_t$

(2) $\text{Log (Real NSDP)}_t = a + b \text{ Log (Sector)}_{t-1}$

where t and t-1 are the incomes originating in the sectors at the current and past respectively. The econometric results are given in Table 4.

Table 4

Estimates of elasticity of real NSDP w.r.t. sectoral/sub-sectoral incomes

Independent Variable	*Current Value*			*Lagged by one Period*		
	Elasticity	*D-W*	*Adj.R^2*	*Elasticity*	*D-W*	*Adj.R^2*
Agriculture	1.80 (15.300)*	1.57	0.95	1.75 (8.186)*	0.67	0.87
Forestry	-0.02 (-0.485)	2.45	0.92	0.03 (0.686)	3.26	0.92
Fishing	-0.06 (-0.188)	2.58	0.91	0.91 (9.566)*	1.66	0.94
Manufacturing	0.73 (18.459)*	1.61	0.97	0.74 (8.692)*	2.06	0.88
Construction	0.37 (5.184)*	1.94	0.97	0.49 (7.380)*	2.13	0.84
Transport, Storage & Communication	0.59 (13.834)*	1.72	0.94	0.51 (4.463)*	2.64	0.94
Trade, Hotels & Restaurants	0.43 (2.381)*	2.56	0.95	0.20 (5.326)*	1.35	0.73
Banking	0.26 (3.388)*	2.44	0.97	0.50 (6.270)*	1.55	0.79
Real Estate	1.06 (16.656)*	2.07	0.96	1.30 (18.837)*	1.73	0.97
Public Administration	0.94 (11.656)*	1.65	0.96	0.84 (7.093)*	2.53	0.83
Other Services	0.87 (11.659)*	1.52	0.92	0.85 (6.746)*	2.11	0.82
FINS	0.73 (19.200)*	1.41	0.99	0.83 (10.540)*	1.60	0.92
CPRS	0.92 (14.988)*	2.04	0.95	0.850 (7.051)*	2.32	0.83
Primary	1.78 (10.612)*	1.64	0.91	1.80 (7.653)*	1.42	0.85
Secondary	0.55 (15.580)*	1.40	0.95	0.57 (8.258)*	2.35	0.87
Tertiary	0.96 (31.779)*	1.20	0.99	0.95 (10.080)*	2.71	0.91

Note: 1. Figures in parentheses indicate value of t statistics.
2.* indicates significant at 1%.

Regarding the estimation results of model (1), we can see that among the broad sectors, it is the primary sector which has the highest impact on the state income. The fact that the real income of Manipur is primary sector elastic can be seen from the column 2 of Table 4 with the coefficient of elasticity of this sector being 1.8 with respect to state income. In this way, despite of its decreasing share in the NSDP of the state, agriculture still occupies an important place in the economy of Manipur in terms of its high significant coefficient of elasticity with respect to the real income of the state. The role of industries in the development process of the state cannot also be neglected because among the sub-sectors in the secondary sector, it has the highest elasticity with 0.73. Among the sub-sector in the tertiary sector, real estate has the highest impact on the state income with coefficient of elasticity of 1.06. The picture will be clearer when we estimate elasticity of the real state income with respect to the past values of the sectors i.e. lagged values of the sectoral incomes by one period (model 2). It is shown in the column 5 of the Table.

Table 5

Estimates of elasticity of growth of Real NSDP w.r.t. Current Values of Sectoral/Sub-Sectoral Incomes

Independent Variable	*Elasticity*	*D-W*	*Adj.R^2*
Agriculture	2.89 (1.065)	2.70	0.02
Forestry	-0.87 (-1.007)	2.52	0.00
Fishing	0.75 (0.452)	2.83	-0.11
Manufacturing	0.70 (0.644)	2.81	-0.07
Construction	0.65 (0.747)	2.75	-0.06
Transport, Storage & Communication	0.37 (0.414)	2.80	-0.11
Trade, Hotels & Restaurants	1.13 (0.489)	2.84	-0.10
Banking	0.46 (0.622)	2.80	-0.08
Real Estate	0.88 (0.501)	2.80	-0.10
Public Administration	1.94 (1.450)	2.49	0.12
Other Services	1.98 (1.536)	2.48	0.14
FINS	0.67(0.548)	2.80	-0.09
SPRS	1.97(1.495)	2.48	0.14
Primary	1.90 (0.53)	2.83	-0.07
Secondary	0.55 (0.54)	2.80	-0.08
Tertiary	1.55 (0.32)	2.70	0.01

Note: Figures in parentheses indicate value of t statistics.

The analysis yield almost identical results with those arrived at in column 2. While fishing sub-sector was having no impact on real NSDP of the state, its past value is found to have positive impact on the state's real income. The past values of primary sector continue to be a main determinant of the state's income in this model also. We also tried to find out impact of the different sectors on the growth of the state income by using the specification Log $(NSDP_t - NSDP_{t-1})$ = a + b log (Sector) but unfortunately, none of them are found to be statistically significant as is shown in the Table 5.

Another exercise is also done by taking the growth of other sectors as explanatory variables. As can be seen from Table 6, only the growth of only one broad sector viz. tertiary sector and only two sub-sectors, one from the primary sector and other from the tertiary sector i.e. agriculture and public administration are found to have impact on the growth of the state income. The results are more or less in conformity with those arrived at in the aforesaid discussions. Thus it is becoming clearer that primary sector in Manipur still forms the backbone of the state economy with increasing diversification of the tertiary sector. The need of good governance in the process of economic development is also reflected in view of the significant impact of growth of public administration on the growth of state income in terms of elasticity. The whole argument has been shown in the Table 6.

Table 6

Estimates of elasticity of growth of Real NSDP w.r.t. Growth of Sectoral/Sub-Sectoral Incomes

Independent Variable	*Elasticity*	*D-W*	*Adj.R^2*
Agriculture	0.57 (2.772) **	2.29	0.53
Forestry	0.01 (0.013)	1.94	-0.50
Fishing	-0.11 (-0.760)	2.41	-0.06
Manufacturing	-0.21 (0.599)	2.94	-0.08
Construction	0.05 (0.144)	2.05	-0.16
Transport, Storage & Communication	0.16 (0.630)	2.81	-0.08

(Contd...)

Independent Variable	*Elasticity*	*D-W*	*Adj.R^2*
Trade, Hotels & Restaurants	0.13 (0.706)	1.51	-0.09
Banking	0.41 (1.824)	2.26	0.25
Real Estate	0.33 (0.266)	2.79	-0.13
Public Administration	0.47 (2.682) **	1.58	0.51
Other Services	0.27 (1.713)	1.05	0.26
FINS	0.60(1.699)	2.63	0.19
SPRS	0.44(2.717)**	1.45	0.51
Primary	0.71 (1.214)	0.81	0.08
Secondary	0.19 (0.613)	2.91	-0.08
Tertiary	0.83 (8.884) *	0.89	0.93

Note: 1. Figures in parenthesis indicate value of t statistics.
2. *& **indicate significant at 1% & 5% respectively.

In so far we have examined the determinants of growth of the state economy with the real income as the dependent variable. In the following exercise, we investigate the determinants of growth of the state economy in terms of the real per capita of the state. The models used here are as follows:

(i) $GRPCI = a + a_1 PPRIM + a_2 PSECD + a_3 PTERT$

(ii) $GRPECI = a + a_1 PPRIM$

(iii) $GRPCI = a + a_1 PSECD$

(iv) $GRPCI = a + a_1 PTERT$

(v) $Log(GRPCI) = a + a_1 Log(PPRIM) + a_2 Log(PSECD) + a_3 Log(PTERT)$

(vi) $Log(GRPECI) = a + a_1 Log(PPRIM)$

(vii) $Log(GRPCI) = a + a_1 Log(PSECD)$

(viii) $Log(GRPCI) = a + a_1 Log(PTERT)$

where the symbols represent growth of real per capita income of the state and real per capita incomes originating in the three broad sectors. The regression results are shown in the following tables.

Table 7
Regression of growth of per capita income

Dependent Variable	*Estimates of*					
	a	a_1	a_2	a_3	*Adj.R^2*	*DW*
GRPCI	228.37	-97504.59	-55674.55	87139.86	-0.22	2.47
	(0.080)	(-0.530)	(-0.562)	(0.907)		
Log(GRPCI)	3.64	-10.62	-17.45	33.62	-0.12	3.21
	(0.031)	(-0.214)	(-1.099)	(0.777)		

Note: Figures in parenthesis indicate value of t statistics.

Table 8
Regression of growth of per capita income

Independent Variable	*Estimates of*			
	a	a_1	*DW*	*Adj. R^2*
PPRIM	-840.64 (-5.773) *	48499.98 (149.688) *	2.60	0.61
PSECD	-183.96 (-0.384)	28159.91 (0.756)	2.67	-0.05
PTERT	-840.64 (-0.909)	31607.94 (1.099)	2.67	0.02
Log(PPRIM)	42.92 (0.588)	9.93 (0.520)	2.50	-0.11
Log(PSECD)	-9.83 (-0.591)	-3.36 (-0.880)	3.07	-0.03
Log(PTERT)	-2.79 (-0.097)	-2.21 (-0.265)	2.92	-0.18

Note: 1. Figs. in parenthesis indicate value of t statistics.
2. * indicates significant at 1%.

The above econometric results yield the following results:

(i) None of the three broad sectors influence the growth of per capita income in the multiple regression framework.

But when examined separately, per capita primary income is found to have a positive impact although the explanatory power of the model is reasonably low.

(ii) In the elasticity model, all the broad sectors have insignificant impact on the growth of per capita income of the state.

Sectoral Correlation Analysis

In the preceding analyses, we have tried to examine the determinants of economic growth of the state by adopting many possible economic models. In the following paragraphs, we will try to examine the inter-relations between the various sectors and sub-sectors of the state by using the appropriate models. To do so a sectoral correlation matrix is constructed.

We have selected four sub - sectors viz. agriculture; industry; public administration and other services; and banking and finance related services representing the corresponding broad sectors i.e. primary, secondary and tertiary sectors to observe sectoral correlation with some other selected sectors and sub-sectors. It is found that all the chosen sub- sectors have high correlation with each others. In view of the above results, the double log model was fitted as follows to observe the degree of inter-relations with amongst them.

$$\text{Log(AGRI)} = a + b \text{ Log } (X) + u$$

$$\text{Log(IND)} = a + b \text{ Log } (X) + u$$

$$\text{Log(SPRS)} = a + b \text{ Log } (X) + u$$

$$\text{Log(FINS)} = a + b \text{ Log } (X) + u, \text{ where } X = \text{correlated variable}$$

The regression results are given in the appendix 2 to 5. Some of the important findings of the above study may be summed up as follows:

(i) Agriculture- Industry relation holds true in the case of Manipur also with agriculture influencing industry and vise-versa.

(ii) The highest impact on agriculture is found in the case of trade sub-sector validating the hypothesis that major trade items of the state comprise mostly of agricultural products.

(iii) All the selected sectors and sub-sectors have high elasticity with respect to the industrial sector of the state except trade sub-sector.

(iv) Agriculture, primary sector, state income, trade have not emerged as significant explanatory variables for financial services.

Conclusion

Manipur has assumed the characteristic of a developed economy by virtue of its small share of primary sector and dominance of tertiary sector. The shares of primary sector and agriculture have fallen considerably over the years. But one striking point is that we cannot neglect at all agriculture in Manipur. Our study has shown that it was more or less only agriculture which emerged as significant variable in almost all the models examined. Another important observation was its high elasticity with the industrial sector in the state. With public administration and private services dominating the tertiary sector coupled with virtual absence of any noticeable industry, agriculture in the state economy will continue to occupy its position for many years to come. The low growth of agriculture therefore needs more detailed analysis.

Decreasing share of trade in the state economy is very unusual at a time when we are talking about programmes like Look East Policy and connecting of the sub-continent with the Asian Tigers. Another important observation was its non significant association with industry in the state. This, among others, is the main reason why the state has been labeled as a mere transit point between the mainland India and south East Asian countries in the ongoing Indo-Myanmar Border trade arrangement.

Regarding industry sector, time has come to think of ways of setting up medium and large industries. The opportunities provided by the markets of South East Asian Countries should not be misused. Better connectivity will enable our industries to reap the benefit of scale economies.

NOTES

1. Figure as given in Kapila, Uma (2008).
2. The state income data supplied by the Central Statistical Organisation (CSO) available in its official website forms the main basis of the present study. All the figures are real incomes originating at 1993-94 prices.
3. Industry here refers to manufacturing sector only.
4. The growth rates are derived by using the linear trend model $LogY_t = a + bt + u_t$ where Y is the variable for which the growth rate is to be determined and t is time trend, u is the error term and applying the formula: Growth Rate = $(e^b - 1) \times 100$.
5. The pattern of growth is determined by using $LogY_t = a + bt + ct^2 + u_t$. If 'c' is statistically significant with positive sign, it is the case of acceleration. If it is statistically significant with a negative sign, it denotes the case for deceleration. The variable grows at constant rate if it statistically insignificant.
6. A similar exercise was done in Singh, S. Brajamani (2003). The elasticity is found out by using the double-log model of the form $logY_t = a + b \log X_t + u_t$. The correction for autocorrelation has been taken care of whenever necessary.

REFERENCES

Bathla, Seema (undated): "Inter-Sectoral Growth Linkages in India: Implications for Policy and Liberalised reforms", Institute of Economic Growth, Delhi.

Bhattacharya, B. B. and A. Mitra, (1989): "Industry- Agriculture Growth Rates: Widening Disparity: An Explanation' *Economic and Political Weekly,* Vol. 24, No. 34, August.

Fuller, V. (1963): "Bargaining in Agriculture and Industry: Comparisons and Contrasts", *Journal of Forum Economics*, Vol. 45, No. 5, Blackwell Publications, December.

Gereffi, G. (1989): "Rethinking Development Theory: Insights from East Asia and Latin America", *Sociological Forum*, Vol. 4, No. 4, Springer Publications, December.

Gupta, D. N. Sen (1993): "Indian Manufacturing Industry: Growth Episode of the Eighties", *Economic and Political Weekly,* Vol. 28, No. 22, May.

Kapila, Uma (2008): "Indian Agriculture: Developments, Issues and Policies" in Uma Kapila (ed.) *Indian Economy Since Independence*, Academic Foundation, New Delhi.

Sastry, D. V. S., B. Singh, K. Bhattarcharya and N. K. Unnikrishnan (2003): "Sectoral Linkages and Growth Prospects : Reflections on the Indian Economy", *Economic and Political Weekly,* Vol. 38, No. 24, June.

Singh, S. Brajamani (2003): *Economic Growth in Manipur,* S. Romesh Singh (Publisher).

Suryahadi, A., D. Suryadarma, S. Sumarto and J. Molyneaux (2006): "Agriculture Demand Linkages and Growth Multiplier in Rural Indonesia", SMERU Research Institute, Jakarta, July.

Vogel, S. J. (1994): "Structural Changes in Agriculture: Production Linkages and Agriculture Demand Led Industrialisation", *Oxford Economic Papers*, New Series, Vol. 46, No. 1, OUP, January.

Appendix 1

Real state income of Manipur (1993-94 Prices)

YEAR	AGRI	FORE	FISH	MANU	REGM	UNRG	CONS	TRAN	TRAO	COMM	TRAD	BANK	REAL	PUBI	OTHR	NSDP	PECI
1994	35599	4041	3587	8437	218	8219	8343	3910	3308	596	13899	1907	4034	15574	13639	114144	5846
1995	33879	3528	3763	8164	240	7924	9097	4016	3367	645	12921	1594	4254	16200	13664	111030	5558
1996	34118	3040	3920	8570	331	8239	11708	4045	3425	615	12972	1528	4476	17197	14376	114737	5616
1997	36686	2916	3931	9269	455	8814	14927	4358	3520	833	14245	2142	4722	18883	15850	125788	6022
1998	38397	6024	4237	9448	209	9239	15576	4894	3903	986	16871	2389	4910	19888	17252	137364	6434
1999	38168	6522	5036	10800	168	10632	14234	5280	4188	1087	17878	2415	5134	18640	15692	139636	6401
2000	40952	2598	5670	13061	92	12969	18254	5463	4376	1082	17748	2722	5363	24929	20859	158117	7097
2001	43163	2993	5872	11683	128	11555	14952	6582	5081	1496	16344	2434	5774	24283	22176	155850	6851
2002	44553	3318	5756	14030	193	13837	19384	7327	5597	1724	18173	3304	6066	28010	22740	173015	7445
2003	43101	3312	5788	14979	276	14703	25117	8103	5992	2106	18125	4104	6386	25775	21585	176555	7446
2004	44427	3307	5820	16093	393	15700	26501	8992	6415	2573	18162	4410	6728	26083	21669	182284	7532
2005	45795	3697	5822	17571	416	17155	31096	9839	6868	2966	18265	5104	7106	28126	25419	197936	8015

Source:- CSO, available at www.mospi.nic.in , accessed on 16/1/2008

AGRI:- AGRICULTURE; FORE:- FORESTRY; FISH:- FISHING ; MANU:- MANUFACTURING (INDUSTRY) ; UNRG:- UNREGISTERED INDUSTRY; CONS:- CONSTRUCTION; TRAN:- TRANSPORTATION; TRAO:- TRANSPORT, STORAGE & COMMUNICATION; COMM:- COMMUNICATION; TRAD:- TRADE, HOTELS & RESTAURANTS; BANK:- BANKING & INSURANCE; REAL:- REAL ESTATE; PUBI:- PUBLIC ADMINISTRATION; OTHER:- OTHER SERVICES; NSDP:- NET STATE DOMESTIC PRODUCT; PECI:- PER CAPITA INCOME

Appendix 2
Estimates of elasticity of agriculture w.r.t. other sectors

Sectors	*Elasticity*	*D-W*	*Adj.* R^2
IND	0.38 (9.406)*	1.65	0.89
NSDP	0.53 (15.301)*	1.61	0.95
SEC	0.29 (7.898)*	1.46	0.85
TERT	0.52 (18.770)*	1.95	0.97
SPRS	0.48 (13.455)*	2.05	0.94
FINS	0.41 (9.232)*	1.01	0.88
TSC	0.31 (9.916)*	1.35	0.90
THR	0.88 (7.383)*	1.29	0.84

Note: 1. Figures in parentheses indicate value of t statistics.
2. * indicates significant at 1%.

Appendix 3
Estimates of elasticity of industry w.r.t. other sectors

Sectors	*Elasticity*	*D-W*	*Adj.* R^2
AGRI	2.41(19.363)*	1.69	0.95
NSDP	1.34(18.459)*	1.65	0.97
PRI	2.29 (7.070)*	1.54	0.82
TERT	1.27 (12.927)*	1.45	0.94
SPRS	1.30 (11.027)*	2.05	0.92
FINS	1.06 (16.554)*	1.81	0.96
TSC	0.78 (13.049)*	2.68	0.94
THR	0.53 (1.403)	2.58	0.89

Note: 1. Figures in parentheses indicate value of t statistics.
* indicates significant at 1%.

Appendix 4
Estimates of elasticity of social & personal related services w.r.t. other sectors

Sectors	*Elasticity*	*D-W*	*Adj. R^2*
AGRI	1.97 (13.456)*	2.13	0.94
IND	0.76 (8.742)*	1.49	0.87
NSDP	1.03 (14.480)*	2.25	0.95
PRI	1.87 (7.346)*	1.91	0.83
SEC	0.55 (9.297)*	1.85	0.92
TERT	1.03 (23.389)*	2.34	0.98
FINS	0.81 (7.681)*	1.27	0.84
TSC	0.62 (7.734)*	1.65	0.84
THR	1.58 (10.520)*	1.37	0.82

Note: 1.Figures in parentheses indicate value of t statistics.
* indicates significant at 1%.

Appendix 5
Estimates of elasticity of banking & finance related services w.r.t. other sectors

Sectors	*Elasticity*	*D-W*	*Adj. R^2*
AGRI	0.47 (1.175)	1.77	0.96
IND	0.91 (16.554)*	1.75	0.96
NSDP	0.68 (2.783)**	1.63	0.97
PRI	0.28 (0.743)	2.00	0.95
SEC	0.70 (20.416)*	2.65	0.97
TERT	1.34 (12.154)*	1.45	0.97
SPRS	1.05 (7.681)*	1.12	0.84
TSC	0.75 (20.732)*	1.99	0.97
THR	0.88 (5.651)*	2.23	0.98

Note: 1. Figs. in parentheses indicate value of t statistics.
2. *& **indicate significant at 1% & 5% respectively.

17

New Wave of Globalization and Hill Village Economy in Manipur: An Observation

Komol Singha

Introduction

Globalization is a process by which the entire world becomes a single unit. It helps in interaction and integration among people, companies, and governments of different nations. The magnitude of globalization is driven by international trade and investment, and aided by information technology. This process has effects on environment, culture, political systems, economic development and prosperity, and human physical well-being in societies around the world.

Ronald Robertson and Habib Haque Khondkher (1998) have analyzed globalization as the process of compression of entire world on the one hand and increase in consciousness of the whole world on the other. The Human Development Report (1999) has elaborated that globalization comprises global market, global technology, global ideas and global solidarity. Jain (2001) observes, "Globalization is understood as an economic idea. It is linked with liberalization. But, at the local level, when globalization comes to a village, it changes a lot. Besides economic changes, there is a cultural change also". Bhagwati

(2004) opines that the economic globalization constitutes integration of national economies into the international economy through trade, FDI, short-term capital flows, international flows of workers and humanity generally, and flows of technology. According to Tomlinson (1999), "Globalization refers to an empirical condition of the complex connectivity involves overcoming cultural distances through penetrating experiences provided through education, employment, consumer culture and the mass media and had been described as being more significant than technological advances and physical mobility". In this way, globalization becomes an inevitable process which we cannot ignore at all in evolution of economic development. To become a winner in this era, harnessing it in a right manner has become the need of the hour.

Considering the importance of globalization, with the help of primary as well as secondary data, this paper is a modest attempt to highlight the impact of globalization in the hill villages. How the *New Wave of Globalization* enters into the hill villages, which could not be explored by the earlier form of globalization, is also discussed in this paper. For the purpose of the study, a primary field survey was conducted through a well-structured questionnaire in the early part of 2006 in a hill tribal village of Manipur (Maram Khullen), under the Tadubi Sub-division of Senapati district. This village is the home of Maram Tribe, the lone primitive tribe in the State.

To highlight the concrete viewpoint of the study, the paper is classified into six parts. With a brief introduction and conceptual definition of globalization in the first part, the second section of the paper discusses the origin of globalization in the tribal economy. In this section, how market and Christianity enter into the tribal hinterlands of North East India (NEI) is also discussed. The third section deals with the idea of New-Wave of globalization which penetrates easily into the hill villages. The next section, i.e. section four, covers the impact of globalization in the hill villages and gives a detail study of positive and negative impact of globalization. In the fifth section, finding of new-wave of globalization in the tribal village is discussed. The last section wraps up with concluding remarks and some possible suggestions to overcome challenges brought about by globalization.

Origin of Globalization

In the pre-modern threefold period (Pre-1500), the key agents of globalization were three-fold, viz. (a) Political and Military empires (b) World religions, and (c) the Migratory movements of Nomadic Groups. In the early modern period (1500- 1800), the rise of the west was regarded as the key agent of globalization. The modern period (1850-1945) witnessed an enormous acceleration in the spread and entrenchment of global networks and flows that had begun in the early modern period. And in the contemporary period from 1950 onwards, globalization is shaped profoundly by the structural consequences of the World War II and the emergence of a worldwide system of nation states, overlaid by multilateral, regional and global systems of regulations and governance. According to Roland Robertson[1], the expansion of the world religions of Islam and Christianity had an important role in the globalization process. Religion became one of the bases for social transformation both at the level of people's everyday lives and at the national level. If religion was seen as one of the most fundamental means of organizing human life, then the seeds of globalization could be found in religion itself[2].

In the village level, globalization has made its entry into the tribal society through the *market* and world *religion* in North East India (NEI) particularly in the hill tribal villages of Manipur. When we trace further more, the origin of globalization in the hill tribal society, *market system* comes at the first even if it is very recent. And on the more important side, the advent of *Christianity* is the beginning of new globalization in the tribal society in NEI. So, for tracing the origin of globalization in the tribal society in NEI particularly in the hill villages of Manipur, we have to look into two dimensions; one, the formation of *Market economy* in the tribal area/villages and two, the *advent of Christianity* in the tribal society.

Market and Tribal Village

Economists have long observed that countries and regions that are linked by common institutions, currencies, or policies, and that enjoy relatively free access to each other's markets, tends to converge to similar levels of income over time (IMF 2006). The earliest form of globalization has been the institution of weekly markets among the tribal (Jain 2001). All over the country there had been weekly markets in one form or the other among the tribal. This weekly markets were beyond the single village but within a cluster of villages. To understand globalization in the context of Indian tribal society, we must conceptualize the primary units of market economy i.e. weekly market, having a record of about 100 years. And therefore, what we call globalization today is only a recast of weekly markets found among the tribal (Jain 2001). When we trace the civilization or integration of the society, we cannot ignore the market system. Globalization has made its entry into the tribal society through the market. Even if the market system is very new in tribal society in NEI, its role through which the society enters into globalization is very much remarkable. Before the advent of this present market system, they maintained subsistence economy. They produced their own essential commodities including food and clothing according to their need without hired labor and also from the locally available resources. It was a period before the advent of monetization and production was in the backward sloping supply shape. If there is any surplus over self-consumption, the balance is bartered or presented to their near and dear ones in the village. This process was not different in the Maram Khullen too. People of the village were making their own clothes from the white cotton planted in the village sufficiently without depending on the market. And till today some of them in the village are having those hand woven clothes. As economy evolves, exceptional needs apart from their own produces in the village were purchased from the nearest market. It was the beginning of socialization and the very socialization changes economic pattern of the society. It is nothing but the beginning of globalization in the tribal society or any other society in this globe.

Christianity and Tribal Village

The advent of Christianity in tribal villages in NEI is one of the most important routes for entering real globalization into their society. Before it, they were living in an isolated world, a single independent economic unit. Tribal communities in NEI were following traditional religion/paganism before the advent of Christianity. And, it is not an exaggeration that the advent of Christianity is the beginning of globalization in the tribal society of NEI. Christianity gives indigenous tribal people new hopes and aspirations. So, we have to thank Christianity and Western Missionary Institutions for imparting English education (which is the most important education system in the modern competitive world) to the tribal people. In the words of B. M. Pugh [3] "the Tribes of NEI today feel greatly indebted to the Missionaries of the West for their work of uplifting them".

Coming to the origin of Christianity in Manipur and then in Maram Khullen in particular, Rev. William Pettigrew, an Englishman born in Edinburgh, Scotland arrived at Imphal for the first time on 6th Jan 1894 for preaching Christianity. On the 5th March 1956 Fr. Ravalio and Peter Bianchi, Roman Catholic priests landed up at Imphal. From 1961, Fr. Bianchi started Don Bosco Missionary work at Mao-Maram area [4]. According to Kangba Raphel, the present local catechist of Maram Khullen village and Karaiba James, a College teacher, Christian village church in Maram Khullen was founded only after 1956. That is so why they were celebrating Golden Jubilee of the village Catholic Church in December 2006 in commemoration of the foundation of the church in the village. Despite being one of the biggest hill villages in Manipur, having around 400 households, there is no proper government educational institution except one lower primary school, which is also not functioning properly now. This phenomenon is more or less the same in the entire hill tribal villages of NEI. And it is not an exaggeration that as much as 99 per cent of educated youths of this village are the products of Missionary Institutions. But, the quality of life of this village is now far better than some other villages in the plains of NEI.

New Wave of Globalization

The earlier integration of the world economy was driven more by technological developments in transportation and communications rather than by policy changes. But today's most drastic change is in the degree to which government have intervened to reduce obstacles to the flow of trade and investments worldwide. And the new information technologies have created a landscape where movements of services and capital are faster by several orders of magnitudes[5]. This is what the author termed as '*New Wave of Globalization*' and branded as '*Globalization by Air*'. Globalization is not new; recast of the early 16th century and the late 19th century. But this era is different (HRD 1999). Globalization has been a boon to electronic communication apart from computer and software. Coming to the study area, recently from 2005, Maram Khullen has entered into a new world by introducing Mobile phone, Internet, DTH television/ radio channel. It is nothing but a *New-Wave of Globalization* in this village.

Globalization is not new, though. For thousands of years, people and, later, corporations have been buying and selling to each other in lands at great distances, such as through the famed Silk Road across Central Asia that connected China and Europe during the middle ages. Likewise, for centuries, people and corporations have invested in enterprises in other countries. In fact, many of the features of the new wave of globalization are slightly different to those prevailing before the outbreak of the World War I becomes in 1914. But policy and technological developments of the past few decades have spurred increases in cross-border trade, investment, and migration so large that many observers believe the world has entered a qualitatively new phase in its economic development. Since 1950, for example, the volume of world trade has increased by 20 times, and from just 1997 to 1999 flows of foreign investment nearly doubled, from $468 billion to $827 billion. Distinguishing this new wave of globalization from earlier ones, Thomas Friedman has said that globalization today is "farther, faster, cheaper, and deeper."

The new wave of globalization is the globalization by *Air* not *by Road* like before. This new wave of globalization is very much different from earlier type of globalization especially in the tribal society of NEI. Old system of globalization could not reach tribal hinterland but this new wave of globalization reaches to every nock and corner of this globe because it is the globalization by air, not by road. Before the advent of this new form of globalization in Maram Khullen, people of this village could not receive any sort of TV and Radio channel properly. Now they can enjoy DTH channel properly and get global information easily. There is no landline telephone connection in this village till today (till the survey was conducted) but after the advent of this new wave of globalization, they can get mobile network properly even if government cannot install land line telephone exchange center or connection in the village. As regards to internet facility, this village can avail 24-hour internet facility in the Don Bosco College (even if it is on commercial basis), which is hardly 4 km from the village. Readers may ask, "Are the facilities mentioned above new in the information and electronic technology? The answer is *big* yes in the case of tribal villages like Maram Khullen. It is the new arrival of global technology i.e. only in 2005-06 particularly in this hill village of Manipur.

Impact of Globalization in the Tribal Village

To begin with, globalization itself is a social phenomenon of systematic proportions, embodying contradictory processes and different crosscurrents. Again, no single variable can explain such a broad and multifaceted phenomenon as the economy. So, the impact of globalization a controversy among the intellectuals and policy makers. There is a big block of anti-globalization movement in the developing nations which sees only pessimistic side of the globalization. And on the other block of the advanced nations, is optimistic side of the globalization looking for big market and global competition. It is still debatable and inconclusive and has got mixed response in India. For the present study, the author analyses globalization and its impacts in this Maram village independently.

When this globalization comes to village level, a question that arises "what will happen to tribal economy/society if it reaches to the grass root level?" This is the core idea of this paper, and tries to draw a conclusion by analyzing micro level village survey. Globalization, when it comes down to a village level particularly in Maram Khullen, its situation is different from the global phenomenon. Whatsoever the reason, the impact of globalization is to be discussed in two different ways: (i) Negative aspects, and (ii) Positive aspects.

Negative Aspects of Globalization

The dean of Marxist economists in India, Prabhat Patnaik offers an exemplary articulation of the contra position. In a wide-ranging attack in which he uses the term "Globalization and Imperialism" alternatively to describe the same phenomenon, Patnaik claims that:

> *The net result, taking the 3rd world as a whole, of surrendering to the process of globalization in this sense is: relative economic stagnation, increased income inequalities leading to a worsening of poverty, a loss of economic and political sovereignty, ... a loss of control over domestic assets and natural resources to metropolitan capital, and the loss of food security.* [6]

With the advent of new wave of globalization, the sense of vulnerability or economic security is arguably greater today than in earlier periods because the growing integration of nations worldwide into the international economy has intensified competitive pressures from actual and potential rivals elsewhere. It is also easily seen that indigenous people have suffered grossly at the hand of bigger and advanced groups. The biggest worry seems to have been that they would lose their lands because the governments of the countries in which the indigenous groups were supplanted by intruding colonialists and settlers in the last two centuries appear to have turned to legal doctrines such as the theory of *terra nullius* (under which communal rights to "unoccupied" land are not recognized). Such doctrines have made it easier to deprive the indigenous groups of their traditional right to deny legal purchase by others of such lands (Bhagwati 2006:114). In this context, Jain (2006) has rightly observed that globalization has also proved to be destructive in some aspect of culture. The western culture tends to dominate over the indigenous culture. It produces a downward pressure for local autonomy and regional reforms. Local culture would always be at the verge of extinction. Not only the culture but the local economy would always be disturbed. For instances, the locally made artifacts and handicrafts would decay at the onslaught of the products made from the outside. This will discourage the initiatives and creativity of the indigenous people in the tribal villages. As a result of which handloom and handicraft goods of tribal people in Manipur became only a show piece in the museum.

Economy flows with the tune of social structure and culture in the society. As the social structure changes, the consumption pattern and the direction of the economy also changes into that direction. With the advent of new wave of globalization, the basic structure of the Maram Khullen village has been displaced (not necessarily positive or negative). Globalization very often leads indigenous communities to westernization, not modernization. Folk culture, songs and traditional music are replaced by the rock and pop music of west. They are attracted by the fashionable dresses, bourgeois life style and consumption habit of the west shown in T. V. and other electronic media. They have all drown in the conspicuous consumption which leads them to impoverishment. There is a wide gap between income and expenditure flow in the tribal economy. It is due to the westernization (not modernization) influenced by the electronic media, T V, cinema and modern globalization[7]. Domestic producing units and cottage industries are compelled to shut down as the economy turns away towards the west. Individualism and materialism became very prominent in the village now. Consumption of daily life in the village from down to dusk is the products of MNCs from outside the village. As Neo-classical economists argue, the balance of payment of Less Developed Nations deteriorates when they have international trade with Developed Nations, village economy suffers when global market penetrates into it. With the influence of new globalization wave, people of this village have accustomed to fashionable dresses, hair fixer, lipstick, perfume, face cream, tobacco and foreign liquor etc. Here the question is "Are not these products consumed in other areas?" No doubt, others are also using these items but this phenomenon is very recent in this particular village. Before the new wave of globalization, people of this village were weaving their own clothes but now-a-days no one is practicing it. Even the local made wine is brought from the *Sekmai* [8] because the quality of Sekmai is far better than those locally brew at home. These are some of the big blows of new wave of globalization in the Maram Khullen/village.

Positive Aspects of Globalization

India has made considerable accommodation to globalization since the last decade of the 20th century if not earlier and more importantly after 1991. Contrary to the position of the critics of globalization who emphasize economic stagnation as its likely outcome, the empirical data on economic growth rates leave no doubt that the opening to globalization has been enormously beneficial for economic growth in India. Rather than economic stagnation, globalization has led to the acceleration of the growth rate on literally every count; criticism of globalization seems groundless (Nayar 2006). In a market economy, employment and wages have been largely influenced by the integration of the labour supply and demand, rather than by government legislation or union pressure. Such flexible markets have encouraged efficient allocation of workers across sectors, higher investment and use of more labour intensive technologies. This has resulted in more rapid output growth, which in turn has enhanced labor demand, employment and wages. The cycle has been reinforced by the high levels of education, vocational training and health care that have allowed the pattern of employment more skilled-intensive, again supporting rising wages and living standards.[9]

Globalization has been a boon to village life. Recently from 2005, Maram Khullen village has entered in to a new world by introducing Mobile phone, Internet, DTH Radio/TV channel. Before it this village could not receive any sort of TV and Radio channel properly. Now after installing DTH dish antenna costing hardly Rs. 2000/- (two thousand) at current market price, they can get world information in this remote village. They can enjoy BBC world service, Headlines, DD news, Ajtak and Gyan Darshan easily. Is not it advancement of electronic technology? Even though Maram Khullen is not getting land line telephone connection till date, they can get mobile network easily from different centres even from Nagaland as it is situated on the high hill top. Road connecting the village to NH 39 which is hardly 4 km was just made motorable only in 2004. Now there is regular passenger Sumo and Mini bus service from village. And as far as quality education is concerned, this village has got one of the best colleges in Manipur[10] offering all the three streams with 24 hr internet service. Thanks to the Western Missionary Institution (Catholic Mission) for imparting quality and English education in this village. There is no proper government educational institution in this village. With the effort of Missionary Institution, this village has got good education and quality life. This village has produced 2 doctors, 6 University/College teachers, 2 Bank Provisional Officer and 1 civil servant (SDO). All these are the gifts of Catholic mission/English education in this village. It is nothing but the gift of globalization.

With the advent of new wave of globalization, this village has entered into a new life style. International organizations like IDA, IFAD and RDFA have started cash crop cultivation in both waste land and community land. They have started using fertilizer during cultivation. Private entrepreneurs have started food processing units in this area. New method of cultivation has been already initiated and old system of shifting cultivation is completely discarded in this village. These are the result of new wave of globalization in this village.

Findings of New-wave of Globalization

In the world of the 21st century, there is no real alternative to globalization. According to S. Rangachar[11], if countries want to develop economically, they have to participate actively in the international exchange of goods, services, technology, money and people. As has been mentioned earlier, globalization is taking place by air not by road (whether we like it or not), and we cannot escape from it. No institution/agent can resist or stop this new wave of globalization. It is an automatic and spontaneous process in the global development movement. We cannot say that no TV network, internet and mobile signal should go through our territory. Whether we utilize it properly or not, it is the most essential infrastructure for long term development in the society. No doubt, it creates some inconveniences in the beginning but this will be automatically corrected by the global market mechanism/ globalization process. One thing is true in this village that the most important investment of long term development i.e. education and basic infrastructure is moving to a right direction. Once the basic infrastructure and knowledge is put, growth/development is spontaneous. This is what we need in the tribal society or in any society who are in the transitional stage. Since this new wave of globalization is inevitable, it is better to harness it before it is too late. Since it is compulsory to embrace sooner or later, why should we delay? Let us embrace it and make use of it in a right manner.

Conclusion

In no uncertain terms globalization together with the global village challenges Maram Khullen in efforts towards attaining global competitiveness. Notwithstanding this, some well thought long-term strategies with implications for education and training would enable Maram Khullen to remain competitive in this emerging environment. In this regard, Bhagwati (2006:221) has remarked that:

> "If what I have written so far has been read with care, it should be clear that, inmany ways globalization will yield better results if it is managed. Globalizationshould not be thought of as a solution to everything. It merely provides opportunities. Those who take advantage, they flourish and those who do not they sink".

Globalization is not supposed to produce equality of outcome but it produces equality of opportunity for those with right mindset. Hence the developing countries/poor village economies have to focus on economic restructuring, building market supporting institutions and creating efficient regulatory mechanisms. Globalization should not be accused for loosing share of the low income poor village economy. These economies suffer from internal problems like ignorance, infrastructure bottlenecks, and lack of investment, lack of market and so on. More access to globalization and its benefits demand that poor economies first put in place a necessary conducive environment to ensure higher returns and larger markets for external investors. To get a share of global capital, technology and output, village economies/ developing countries have to upgrade their social and economic institutions through administrative, legislative and legal reforms.[12] In this context, new wave of globalization gives a new vista to Maram

Khullen. And this phenomenon is more or less same to all the tribal villages in NEI. We can develop the traditional artifacts, hand loom and handicrafts in the tune to new system. Keeping in the mind "think globally and act locally", we should not to be drown in the western life style. We can imitate the work culture of the west first then life style and consumption pattern. Very often, we are attracted by the lifestyle of west shown in the cinema and TV. Let our life be guided by the knowledge and value. In this regard, father of the nation, M.K. Gandhi has rightly said:

> "I do not want my house to be walled in on all sides and windows stuffed. I want the cultures of all the lands to be blown about my house as freely as possible. But I refuse to be blown of my feet. I refuse to live in other's houses as an interloper, a beggar or a slave."

NOTES

1. As used by Leela D'Souza (2003).
2. See more detail from Leela D'Souza's paper "Globalization and Religious Fundamentalist Movements: A Search for Identity" in PG Jogdand and S M Michael (2003 eds.), *Globalization and Social Movements: Struggle for Humane Society,* Rawat Publication, Jaipur. p.55 & 63.
3. As used by Jeyaseelam (1996).
4. See Jeyaseelam (1996): *Impact of the Missionary Movement in Manipur*, Scholar Publishing House Pvt. Ltd. New Delhi. p. 74.
5. Jagdish Bhagwati (2006): *In Defense of Globalization*, Oxford University Press, New Delhi. pp. 11-12.
6. Baldev Raj Nayar (2000): *India's Globalization: Evaluating the Economic Consequences*, East-West Center, Washington D.C., pp. 2-3.
7. It is abstracted from the author's article "Demonstration Effect in Economic Development in Tribal Economy" on 21st April 2005 in local daily *The Sangai Express*, Imphal.
8. It is an area known for producing best quality of local made liquor in the state and they are legally permitted.

9. Detail text of this part was heavily depended to G Raju (2001): "How the Liberalization Works for the Rural Poor", *Southern Economist*, Sept. 1.

10. One of the best colleges in Manipur "Don Bosco College" is just below the Maram Khullen foothill.

11. S. Rangachar is a former staff member of the World Bank, Washington D C, USA.

12. See in detail from M Mallick and J Lenka (2006) "Globalization and Development: Disaggregate Dynamics" *Southern Economist*, 15 Jan.

REFERENCES

Bhagwati, Jagdish (2006): *In Defense of Globalization*, Oxford University Press, New Delhi.

Doshi, S. L. and P.C. Jain (1999): *Rural Sociology*, Rawat Publications, New Delhi.

Gudeman, Stephen (2004): *The Demise of a Rural Economy: From Subsistence to Capitalism in a Latin American Village*, Routledge, London.

Ganguly, J. B. (ed)(1995): *Urbanization and Development in NE India: Trends and Policy Implications*, Deep & Deep Publications, New Delhi.

Jain, P. C. (2001): *Globalization and Tribal Economy*, Rawat Publications, New Delhi.

Jogdand, P. G. and S. M. Michael (eds.) (2003): *Globalization and Social Movements—Struggle for Humane Society*, Rawat Publications, Jaipur.

Jaya Seelam, L. (1996): *Impact of Missionary Movement in Manipur*, Scholar Publishing House (P) Ltd, New Delhi.

Joshi, Satyakam (1999): "Tribals, Missionaries and Sadhus- Understanding Violence in the Dangs", *Economic and Political Weekly*, September 11.

Keith, Griffin (1974): *The Political Economy of Agrarian Change*, Harvard University Press.

Mallick, M. and J. Lenka (2006): "Globalization and Development: Disaggregate Dynamics", *Southern Economist*, 15 Jan., p.14.

Nayar, Baldev Raj (2006): *India's Globalization: Evaluating the Economic Consequences*, East-West Center, Washington.

Ramamani, V. S. (1988): *Tribal Economy: Problems and Prospects*, Chugh Publication, Allahabad.

Raju, G. (2001): "How Liberalization Works for the Rural Poor", *Southern Economist*, Sept 1, 2001. Bangalore. Pg. 12.

Rangachar, S. (2006): "Globalization: Issues & Challenges", *Southern Economist*, April 1 & 15, p.9.

Raman, H. (2001): "Globalization: Impact on Economic Development Strategy of India", *Southern Economist*, May 15, p. 5.

Robertson, Roland and K.H. Haque (1998): "Discourses of Globalization", *International Sociology*, XIII (1): 29 March.

Sen, S. and S. Raju (2006): "Globalization and Expanding Markets for cut flowers: Who benefits?", *Economic and Political Weekly*, 30 June, pp. 2725-2730.

Sikidar, Sujit (1990): *Economic Development of Tribal India*, Ashish Publishing House, New Delhi.

Sharma, B. D. (1978): *Tribal Development—The Concept and the Frame*, Prachi Prakashan, New Delhi.

Taylor, E. J. and Irma Adelman (1996): *Village Economies*, Cambridge University Press, Cambridge.

Tomlinson, John (1999): *Globalization and Culture,* Chicago University Press, Chicago.

18

Economic Liberalization in Manipur: A Critical Understanding

H. Isworchandra Sharma

Introduction

Economic reforms of the 1990's can be regarded as the watershed in the Indian economic history not necessarily for its success or failure, but for it is the 'ground zero' for all the contemporary development debates on Indian economy. Economic reform of 1990's is the fall out of interplay between the external compulsion and volatile domestic condition. The late 80's and early 90's were marked by changing world economic order with the end of cold war (collapse of Soviet Union) and it was also marked by tide of 'neoliberalism'[1] as the new development mantra. On the other hand India's internal economy was marred by massive BOP deficit, fiscal deficit, stagnant growth of output and employment, inequality, etc. Both these external and internal scenarios have prompted to take the World Bank-IMF prescription of economic reforms (stabilization and structural adjustment). India is now in the 'second generation' reform and success and failure story of reforms have been coming up. The essay will survey the underlying contours of economic liberalization in India and critically look at its impact on Manipur, which has been a peripheral economy from the time of its merger to the Indian Union.

Economic Liberalization: A Synoptic View

Economic liberalization has two basic but interrelated components: (1) program of macro-economic stabilization with fiscal adjustment (of IMF type), and (2) program of micro-economic structural adjustment (of World Bank type).

Macro-economic Stabilization

Looking at the history of developing countries which adopted economic liberalization, the stabilization programme generally preceded or was the pre-condition for the adoption of the economic reforms. These countries suffered from inconsistency between internal policies and external balance saddled with non-sustainable capital flows. These were the countries which implemented stabilization programme to re-establish external balance in the short run through demand management even at the cost of economic growth (Conway 1991). Macro-economic stabilization tries to cure in a short term period, an economy in deep crisis. Its successful implementation will act as a pre-condition to facilitate the adoption of economic reforms.

It generally has two fundamental objectives, viz. (i) to reduce current account deficit as much as possible to eventually avoid a BOP problem, and (ii) to control inflation. For achieving these objectives, it uses two instruments - fiscal policy of the government (taxation and expenditure in the central budget) and monetary policy of the central bank (interest rates and credit controls). Both these measures are used to curve aggregate demand especially generating from government in the economy.

The essence of macro-economic stabilization is demand compression. It uses both instruments for effecting demand compression so as to reduce the gap between aggregate demand and short-run aggregate supply in the economy. It tries to bring inflation under control through a restrictive monetary policy. Interest rates may be hiked to reduce investment demand and to increase savings. Further, along with the above, government deficit finance may be shifted from banking system to private bond holders to enable stricter control of money supply. On the fiscal front, fiscal deficits may be checked by curving government expenditures, particularly subsidies and other non-essential spending. Increases in the prices of government supplied goods like food and infrastructure and tax reforms, both of which may augment revenues, are required to cut down fiscal deficits.

Further, IMF-World Bank prescribes devaluation of national currencies (in a fixed exchange rate regime) for improving BOP's. According to them, first, the existing exchange rate may be unsustainable. Second devaluation makes the domestic currency relatively cheaper, thus providing an incentive to exports and disincentive to imports. As a result, current account deficit may come down. The devaluation should be accompanied by import liberalization and a transition to floating exchange rates.

India implemented these policies in July 1991 to manage and solve the impending debt crisis. The package contained a sharp reduction in fiscal deficits, a tight monetary policy along with a substantial devaluation of the rupee. The government identified a number of means for dealing with the fiscal deficit (Chandrasekhar and Ghosh 2000: 21). The first was to reduce expenditures other than those on interest payments, especially the expenditures of the government on subsidies and administration, both of which were considered excessive and reflective of inefficiency. The other, capital expenditure was cut back even more drastically. Regarding devaluation, the rupee was devalued twice, on July 1 and on July 3 in 1991 resulting in devaluation by 18 percent.

Structural Adjustment Programme

Micro-economic structural programme was another part of policy prescription of WB-IMF. The principle aim of the structural adjustment policies adopted as a part of the reform process were: (i) to do away with or substantially reduce controls on capacity creation, production and prices, and let market forces influence the investment and operational decisions of domestic and foreign economic agents within the domestic tariff area; (ii) to allow international competition and therefore international relative prices to influence the decisions of these agents; (iii) to reduce the presence of state agencies in production and trade, except in areas where market failure necessitates state entry; and (iv) to liberalize the financial sector by reducing controls on the banking system allowing for the proliferation of financial institutions and instruments and permitting foreign entry into the financial sector. To sum up, structural adjustment programme emphasized on deregulation, marketization and privatization for bringing more efficiency and dynamism to the economy (Chandrashekhar and Ghosh 2000: 21-22).

In compliance with the stabilization and structural adjustment prescription of the IMF and World Bank, the Government of India in July 1991 introduced significant structural policy changes in (a) the industrial sector (b) the trade regime (c) foreign investment (d) foreign technology (e) public sector and (f) the financial sector.

Reforms in Industrial Policy: The dismantling of the complex system of controls has been carried out. Investment decisions no longer need government approval. New firms have free entry now. Existing firms can increase its size without limit. Except for specified few, industrial licensing has been abolished. Big houses no longer need prior government approval for capacity expansion, capacity creation, amalgamation, mergers or takeovers.

Trade Policy Reform: It wanted to remove controls on imports, to reduce the production in domestic industry, and to bring domestic prices closer to world prices. To achieve the above objectives, it dismantled quotas on imports and exports, substantially reduced tariffs on imports and abolished subsidies on exports. The exchange rate was adjusted downwards. These steps would shift resources from non-traded goods to traded goods, while exposure to international competition would make domestic firms more efficient.

Policy Regime for Foreign Investment and Foreign Technology: Now, prior government approval for getting foreign investment is the exception and not the rule. Government wanted to get more non-debt creating foreign capital. Technology acquisition seems to be a secondary objective.

Public Sector Reform: The government wanted the public sector to focus only on strategic, high-technology areas and essential infrastructure. It wanted to close the lose-making units, to lessen the public sector's burden on the exchequer and to reduce the activities of the public sector. Most important, there has been considerable disinvestment of government equity up to 20% which was subsequently extended to 49%.

Financial Sector Reform: The government felt that the commercial banking system and the domestic capital market were over-regulated and under-governed. It deregulated both systems, to improve profitability of the state-owned commercial banks and better functioning of the domestic capital market. Commercial banks' complex interest rates have been simplified. Interest rates in the domestic capital market have been deregulated. The reforms in the capital market seek to finance investment in the private sector to attract foreign portfolio capital (Bhaduri and Nayyar 1996). Thus, far reaching reforms were introduced in the above sectors.

Debates surrounding the success and failures of reforms are numerous and endless. Advocates of reform place it in high esteem for attaining high growth rate which was not experienced in other countries especially Asian economies during the post 1990's, for attaining a sound external sector, service sector revolutions etc. On the other hand critics of reforms have their equal arguments; blame the reforms for stagnant agriculture, poverty, unemployment, inequality, failure in social sector etc. But the important question arises is that does the national level debates over the liberalization sounds good for our state, does liberalization has affected our state negatively or positively or what are the impacts of the reforms in our state. These are some crucial question that needs to be addressed judiciously.

Pre-liberalization Economy of Manipur

Pre-liberalization economy of the state can be divided in two phases—first, centralized economy of pre-statehood period and post-statehood economy phase up to 1991. The economy of the state was throng in the lap of centralized planning immediately after the merger with the Indian Union. The centralized planning in the first four FYP during the pre-statehood period concentrates more on transport and communication and social and community services neglecting the vital sector of agriculture, industry, irrigation and power. The scene was different for all India pattern as the period was focusing on lading a strong industrial base. Thus the two sectors viz. transport-communication and social-community services accounted for 91, 73, 77, and 66 per cent of the total outlay in the 1st, 2nd, 3rd, and 4th plan of Manipur respectively. Juxtaposition with all India patterns of 50, 46, 20 and 38 per cent in the same sectors reveals the lopsided and disproportionate nature of Manipur's plan outlays. In a state where 90 per cent of the area is hills, concern for transport and communication is understandable. However no stretch of imagination can reconcile the grossly disproportionate investment in the transport and communication sectors to the ruinous neglect of agriculture (Chongtham 1985).

Perpetuation of Manipur' status after the merger as a peripheral economy is quite evident from the pattern of plan outlays of the state. Nothing was done during the centralized planning to strengthen the productive base of the economy. The state was reduced to a captive market for the indigenous capitalist class of India which had already made significant inroads during the British rule. Centralized Indian planning concentrated development and advancement in certain metropolitan (core) economy and left the North East outside its development frame. The political economy of India's development on the capitalist path of development found a corollary in the underdevelopment of Manipur and North East region (Ahmad and Biswas 2005). During this period the Indian Government followed state-backed industrialization for nurturing and strengthening the indigenous capitalist class. The period is also marked by a policy of import substitution; the share of consumer goods, which were imported, was already low at the beginning of 1950's. By the end of 1960, India imported practically no consumer goods (Sodersten 1984). On the other hand, the period also witnessed Manipur's increasing dependence on core economy for food grains and other consumer goods.

Attainment of statehood brought some changes in the development approach. The state started giving attention on agriculture and industry focusing on major irrigation projects and establishment of PSUs. The first major irrigation project, the Loktak Lift irrigation Project, was taken up in the year 1973-74. It was followed by medium river irrigation projects viz. Imphal barrage, Sekmai barrage, Khoupum Dam, Singda Project and a number of minor irrigation projects. By the time Manipur attained statehood, Green Revolution was already in place in other parts of the country. Post-statehood agricultural scenario witnessed intensified use of HYV, chemical fertilizers and irrigation. The result has been the state's modest participation in Green Revolution. Both production and productivity of the staple crop, rice has increased substantially. However the state did not reach the comfort zone of self sufficiency in food grains.

State backed industrialization also commenced after the attainment of statehood with the incorporation of the Manipur Spinning Mill in 1974. It was followed by the establishment of a number of public sector undertakings viz. Manipur Cycle Corporation Ltd., Manipur Cement Ltd., Manipur Pulps and Allied Products Ltd., Manipur Food Industries Corporation Ltd., Manipur State Drugs and Pharmaceuticals Ltd., Manipur Vanaspati and Allied Industries Ltd., Manipur Handloom and Handicraft Development Corporation Ltd., Manipur Electronics Development Corporation Ltd. and Manipur Industrial Development Corporation Ltd. From its inception these PSU had been surrounded by plethora of problems.

A cursory glance at composition of net state domestic product (NSDP) (Table 1) and workforce participation (Table 2) will portray the state of the economy of Manipur. In terms of structural change the state does not witnessed the 'classic industrialization pattern'[2], moving from primary to manufacturing activities. Though the usual trend of falling income shares of primary sector especially agriculture to the total income as the economy progresses is also witnessed in the context of Manipur's economy; the decline is very disturbing, as it has not been accompanied by a matching fall in the workforce dependent on agriculture indicating persistence low productivity of labour in the primary sector.

Table 1
Composition of NSDP of Manipur by major sector at constant prices (1980-81)

(per cent)

Sector	*1960-61*	*1970-71*	*1980-81*	*1990-91*
Primary	53.62	49.69	49.11	38.02
Secondary	6.26	6.42	7.65	10.20
Tertiary	40.12	43.89	43.24	51.78

Source: Various estimates of NSDP by DES, GOM.[3]

Table 1 shows the percentage composition of NSDP by major sector from 1960-61 to 1990-91. The share of primary sector to NSDP uninterruptedly declines from 53.62 per cent in 1960-61 to 38.02 percent in 1990-91. The growth of secondary sector is very slow from 6.26 percent in 1960-61 to 10.20 percent in 1990-91. The tertiary sector registered a high growth from 40.12 per cent in 1960-61 to 51.78 per cent in 1990-91. A very high percentage of primary sector i.e 53.62 percent and tertiary sector i.e 40.12 per cent and a low secondary sector 6.26 per cent in the initial stage (1960-61) indicate an agrarian economy with weak industrial base and an inflated tertiary sector. From early stage of pre-liberalization, the state had been inclining towards a dependent economy.

Table 2
Distribution of workforce in Manipur by occupational sector

(per cent)

Census Year	*Primary Sector*	*Secondary Sector*	*Tertiary Sector*
1961	66.26	23.05	10.69
1971	71.27	14.53	14.20
1981	68.59	9.68	21.73
1991	69.97	9.69	20.34

Source: Census Report as Compiled by the DES, GOM and published in Statistical Abstract of Manipur 2004.

Table 2 shows percentage distribution of workforce in Manipur by occupational sector. The fall in the contribution of primary sector to the NSDP not been accompanied by a matching fall in the workforce dependent on agriculture; contribution of primary sector to the total workforce registered an increased from 66.26 per cent in 1961 to 69.97 per cent in 1991. The state has an 'overpopulated and unproductive' labour force in the primary sector. On the other hand, contribution of secondary sector to total workforce declines by a huge margin from 23.05 per cent in 1961 to 9.69 per cent in 1991; a scene of deindustrialization and retroversion. This is in spite of the industrialization process carried out in the pre-liberalization period. The industrialization process was not able to absorb the growing workforce from the primary sector owing to inherent weakness of the industrialization and structural constraints.

Pre-liberalization economy witnessed a shrinking manufacturing sector and the economy was going slowly but surely towards a very highly tertiarised economy. Though attention was paid to agriculture and industry, there was no success story in these two important sectors. The economy was increasingly going through a parasitic development process.

Economic Liberalization vis-a-vis Manipur's Economy

Economic liberalization imparted drastic structural changes and exacerbates the already feeble economy. It brought all the economic ailments in the state- deindustrialization, agricultural stagnation, and unemployment. In post 1990's, neither agricultural nor manufacturing become the accelerator of economy. Heighten tertiarization is the order of the day in the liberalization phase. Table 3, 4, 5 and 6 shows the structural transformation and components of the economy in the liberalization phase.

Table 3
Share of agriculture and other sectors in NSDP in Manipur (% share) at constant prices

Year	*Agriculture*	*Secondary*	*Tertiary*
1990	32.01	9.48	52.25
2000	25.90	20.12	48.75
2005	23.14	24.64	47.42

Source: Calculated from EPW and CSO

Table 3 shows share of agriculture, secondary and tertiary sectors in NSDP in Manipur from 1990. Agriculture shows a falling share in NSDP i.e from 32.01 per cent in 1990 to 23.14 per cent in 2005. The secondary sector shows a handsome improvement in NSDP i.e. 9.48 per cent in 1990 to 24.64 per cent in 2005. The tertiary sector registers a marginal fall i.e. 52.25 per cent in 1990 to 47.42 per cent in 2005. But one should not be carried away by improvement in secondary sector as secondary sector growth is construction led not by manufacture propelled. This will be cleared by looking at Table 4, which shows contribution of secondary sector components to state's NSDP. The share of construction records an increased from 7.91 per cent in 1990 to 15.71 per cent in 2005. This is the result of Government attention in construction; showcasing it as a development process.

Table 4

Secondary sector and its components in NSDP in Manipur (% share) at constant prices

Year	*Manufacturing*			*Construction*	*Electricity, gas & water supply*	*Total*
	Regd.	*Unregd.*	*Total*			
1990	0.08	5.68	5.76	7.91	-4.18	9.48
2000	0.06	8.20	8.26	11.54	0.31	20.12
2005	0.21	8.67	8.88	15.71	0.05	24.64

Source: Calculated from EPW and CSO.

Another important and crucial aspect of secondary sector composition is the growth of unregistered manufacturing. The contribution of registered manufacturing cannot touch the 1 percent mark but the contribution of unregistered manufacturing increases from 5.76 percent in 1990 to 8.88 per cent in 2005. This is an indication of 'informalisation' of economy in manufacturing sector. With the advent of liberalization, imported cheap or low priced goods are flooding the local market which has a negative impact in the growth of registered manufacturing sector. There is growing emphasis for cost-cutting strategy; the manufacturing units resort to self-employed, home workers or casual labours to run their units and increasing number of unregistered manufacturing units whose operating costs are much lower.

Table 5
Tertiary sector and its components in NSDP in Manipur (% share) at constant prices

Year	*Transport, storage & communication*	*Trade, hotels & restaurants*	*Banking & insurance*	*Public administration*	*Total*
1990	4.73	4.01	2.31	12.40	23.45
2000	3.46	11.22	1.72	15.77	32.17
2005	4.97	9.23	2.58	14.21	30.99

Source: Calculated from EPW and CSO.

Table 5 shows tertiary sector and its components of NSDP in Manipur. The tertiary sector accounts for almost half of the NSDP. There is nothing to cheer about its high percentage as important sectors viz. transport & communication and banking & insurance have very small share. Bulk of the share comes from public administration i.e. 12.40 per cent in 1990, 15.77 per cent in 2000 and 14.21 per cent in 2005.

Table 6
Distribution of workers/non-workers

Type of Worker	*1991*	*2001*	*Percentage Rise/Decline*
Main Workers	7,08,283	6,59,364	- 6.9 %
Marginal Workers	66,621	2,85,849	329 %
Non Workers	8,07,145	10,62,245	31 %
Total Workers	18,37,149	21,66,788	15 %

Source: GOM (2005), Statistical Abstract: Manipur 2004, DES.

Liberalization also brings about negative impact on the employment scenario of the state. This is visible by looking at Table 6 and 7. Table

6 shows distribution of workers/non workers by 1991 and 2001 census. Liberalization has resulted in increases in unemployment rate and marginalization of labour force. Non workers have increased by 31 per cent and marginal workers have registered a mammoth 329 per cent. The main workers show a decline of 6.9 per cent. A high percentage increase of marginal workers indicates 'casualization and informalisation' of labour force in the state.

Table 7
Main workers by industrial categories

(per cent)

Type of Worker	*1991*	*2001*	*Percentage Rise/ Decline*
Cultivator	61.76	43.76	-34.67
Agricultural Labourer	6.69	6.55	-11.68
Manufacturing, Processing, Servicing, Repairing	8.10	6.34	-24.84
Other Services	23.43	43.34	73

Source: GOM (2005), *Statistical Abstract: Manipur 2004,* DES.

Table 7 shows main workers by industrial categories. Important type of workers viz. cultivator, agricultural labourer, manufacturing, processing, servicing and repairing show a decline - cultivator (34.67 percent), agricultural labourer (11.68 percent), manufacturing, processing, servicing, and repairing (24.84 percent). The fall in workforce in the agricultural sector is not accompanied by rise in the secondary sector; the growing labour force in the primary sector is not absorbed by manufacturing sector rather the workforce engaged in the secondary sector also declines. This is the result of the deindustrialization phase after liberalization. The trouble befalling the two important sectors after liberalization is quite visible. Other services registered a high percentage of growth.

The fall in the cultivator and agricultural labourer or more precisely primary sector is not the result of 'pull factor' but of 'push factor'.

In other words the labour force are moving out of agriculture not because of they are becoming more productive or attracted by other activity but rather non-availability of employment in agriculture. It only highlights the dissatisfaction of the farmers with their profession and their uncertain future. Though the economic reforms did not include any specific design for agriculture, there are certain elements such as - financial liberalization measures, including reducing priority sector lending by banks, which effectively reduced the availability of rural credit, and thus made farm investment more expensive and more difficult, especially for smaller farmers, liberalization and removal of restrictions on internal trade in agricultural commodities, across states within India - have far reaching implication on Manipur. Liberalization has resulted in accelerating influx of agricultural goods that too at low prices which has given less incentive to the farmers in the state. Government attitude also undermines the situation in Manipur. It is giving less attention to agriculture as the state does not have a draft agricultural policy and succumbed to the forces of the market which has not yielded the desired result. Subsistence level of agriculture is so high in the state that it has become a secondary occupation for many part time farmers. Liberalization has brought more adversity than opportunity to agriculture in the state.

The immediate effect of liberalization on the industrialization process in the state has been the closing down of most of the PSUs. India's economic liberalization of the 90's turned out to be the last nail on the coffin for the already ailing public sector undertakings of the state. Liberalization subserved the interest of advanced capitalism of the core economy of the mainland against underdeveloped peripheral economies like Manipur. Though the PSUs of the state were suffering from endogenous factors like infrastructural bottlenecks, the deathblow was given by the strong exogenous factor of economic liberalization. Huge inflow of cheap products from mainland India and Southeast Asia in the liberalization period virtually led to the closure of many manufacturing units ranging from large to small due to their inability to withstand the competition. Going in tune with the national trend of closing down of PSUs and disinvestment, the State Government adopted the ideology of privatization without taking into account the ground reality of the state's economy in keeping with the policy prescriptions of New Delhi under the plea of fiscal streamlining (Hanjabam 2007). The state government has shut down most of the PSUs established during the pre-liberalization period. Deindustrialization rather than industrialization is the current trend in Manipur. The state is nowhere on the industrial map of India. The state remains as an industrially backward state with all the districts under the category of 'No Industry District' by all India standards.

Indo-Myanmar border trade, the apostle of liberalization in Manipur has also added misery to the state's economy. The trade was officially launched on 12th April 1995 as a corollary to India's economic liberalization. It has completed a decade and fails to reach the expectation of people as it cannot boost the industrial sector and generate gainful employment and income in the state. The Indo-Myanmar Border Trade has completed a decade, a decade of meretricious trade (Hanjabam 2006: 60). It largely undermines the development of substantial productive base in the state. In the face of the existing incongruities, a decade of border trade shows a declining trend in the official volume of trade. According to official data, goods worth Rs.31,70,51,137 were exported when the import volume was Rs. 15,17,64,137 during 1996-97 but in 2004-05 it dwindled to just Rs. 5,64,45,050 in export and Rs. 5,00,81,749 in import (*The Sangai Express, 1st Aug 2006*). But trade in unofficial item is going on smoothly without interruption. Products ranging from clothes, electronic goods, edible items, detergent and other consumer items imported from Myanmar have flooded the local market. It is estimated that in 2004-05 goods amounting to Rs. 186 crores were imported from Myanmar through informal trade (Thongam 2008). The burgeoning imports from Myanmar along with the products from mainland India have significantly crippled the fledging productive units in Manipur. Instead of strengthening the industrial base of Manipur, border trade has increased the degree of tertiarization (Hanjabam 2006: 61). Border trade has only managed to mould a 'petty trading class' in the state in lieu of gainful and quality employment.

Conclusion

Liberalization process of India was also initiated to integrate the indigenous capital class to metropolitan capitalist; it does not deliberate about integration of sub-regional or regional economy to the national economy. Peripheral economy like Manipur has been serving as a 'captive market' for India's indigenous capitalist class. Convergence of western metropolitan capitalist and India's indigenous capitalist class as a sequel to liberalization furthers Manipur's status as a captive market. It has been widely argued that the Indian state failed to discard the legacy of colonial development in 'decolonized' India as a result of the interplay of the alliance between Western metropolitan capital and the indigenous capital class (Patnaik 2001). The so call socialist path of development in the pre-liberalization period has done nothing for the development of the region and liberalization only worsens the already fragile economy. Just as there was nothing socialist in the socialist pattern of society, there is hardly anything liberal in the liberalization phase (Srikanth 1998). Liberalization phase witnessed Manipur's economy highly integrated to world capital market with a very weak productive base internally. Liberalization brings more lacunae and lapses to the region's economy - stagnant agriculture, deindustrialization, unemployment, inequality, proletarization, etc.

NOTES

1. Under Neoliberalism, the central objective of economic growth is to be achieved though structural reform, deregulation, liberalization and privatization. See Jan Nederveen Pieterse (2001), *Development Theory: Deconstruction/Reconstruction,* Vistaar Publication, New Delhi.
2. A phrase borrowed from Chandrasekhar and Ghose (2007).
3. Directorate of Economics and Statistics (DES), Government of Manipur (GOM).

REFERENCES

Ahmad, Raiful and Prasenjit Biswas (2004): *Political Economy of the Underdevelopment of North East India*, Akansha Publishing House, New Delhi.

Bhaduri, A and D. Nayyar(1996): *The Intelligent Person's Guide to Liberalization*, Penguin India (P) Ltd.

Chandrasekhar, C.P. and Jayati Ghosh (2000): *The Market That Failed - Neoliberal Economic Reforms in India,* Leftword Books, New Delhi.

———— (2007) "Recent Employment Trends in India and China: An Unfortunate Convergence" National Conference on *Making Growth Inclusive with Reference to Employment Generation,* 28-29th June, Jawaharlal Nehru University, New Delhi, 20th September 2007.

Chongtham, Priyoranjan (1985) "Aspects of the State Economy and Planning for 2000 AD", Seminar Paper Manipur 2000 AD October, Manipur University, Imphal.

Conway, P. (1991) "A theoretic Evaluation of Success in Stabilization in Developing Countries", Working Papers, Trade Policy, Country Economic Development, The World Bank, March, WPS 629.

EPW (2003): *Domestic Product of States of India 1960-61 to 2000-01*, EPW Research Foundation, Mumbai.

Government of Manipur (2005): *Statistical Abstract Manipur 2004*, Department of Economics and Statistics, Imphal.

Hanjabam, Isworchandra (2006): "India's Look East Policy and Manipur's Economy: A Critical Scrutiny", *Alternative Perspectives* ,Vol. I, Issue IV, July-September.

———— (2007) "Post-Statehood Economy of Manipur: A Critical Analysis", *Alternative Perspectives,* Vol. II Issue III, April-June.

Patnaik, Prabhat (2001): *Whatever Happened to Imperialism and Other Essays*, Tulika, New Delhi.

Sodersten, Bo. (1984): *International Economics*, McMillan Publisher, London.

Srikanth, H. (1998): "Liberalization and Development of India's North East: Learning from Experience" in Das, Gurudas and R.K. Purkayastha (eds) *Liberalization and India's North-East*, Commonthwealth Publishers, New Delhi.

Thongam, Priyokumar (2008): "Informal Trade Along Myanmar- Manipur (India) Border: Magnitude and Composition of Trade Flows" in Singh, E.BK. and Ksh. Jhaljit Singh (eds) *Challenges of Economic Policy in Manipur- Essays in Honour of Prof. M. Iboton Singh*, Akansha Publishing House, New Delhi.

Index

■■■